THE *Constitution* — AND THE — *Nation*

TEACHING TEXTS IN LAW AND POLITICS

David A. Schultz
General Editor

Vol. 23

PETER LANG
New York • Washington, D.C./Baltimore • Bern
Frankfurt am Main • Berlin • Brussels • Vienna • Oxford

Christopher Waldrep
& Lynne Curry

THE Constitution AND THE Nation

The Civil War and American Constitutionalism, 1830–1890

PETER LANG
New York • Washington, D.C./Baltimore • Bern
Frankfurt am Main • Berlin • Brussels • Vienna • Oxford

Library of Congress Cataloging-in-Publication Data

Waldrep, Christopher.
The constitution and the nation. The Civil War and American constitutionalism, 1830–1890 / Christopher R. Waldrep, Lynne Curry.
p. cm. — (Teaching texts in law and politics; v. 23)
Includes bibliographical references and index.
1. Constitutional history—United States. I. Title: Civil War and American constitutionalism, 1830–1890.
II. Curry, Lynne. III. Title. IV. Series.
KF4541.W352 342.73'029—dc21 2002155897
ISBN 0-8204-5731-0
ISSN 1083-3447

Bibliographic information published by **Die Deutsche Bibliothek**.
Die Deutsche Bibliothek lists this publication in the "Deutsche Nationalbibliografie"; detailed bibliographic data is available on the Internet at http://dnb.ddb.de/.

Cover design by Lisa Barfield

The paper in this book meets the guidelines for permanence and durability of the Committee on Production Guidelines for Book Longevity of the Council of Library Resources.

275 Seventh Avenue, 28th Floor, New York, NY 10001
www.peterlangusa.com

Printed in the United States of America

TABLE OF CONTENTS

INTRODUCTION

While few Americans recall details about their Constitution, most have absorbed the great document's basic principles. A few think the Constitution hopelessly flawed or bigoted, but most agree the framers simply created an imperfect document. This book is one of four volumes about the changing Constitution, its evolution from a slaveholders' compact to a modern guarantor of individual rights. In other words, we plan to study the Constitution *historically* as the product of change over time. Often law is not studied historically. To anyone at all familiar with the chronologically organized texts that line the walls of any law library, this statement might seem paradoxical. Yet, historians have only studied the law and constitutionalism for three generations. Social and cultural historians even today doubt law really gets at the core of what makes society function. The Constitution often makes only a brief appearance in many U.S. history survey courses.

Law at its most potent presents itself as timeless, immutable, above social change. Law embodies fundamental, unchanging rules. Some lawyers today display the Ten Commandments and evoke Moses in a reflection of such beliefs. History, by contrast, assumes change. History is the study of change over time; other disciplines seek unchanging values, but not history. The political scientist reads Machiavelli to find truths usable in any political situation; the historian reads Machiavelli to learn about the Renaissance. To see law as historical makes powerful assumptions: law does change, law reflects its time, political forces mold law.

A constitution is law, but everyone realizes that constitutional law differs from the sort of law that regulates highway speeds and parking. Constitutional law is fundamental; it is often said to be organic. Constitutional beliefs do not change easily but do change. Americans understand constitution as a construct that restricts power. Constitutions also distribute power, prescribing the extent and manner of the exercise of power, but constitutions also enshrine the society's most basic and cherished beliefs. Without constitutionalism, constitutions are meaningless. Constitutionalism is the belief that the constitution restricts power. For a constitution to effectively limit arbitrary authority, the people must imagine it has force. In the United States, it must be said, constitutionalism is contested. Some Americans genuinely believe their Constitution limits the exercise of power by government and even by the people themselves, but others do not.

The power limited by the Constitution is sovereign power, the absolute, unlimited, uncontrollable power by which the state is governed. Federalism is a particular arrangement of power that divides sovereignty between the central authority and regional power centers. The U.S. Constitution divides power between the national government and the states. Readers of this book should remember that it studies the evolution of the distribution of power in the United States.

In editing these documents we have retained original spelling, punctuation, use of italics, and capitalization except when changes proved necessary for sense.

We must begin also with thanks to all our students who inspired this book with their interest, questions, doubts, and affirmations. We must thank also our colleagues who offered suggestions or read portions of the manuscript: Richard B. Bernstein, Sally Hadden, Tim Huebner, and Judy Schafer. Tom Schwartz helped us obtain permissions for the Lincoln texts. Rachel Van helped immeasurably with the preparation of the text for publication.

1.

Jacksonian Constitutionalism

Very few candidates can claim to have "won" three presidential elections. Yet Andrew Jackson garnered most of the popular votes in 1824, 1828, and 1832. In 1824, Jackson won 153,740 votes, beating his closest rival, John Quincy Adams, by 45,000 votes. Jackson also won most of the electoral votes (99 to Adams's 84) but the country lurched into a crisis because Jackson did not win a majority of the electoral votes, and the election went to the House of Representatives. The House picked the president, choosing Adams even though Jackson had won most of the popular votes.

In 1828, Jackson ran again, winning decisively this time with 56 percent of the vote. It might be said that the 1828 election launched the "Age of Jackson." During Jacksonian America, the Revolutionary generation with its commitment to republicanism faded, and a new generation, dedicated to competitive individualism, stepped forward. Thus for the first time in history it can be said—perhaps accurately—that a privileged elite did not pick the president. Jacksonian democracy came to mean an easing of voting restrictions, equality over privilege, and entrepreneurship over vested interests.

Constitutionally, Jackson both rebuffed aggressive assertions of states' rights (in South Carolina) and supported them (in Georgia). Confronted with an effort to nullify a federal law, Jackson soared to rhetorical heights, promoting arguments on behalf of a perpetual union that Abraham Lincoln could use. In Georgia, Jackson's racism and hostility to Native Americans apparently blinded him to the state defiance he found so repulsive in South Carolina.

Jackson also made war on the Bank of the United States. Jackson's policies scattered the national treasury in a large number of state banks and convinced a generation that the national government should not rely on paper money.

Jackson's thinking, then, promoted a Unionist sentiment that would ultimately prove useful in combating state secession. But he left office with the states' rights dogma that poisoned American nationalism not only intact but, in some ways, strengthened. And he so fundamentally destroyed the notion of a centralized national banking system that he left the nation ill prepared to finance its fight against slavery and for the Union in 1861.

Jackson's First Annual Message to Congress (1829)

Supreme Court Chief Justice John Marshall grew up thinking of Native Americans as "savages." At the same time, Marshall could extend kindnesses to Native American peoples. As a young lawyer, he once successfully argued that Virginia law forbade the enslavement of Native Americans. In 1828, Marshall explained that when Native Americans posed a genuine threat, they had to be resisted, even cruelly resisted, but, when they no longer endangered white interests, morality no longer had to be jettisoned in the name of public safety. When Georgia forced Creek Indians out of the state in 1824, Marshall was indignant. Georgia alarmed Marshall when it began to force the Cherokees from lands occupied under treaties negotiated in 1785 and 1791. In 1828 and 1829 the Georgia legislature passed laws challenging the 1791 Treaty of Holston. Just as surely as South Carolina, Georgia defied federal law in a bid to establish states' rights.

Such assertions of states' rights elsewhere would outrage President Andrew Jackson. In this case, Old Hickory sided with Georgia. Jackson's followers dominated Congress, which passed the Indian Removal Act in 1830. Like all previous presidents going back to Thomas Jefferson, Jackson made it his policy to eliminate all Native Americans east of the Mississippi River. In his first annual message to Congress, President Andrew Jackson asked the national legislature to set aside land west of the Mississippi River to which eastern Indian tribes could be removed. Congress passed the Indian Removal Act the following year. Despite an impassioned plea from the Cherokee Nation, some 16,000 Native Americans were removed from Georgia in an event that has since become known as the Trail of Tears.

December 8, 1829

The condition and ulterior destiny of the Indian tribes within the limits of some of our States have become objects of much interest and importance. It has long been the policy of government to introduce among them the arts of civilization, in the hope of gradually reclaiming them from a wandering life. This policy has, however, been coupled with another wholly incompatible with its success. Professing a desire to civilize and settle them, we have at the same time lost no opportunity to purchase their lands and thrust them farther into the wilderness....

Our conduct toward these people is deeply interesting to our national character. Their present condition, contrasted with what they once were, makes a most powerful appeal to our sympathies. Our ancestors found them the uncontrolled possessors of these vast regions. By persuasion and force they have been made to retire from river to river and from mountain to mountain, until some of the tribes have become extinct and others have left but remnants to preserve for awhile their once terrible names. Surrounded by the whites with their arts of civilization, which by destroying the resources of the savage doom him to weakness and decay, the fate of the Mohegan, the Narragansett, and the Delaware is fast overtaking the Choctaw, the Cherokee, and the Creek. That this fate surely awaits them if they remain within the limits of the states does not admit of a doubt. Humanity and national honor demand that every effort should be made to avert so great a calamity....

As a means of effecting this end, I suggest for your consideration the propriety of setting apart an ample district west of the Mississippi, and without the limits of any state or territory now formed, to be guaranteed to the Indian tribes as long as they shall occupy it, each tribe having a distinct control over the portion designated for its use. There they may be secured in the enjoyment of governments of their own choice, subject to no other control from the United States than such as may be necessary to preserve peace on the frontier and between the several tribes. There the benevolent may endeavor to teach them the arts of civilization, and, by promoting union and harmony among them, to raise up an interesting commonwealth, destined to perpetuate the race and to attest the humanity and justice of this Government.

This emigration should be voluntary, for it would be cruel and unjust to compel the aborigines to abandon the graves of their fathers and seek a home in a distant land. But they should be distinctly informed that if they remain within the limits of the states they must be subject to their laws....

Source: James D. Richardson, ed., *A Compilation of the Messages and Papers of the Presidents* (New York, 1897), 3:1019–1020, 1021, 1022.

Address of the Cherokee Nation (1830)

Address of the committee and council of the Cherokee nation, in general council convened, to the people of the United States.

We are aware, that some persons suppose it will be for our advantage to remove beyond the Mississippi. We think otherwise. Our people universally think otherwise. Thinking that it would be fatal to their interests, they have almost to a man sent their memorial to congress, deprecating the necessity of a removal. . . . It is incredible that Georgia should ever have enacted the oppressive laws to which reference is here made, unless she had supposed that something extremely terrific in its character was necessary in order to make the Cherokees willing to remove. We are not willing to remove; and if we could be brought to this extremity, it would be not by argument, nor because our judgment was satisfied, not because our condition will be improved; but only because we cannot endure to be deprived of our national and individual rights and subjected to a process of intolerable oppression.

We wish to remain on the land of our fathers. We have a perfect and original right to remain without interruption or molestation. The treaties with us, and laws of the United States made in pursuance of treaties, guaranty our residence, and our privileges and secure us against intruders. Our only request is, that these treaties may be fulfilled, and these laws executed.

But if we are compelled to leave our country, we see nothing but ruin before us. The country west of the Arkansas territory is unknown to us. From what we can learn of it, we have no prepossessions in its favor. All the inviting parts of it, as we believe, are preoccupied by various Indian nations, to which it has been assigned. They would regard us as intruders.... The far greater part of that region is, beyond all controversy, badly supplied with wood and water; and no Indian tribe can live as agriculturists without these articles. All our neighbors...would speak a language totally different from ours, and practice different customs. The original possessors of that region are now wandering savages lurking for prey in the neighborhood.... Were the country to which we are urged much better than it is represented to be...still it is not the land of our birth, nor of our affections. It contains neither the scenes of our childhood, nor the graves of our fathers.

...We have been called a poor, ignorant, and degraded people. We certainly are not rich; nor have we ever boasted of our knowledge, or our moral or intellectual elevation. But there is not a man within our limits so ignorant as not to know that he has a right to live on the land of his fathers, in the possession of his immemorial privileges, and that this right has been acknowledged and guaranteed by the U. States; nor is there a man so degraded as not to feel a keen sense of injury, on being deprived of his right and driven into exile....

Source: *Niles Weekly Register*, August 21, 1830.

Worcester v. Georgia (1832)

The Cherokees received no solace from the executive or legislative branches. Their only hope lay in the judiciary. In Cherokee Nation v. Georgia *(1831), the Native Americans asked Marshall's Court to order the state to stop enforcing its laws against the Cherokees. Marshall decided in their favor, but he wrote an uncharacteristically timid opinion and failed to rally his fellow justices to his decision. Marshall still mourned the recent death of his wife and battled the gallbladder problems that would ultimately kill him. It seemed Marshall could no longer vigorously lead the Court.*

In Worcester v. Georgia *Marshall produced a deeply researched opinion that won every justice but one to his side. Georgia authorities had imprisoned Worcester under state law in defiance of federal treaties that gave the Indians – not Georgia – sovereignty over their lands. Marshall decided that the United States government had the exclusive authority to negotiate relations with Native Americans. He also found that Native American tribes had the authority to independently govern themselves.*

Jacksonians blasted the decision. The president, though, reacted silently. He never uttered the famous words attributed to him: "John Marshall has made his decision, now let him enforce it." Jackson's silence, of course, showed his feelings. Marshall probably hurried the litigation through in hopes of making it an issue in the 1832 election campaign. Given his health, Marshall knew that the man elected president would appoint his successor. Unfortunately for Marshall, the voters returned Jackson to office. Marshall's enemy would pick the next chief justice.

MR. CHIEF JUSTICE MARSHALL delivered the opinion of the Court.

This cause, in every point of view in which it can be placed, is of the deepest interest.

The defendant is a state, a member of the union, which has exercised the powers of government over a people who deny its jurisdiction, and are under the protection of the United States.

The plaintiff is a citizen of the state of Vermont, condemned to hard labour for four years in the penitentiary of Georgia; under colour of an act which he alleges to be repugnant to the constitution, laws, and treaties of the United States.

The legislative power of a state, the controlling power of the constitution and laws of the United States, the rights, if they have any, the political existence of a once numerous and powerful people, the personal liberty of a citizen, are all involved in the subject now to be considered....

The indictment charges the plaintiff in error, and others, being white persons, with the offence of "residing within the limits of the Cherokee nation without a license," and "without having taken the oath to support and defend the constitution and laws of the state of Georgia." ...

...The prisoner, being arraigned, plead not guilty. The jury found a verdict against him, and the court sentenced him to hard labour, in the penitentiary, for the term of four years....

It has been said at the bar, that the acts of the legislature of Georgia seize on the whole Cherokee country, parcel it out among the neighbouring counties of the state, extend her code over the whole country, abolish its institutions and its laws, and annihilate its political existence.

If this be the general effect of the system, let us inquire into the effect of the particular statute and section on which the indictment is founded.

It enacts that "all white persons, residing within the limits of the Cherokee nation on the 1st day of March next, or at any time thereafter, without a license or permit from his excellency the governor, or from such agent as his excellency the governor shall authorise to grant such permit or license, and who shall not have taken the oath hereinafter required, shall be guilty of a high misdemeanour, and, upon conviction thereof, shall be punished by confinement to the penitentiary, at hard labour, for a term not less than four years."

The eleventh section authorises the governor, should he deem it necessary for the protection of the mines, or the enforcement of the laws in force within the Cherokee nation, "to raise and organize a guard," &c.

The thirteenth section enacts, "that the said guard or any member of them, shall be, and they are hereby authorised and empowered to arrest any person legally charged with or detected in a violation of the laws of this state, and to convey, as soon as practicable, the person so arrested, before a justice of the peace, judge of the superior, or justice of inferior court of this state, to be dealt with according to law."

The extra-territorial power of every legislature being limited in its action, to its own citizens or subjects, the very passage of this act is an assertion of jurisdiction over the Cherokee nation, and of the rights and powers consequent on jurisdiction.

The first step, then, in the inquiry, which the constitution and laws impose on this court, is an examination of the rightfulness of this claim....

From the commencement of our government, congress has passed acts to regulate trade and intercourse with the Indians; which treat them as nations, respect their rights, and manifest a firm purpose to afford that protection which treaties stipulate. All these acts, and especially that of 1802, which is still in force, manifestly consider the several Indian nations as distinct political communities, having territorial boundaries, within which their authority is exclusive, and having a right to all the lands within those boundaries, which is not only acknowledged, but guaranteed by the United States....

The treaties and laws of the United States contemplate the Indian territory as completely separated from that of the states; and provide that all intercourse with them shall be carried on exclusively by the government of the union....

The Indian nations had always been considered as distinct, independent political communities, retaining their original natural rights, as the undisputed possessors of the soil, from time immemorial, with the single exception of that imposed by irresistible power, which excluded them from intercourse with any other European potentate than the first discoverer of the coast of the particular region claimed: and this was a restriction which those European potentates imposed on themselves, as well as on the Indians. The very term "nation," so generally applied to them, means "a people distinct from others." The constitution, by declaring treaties already made, as well as those to be made, to be the supreme law of the land, has adopted and sanctioned the previous treaties with the Indian nations, and consequently admits their rank among those powers who are capable of making treaties. The words "treaty" and "nation" are words of our own language, selected in our diplomatic and legislative proceedings, by ourselves, having each a definite and well understood meaning. We have applied them to Indians, as we have applied them to the other nations of the earth. They are applied to all in the same sense.

Georgia, herself, has furnished conclusive evidence that her former opinions on this subject concurred with those entertained by her sister states, and by the government of the United States. Various acts of her legislature have been cited in the argument, including the contract of cession made in the year 1802, all tending to prove her acquiescence in the universal conviction that the Indian nations possessed a full right to the lands they occupied, until that right should be extinguished by the United States, with their consent: that their territory was separated from that of any state within whose chartered limits they might reside, by a boundary line, established by treaties: that, within their boundary, they possessed rights with which no state could interfere: and that the whole power of regulating the intercourse with them, was vested in the United States. A review of these acts, on the part of Georgia, would occupy too much time, and is the less necessary, because they have been accurately detailed in the argument at the bar. Her new series of laws, manifesting her abandonment of these opinions, appears to have commenced in December 1828.

In opposition to this original right, possessed by the undisputed occupants of every country; to this recognition of that right, which is evidenced by our history, in every change through which we have passed; is placed the charters granted by the monarch of a distant and distinct region, parcelling out a territory in possession of others whom he could not remove and did not attempt to remove, and the cession made of his claims by the treaty of peace.

The actual state of things at the time, and all history since, explain these charters; and the king of Great Britain, at the treaty of peace, could cede only what belonged to his crown. These newly asserted titles can derive no aid from the articles so often repeated in Indian treaties; extending to them, first, the protection of Great Britain, and afterwards that of the United States. These articles are associated with others, recognizing their title to self government. The very fact of repeated treaties with them recognizes it; and the settled doctrine of the law of nations is, that a weaker power does not surrender its independence—its right to self government, by associating with a stronger, and taking its protection. A weak state, in order to provide for its safety, may place itself under the protection of one more powerful, without stripping itself of the right of government, and ceasing to be a state. Examples of this kind are not wanting in Europe. "Tributary and feudatory states," says Vattel, "do not thereby cease to be sovereign and independent states, so long as self government and sovereign and independent authority are left in the administration of the state." At the present day, more than one state may be considered as holding its right of self government under the guarantee and protection of one or more allies.

The Cherokee nation, then, is a distinct community occupying its own territory, with boundaries accurately described, in which the laws of Georgia can have no force, and which the citizens of Georgia have no right to enter, but with the assent of the Cherokees themselves, or in conformity with treaties, and with the acts of congress. The whole intercourse between the United States and this nation, is, by our constitution and laws, vested in the government of the United States.

The act of the state of Georgia, under which the plaintiff in error was prosecuted, is consequently void, and the judgment a nullity. Can this court revise, and reverse it?

If the objection to the system of legislation, lately adopted by the legislature of Georgia, in relation to the Cherokee nation, was confined to its extra-territorial operation, the objection, though complete, so far as respected mere right, would give this court no power over the subject. But it goes much further. If the review which has been taken be correct, and we think it is, the acts of Georgia are repugnant to the constitution, laws, and treaties of the United States.

They interfere forcibly with the relations established between the United States and the Cherokee nation, the regulation of which, according to the settled principles of our constitution, are committed exclusively to the government of the union.

They are in direct hostility with treaties, repeated in a succession of years, which mark out the boundary that separates the Cherokee country from Georgia; guaranty to them all the land within their boundary; solemnly pledge the faith of the United States to restrain their citizens from trespassing on it; and recognize the pre-existing power of the nation to govern itself.

They are in equal hostility with the acts of congress for regulating this intercourse, and giving effect to the treaties.

The forcible seizure and abduction of the plaintiff in error, who was residing in the nation with its permission, and by authority of the president of the United States, is also a violation of the acts which authorise the chief magistrate to exercise this authority.

Will these powerful considerations avail the plaintiff in error? We think they will. He was seized, and forcibly carried away, while under guardianship of treaties guarantying the country in which he resided, and taking it under the protection of the United States. He was seized while performing, under the sanction of the chief magistrate of the union, those duties which the humane policy adopted by congress had recommended. He was apprehended, tried, and condemned, under colour of a law which has been shown to be repugnant to the constitution, laws, and treaties of the United States. Had a judgment, liable to the same objections, been rendered for property, none would question the jurisdiction of this court. It cannot be less clear when the judgment affects personal liberty, and inflicts disgraceful punishment, if punishment could disgrace when inflicted on innocence. The plaintiff in error is not less interested in the operation of this unconstitutional law than if it affected his property. He is not less entitled to the protection of the constitution, laws, and treaties of his country....

It is the opinion of this court that the judgment of the superior court for the county of Gwinnett, in the state of Georgia, condemning Samuel A. Worcester to hard labour, in the penitentiary of the state of Georgia, for four years, was pronounced by that court under colour of a law which is void, as being repugnant to the constitution, treaties, and laws of the United States, and ought, therefore, to be reversed and annulled.

Source: 31 U.S. (6 Peters) 515 (1832).

"South Carolina Exposition" (1828)

John C. Calhoun

The Tariff of 1828, known in South Carolina as the "Tariff of Abominations," led southern extremists to question whether they could maintain their economic interests within the Union. States' rights advocates embraced John C. Calhoun's theory of state sovereignty and nullification, delineated in his essay, "South Carolina Exposition." In this essay, Calhoun argued that a state could nullify a federal law if the law was deemed to be injurious to its welfare.

Through the first five decades of the nineteenth century, South Carolina remained trapped in a colonial economy. Colonies produce raw materials for the "mother country" to turn into finished products. This situation, which helped drive the colonies to war with Great Britain, was exactly replicated in the antebellum South. The state grew cotton, but manufacturers in other states turned it into cloth. South Carolina farmers could not dictate the price their raw cotton fetched, nor could they control the price of their own cotton when they bought it back in the form of cloth. The more populated and industrialized northern states pushed tariffs through Congress designed to protect northern manufacture from foreign competition. These tariffs drove up the prices consumers paid for products such as clothing.

Resolved, That it is expedient to protest against the unconstitutionality and oppressive operation of the system of protecting duties, and to have such protest entered on the Journals of the Senate of the United States—Also, to make a public exposition of our wrongs, and of the remedies within our power, to be communicated to our sister States, with a request that they will co-operate with this State in procuring a repeal of the Tariff for protection, and an abandonment of the principle; and if the repeal be not procured, that they will co-operate in such measures as may be necessary for arresting the evil....

The Special Committee, to whom the above Resolution was referred, beg leave to report the following Exposition and Protest—

Exposition

The General Government is of specific powers, and it can rightfully exercise only the powers expressly granted, and those that may be "necessary and proper" to carry them into effect; all others being reserved expressly to the States, or to the people. It results necessarily that those who claim to exercise a power under the Constitution, are bound to shew that it is expressly granted, or that it is necessary and proper as a means to some of the granted powers. The advocates of the Tariff have offered no such proof. It is true, that the third section of the first article of the constitution of the United States authorizes Congress to lay and collect an impost duty, but it is granted as a tax power, for the sole purpose of revenue; a power in its nature essentially different from that of imposing protective or prohibitory duties....

The committee feel, on entering on this branch of the subject, the painful character of the duty they must perform. They would desire never to speak of our country, as far as the action of the general government is concerned, but as one great whole, having a common interest, which all the parts ought zealously to promote. Previously to the adoption of the Tariff system, such was the unanimous feeling of this State; but in speaking of its operation, it will be impossible to avoid the discussion of sectional interest, and the use of sectional language. On its authors, and not on us, who are compelled to adopt this course in self-defence, by injustice and oppression of their measures—be the censure. So partial are the effects of the system, that its burdens are exclusively on one side and its benefits on the other. It imposes on the agricultural interest of the South, including the South West, and that portion of the commerce and navigation engaged in foreign trade, the burden not only of sustaining the system itself, but that also of sustaining government....

If there be a political proposition universally true, one which springs directly from the nature of man, and is independent of circumstances, it is, that irresponsible power is inconsistent with liberty and must corrupt those who exercise it. On this great principle our political system rests. We consider all powers as delegated from the people, and to be controlled by those who are interested in their just proper exercise; and our governments, both state and general, are but a system of judicious contrivances to bring this fundamental principle into fair practical operation. Among the most permanent of these is the responsibility of representatives to their constituents, through frequent periodical elections, in order to enforce a faithful performance of their delegated trust. Without such a check on their powers, however clearly they may be defined and distinctly prescribed, our liberty would be but a mockery. The government, instead of being devoted to the general good, would speedily become but the instrument to aggrandize those who might be intrusted with its administration. On the other hand, if laws were uniform in their operation; if that which imposed a burden on one, imposed it alike on all; or that which acted beneficially for one, should act so for all, the responsibility of representatives to their constituents, would alone be sufficient to guard against abuse and tyranny, provided the people be sufficiently intelligent to understand their interests, and the motives and conduct of their public agents....

Our system then consists of two distinct and independent sovereignties. The general powers, expressly delegated to the general government, are subject to its sole and separate control, and the States cannot, without violating the constitution, interpose their authority to check, or in any manner to counteract its movements, so long as they are confined to its proper sphere; so also the peculiar and local powers reserved to the States are subject to their exclusive control, nor can the general government interfere, in any manner, with them, without violating the constitution....

Universal experience, in all ages and countries...teaches that power can only be met by power and not by reason and justice, and that all restrictions on authority, unsustained by an equal antagonist power, must forever prove wholly insufficient in practice. Such also has been the decisive proof of our own short experience. From the beginning, a great and powerful minority gave every force of which it was susceptible, to construction, as a means of restraining a majority of Congress to the exercise of its proper powers; and though that original minority, through the force of circumstances, has had the advantage of becoming a majority, and to possess, in consequence, the administration of the general government, during the greater portion of its existence, yet we this day witness, under these most favourable circumstances, an extension of the powers of the general government, in spite of mere construction, to a point so extreme as to leave few powers to the States worth possessing. In fact, that very power of construction, on which reliance is placed to preserve the rights of the States, has been wielded, as it ever will and must be, if not checked, to destory those rights. If the minority has a right to select *its* rule of construction, a majority will exercise the same, but with this striking difference, that the power of the former will be a mere nullity, against that of the latter. But that protection, which the minor interests ever fails to find in any technical system of construction, where alone in practice it has heretofore been sought, it may find in the reserved rights of the States themselves, if they be properly called into action; and there only will it ever be found of sufficient efficacy. The constitutional power to protect their rights as members of the confederacy, results, necessarily, by the most simple and demonstrable arguments, from the very nature of the relation subsisting between the States and general government. If it be conceded, as it must by every one who is the least conversant with our institutions, that the sovereign power is divided between the States and general government, and that the former hold their reserved rights, in the same sovereign capacity, which the latter does its delegated rights; it will be impossible to deny to the States the right of deciding on the infraction of their rights, and the proper remedy to be applied for the correction.... the existence of the right of judging their powers, clearly established from the sovereignty of the States, as clearly implies a veto, or controul on the action of the general government, on contested points of authority; and this very controul is the remedy, which the constitution has provided to prevent the encroachment of the general government on the reserved rights of the States....

Source: Thomas Cooper, ed., *The Statutes at Large of South Carolina* (Columbia, 1836), 1:248, 249, 260, 263–264.

South Carolina Ordinance of Nullification (1832)

In South Carolina, northern economic exploitation seemed intolerable. In 1832, the "Nullies" captured the South Carolina legislature, which then called for a convention to discuss the tariff issue. Taking action on Calhoun's theory, the convention adopted an ordinance declaring the tariff of 1832 to be null and void, prohibited the federal government from collecting tariff revenues within the state, and authorized the raising of an army.

AN ORDINANCE TO NULLIFY CERTAIN ACTS OF THE CONGRESS OF THE UNITED STATES, PURPORTING TO BE LAWS LAYING DUTIES AND IMPOSTS ON THE IMPORTATION OF FOREIGN COMMODITIES.

Whereas, the Congress of the United States, by various acts, purporting to be acts laying duties and imposts on foreign imports, but in reality intended for the protection of domestic manufactures, and the giving of bounties to classes and individuals engaged in particular employments, at the expense and to the injury and oppression of other classes and individuals, and by wholly exempting from taxation certain foreign commodities, such as are not produced or manufactured in the United States, to afford a pretext for imposing higher and excessive duties on articles similar to those intended to be protected, hath exceeded its just powers under the Constitution, which confers on it no authority to afford such protection, and hath violated the true meaning and intent of the Constitution, which provides for equality in imposing the burdens of taxation upon the several States and portions of the Confederacy: *And whereas,* the said Congress, exceeding its just power to impose taxes and collect revenue for the purpose of effecting and accomplishing the specific objects and purposes which the Constitution of the United States authorizes it to effect and accomplish, hath raised and collected unnecessary revenue, for objects unauthorized by the constitution.

We, therefore, the people of the State of South Carolina in Convention assembled, do Declare and Ordain, and it is hereby Declared and Ordained, That the several acts and parts of acts of the Congress of the United States, purporting to be laws for the imposing of duties and imposts on the importation of foreign commodities, and now having actual operation and effect within the United States, and, more especially, an act entitled "an act in alteration of the several acts imposing duties on imports," approved on the nineteenth day of May, one thousand eight hundred and twenty-eight, and also an act entitled "an act to alter and amend the several acts imposing duties on imports," approved on the fourteenth day of July, one thousand eight hundred and thirty-two, are unauthorized by the Constitution of the United States, and violate the true meaning and intent thereof, and are null, void, and no law, nor binding upon this State, its officers, or citizens; and all promises, contracts and obligations made or entered into, or to be made or entered into, with the purpose to secure the duties imposed by the said acts, and all judicial proceedings which shall be hereafter had in affirmance thereof, are and shall be held utterly null and void....

And we, the People of South Carolina, to the end that it may be fully understood by the Government of the United States, and the People of the co-States, that we are determined to maintain this, our ordinance and declaration, at every hazard, *Do further declare,* that we will not submit to the application of force on the part of the Federal Government, to reduce this State to obedience; but that we will consider the passage, by Congress, of any act authorizing the employment of any military or naval force against the State of South Carolina, her constituted authorities or citizens, or any act abolishing or closing the ports of this State, or any of them, or otherwise obstructing the free ingress or egress of vessels, to and from the said ports, or any other act, on the part of the federal government to coerce this State, shut up her ports, destroy or harass her commerce, or to enforce the acts hereby declared to be null and void, otherwise than through the civil tribunals of the country, as inconsistent with the longer continuance of South Carolina in the Union: and that the People of this State will thenceforth hold themselves absolved from all further obligation to maintain or preserve their political connection with the people of the other States, and will forthwith proceed to organize a separate Government, and do all other acts and things which sovereign and independent States may of right do.

Source: Thomas Cooper, ed., *The Statutes at Large of South Carolina* (Columbia, 1836), 1:329-231.

Veto of the Bank Bill (1832)

Andrew Jackson

In 1791, President George Washington signed into law a bill passed by Congress creating the First Bank of the United States. This new law represented the fervent hopes of America's most passionate nationalists. The Bank, Alexander Hamilton and others expected, would centralize control of the currency, allowing the United States to become a superpower. Hamilton's political opponents disliked the Bank, believing it unconstitutional. In 1811, when the 1791 charter expired, Thomas Jefferson's supporters controlled the Congress and the White House. The Bank died when Congress failed to renew its charter.

In 1816, Congress chartered a new Bank of the United States. In 1823, the brilliant and handsome Nicholas Biddle took charge of the Bank as its president. Under Biddle's leadership, the Second Bank of the United States flourished, doing seventy million dollars of business each year and maintaining branches in twenty-nine cities. The Bank printed its own money and circulated twenty-one million dollars in bank notes. Within five years, Biddle turned the Bank into a financial behemoth.

The charter of the Second Bank of the United States was due to expire in 1836, but friends of the Bank petitioned Congress for early renewal in 1832. Supporters of the Bank believed – quite wrongly – that President Jackson would be less likely to oppose the renewal in an election year. Congress passed the renewal legislation. Because so many regarded the Bank of the United States to be a tool of special privilege, Jackson's veto of the bank bill was popular with much of the nation. He made a demagogic attack on foreigners and staked out a class argument against the rich and the powerful. His veto message then asked voters for a mandate – by taking a strong position in an election year, Jackson could claim, after he won the election, that most voters supported his position. He could then move boldly to destroy the Bank and put the treasury of the United States in state banks. Jackson, in this case, acted for states' rights.

July 10, 1832

To the Senate:

The present corporate body, denominated the president, directors, and company of the Bank of the United States, will have existed at the time this act is intended to take effect twenty years. It enjoys an exclusive privilege of banking under the authority of the

General Government, a monopoly of its favor and support, and, as necessary consequence, almost a monopoly of the foreign and domestic exchange. The powers, privileges, and favors bestowed upon it in the original charter, by increasing the value of the stock far above its par value, operated as a gratuity of many millions of the stockholders....

Every monopoly and all exclusive privileges are granted at the expense of the public, which ought to receive a fair equivalent. The many millions which this act proposes to bestow in the stockholders of the existing bank must come directly out of the earnings of the American people....

It is maintained by the advocates of the bank that its constitutionality in all its features ought to be considered as settled by precedent and by the decision of the Supreme Court. To this conclusion I can not assent. Mere precedent is a dangerous source of authority, and should not be regarded as deciding questions of constitutional power except where the acquiescence of the people and the States can be considered as well settled. So far from this being the case on this subject, an argument against the bank might be based on precedent. One Congress, in 1791, decided in favor of a bank; another, in 1811, decided against it. One Congress, in 1815, decided against a bank; another, in 1816, decided in its favor. Prior to the present Congress, therefore, the precedents drawn from that source were equal. If we resort to the States, the expressions of the legislative, judicial, and executive opinions against the bank have been probably to those in its favor as 4 to 1. There is nothing in precedent, therefore, which, if its authority were admitted, ought to weigh in favor of the act before me.

If the opinion of the Supreme Court covered the whole ground of this act, it ought not to control the coordinate authorities of this Government. The Congress, the Executive, and the Court must each for itself be guided by its own opinion of the Constitution. Each public officer who takes an oath to support the Constitution swears that he will support it as he understands it, and not as it is understood by others. It is as much the duty of the House of Representatives, of the Senate, and of the President to decide upon the constitutionality of any bill or resolution which may be presented to them for passage or approval as it is of the supreme judges when it may be brought before them for judicial decision. The opinion of the judges has no more authority over Congress than the opinion of Congress has over the judges, and on that point the President is independent of both. The authority of the Supreme Court must not, therefore, be permitted to control the Congress or the Executive when acting in their legislative capacities, but to have only such influence as the force of their reasoning may deserve....

A bank is constitutional, but it is the province of the Legislature to determine whether this or that particular power, privilege, or exemption is "necessary and proper" to enable the bank to discharge its duties to the Government, and from their decision there is no appeal to the courts of justice. Under the decision of the Supreme Court, therefore, it is the exclusive province of Congress and the President to decide whether the particular features of this act are *necessary* and *proper* in order to enable the bank to perform conveniently and efficiently the public duties assigned to it as a fiscal agent, and therefore constitutional, or *unnecessary* and *improper*, and therefore unconstitutional....

This act authorizes and encourages transfers of stock to foreigners and grants them an exemption from all State and national taxation. So far from being "*necessary and proper*" that the bank should possess this power to make it a safe and efficient agent of the Government in its fiscal operations, it is calculated to convert the Bank of the United States into a foreign bank, to impoverish our people in time of peace, to disseminate a foreign influence through every section of the Republic, and in war to endanger our independence....

The Government of the United States have no constitutional power to purchase lands within the States except "for the erection of forts, magazines, arsenals, dockyards, and other needful buildings," and even for these objects only "by consent of the legislature of the State in which the same shall be." By making themselves stockholders in the bank and granting to the corporation the power to purchase lands for other purposes they assume a power not granted in the Constitution and grant to others what they do not themselves possess...it is not *proper* that Congress should thus enlarge the powers delegated to them in the Constitution....

The Government is the only "*proper*" judge where its agents should reside and keep their offices, because it best knows where their presence will be "*necessary*." It can not, therefore, be "*necessary*" or "*proper*" to authorize the bank to locate branches where it pleases to perform the public service....

It can not be *necessary* to the character of the bank as a fiscal agent of the Government that its private business should be exempted from that taxation to which all the State banks are liable, nor can I conceive it "*proper*" that the substantive and most essential powers reserved by the States shall be thus attacked and annihilated as a means of executing the powers delegated to the General Government....

It is to be regretted that the rich and powerful to often bend the acts of government to their selfish purposes. Distinctions in society will always exist under every just government. Equality of talents, of education, or of wealth can not be produced by human institutions. In the full enjoyment of the gifts of Heaven and the fruits of superior industry, economy, and virtue, every man is equally entitled to protection by law; but when the laws undertake to add to these natural and just advantages artificial distinctions, to grant titles, gratuities, and exclusive privileges, to make the rich richer and the potent more powerful, the humble members of society—the farmers, mechanics, and laborers—who have neither the time nor the means of securing like favors to themselves, have a right to complain of the injustice of their Government. There are no necessary evils in government. Its evils exist only in its abuses. If it would confine itself to equal protection, and, as Heaven does its rains, shower its favors alike on the high and the low, the rich and the poor, it would be an unqualified blessing. In the act before me there seems to be a[n]...unnecessary departure from these just principle....

I have now done my duty to my country. If sustained by my fellow citizens, I shall be grateful and happy; if not, I shall find in the motives which impel me ample grounds for contentment and peace....

Source: James D. Richardson, comp., *A Compilation of the Messages and Papers of the Presidents* (New York, 1897), 3:1139, 1140, 1144–1145, 1146, 1147–1148, 1151, 1153, 1154.

Seneca Falls Declaration (1848)

In 1848, the tiny town of Seneca Falls, New York, witnessed the first convention devoted to the advancement of women's rights. One of the convention's organizers was Elizabeth Cady Stanton, who along with her husband, Henry Stanton, had been active in the American Antislavery Society. Some had begun to argue that the emancipation of slaves and the emancipation of women represented two sides of the same ideological coin, and agitation on behalf of both causes, therefore, should be linked. Others disagreed, countering that expanding the antislavery movement's scope to include women's rights would merely dilute their message. At the convention, Stanton introduced a "Declaration of Sentiments" which outlined a platform of women's rights issues. In modeling this document after the Declaration of Independence, Stanton emphasized her belief that women were entitled to the same natural and inalienable rights enjoyed by men. She also attacked the Common Law notion, as stated by Blackstone, that married women were civilly "dead," having no independent right to property.

"Declaration of Sentiments"

When, in the course of human events, it becomes necessary for one portion of the family of man to assume among the people of the earth a position different from that which they have hitherto occupied, but one to which the laws of nature and of nature's God entitle them, a decent respect to the opinions of mankind requires that they should declare the causes that impel them to such a course.

We hold these truths to be self-evident: that all men and women are created equal; that they are endowed by their Creator with certain inalienable rights, that among these are life, liberty, and the pursuit of happiness; that to secure these rights governments are instituted, deriving their just powers from the consent of the governed. Whenever any form of government becomes destructive of these ends, it is the right of those who suffer from it to refuse allegiance to it, and to insist upon the institution of a new government, laying its foundation on such principles, and organizing its powers in such form as to them shall seem most likely to effect their safety and happiness. Prudence, indeed, will dictate that governments long established should not be changed for light and transient causes; and accordingly, all experience hath shown that mankind are more disposed to suffer, while evils are sufferable, than to right themselves by abolishing the forms to which they were accustomed. But when a long train of abuses and usurpations, pursuing invariably the same object evinces a design to reduce them under absolute despotism, it is their duty to throw off such government, and to provide new guards for their future security. Such has been the patient sufferance of the women under this government, and such is now the necessity which constrains them to demand the equal station to which they are entitled.

The history of mankind is a history of repeated injuries and usurpations on the part of man toward woman, having in direct object the establishment of an absolute tyranny over her. To prove this, let facts be submitted to a candid world.

He has never permitted her to exercise her inalienable right to the elective franchise.

He has compelled her to submit to laws, in the formation of which she had no voice.

He has withheld from her rights which are given to the most ignorant and degraded men—both natives and foreigners.

Having deprived her of this first right of a citizen, the elective franchise, thereby leaving her without representation in the halls of legislation, he has oppressed her on all sides.

He has made her, if married, in the eye of the law, civilly dead.

He has taken from her all right in property, even to the wages she earns.

He has made her, morally, an irresponsible being, as she can commit many crimes with impunity, provided they be done in the presence of her husband. In the covenant of marriage, she is compelled to promise obedience to her husband, he becoming, to all intents and purposes, her master—the law giving him power to deprive her of her liberty, and to administer chastisement.

He has so framed the laws of divorce, as to what shall be the proper causes; and in case of separation, to whom the guardianship of the children shall be given; as to be wholly regardless of the happiness of women—the law, in all cases, going upon a false supposition of the supremacy of man, and giving all power into his hands.

After depriving her of all rights as a married woman, if single and the owner of property, he has taxed her to support a government which recognizes her only when her property can be made profitable to it.

He has monopolized nearly all the profitable employments, and from those she is permitted to follow, she receives but a scanty remuneration. He closes against her all the avenues to wealth and distinction, which he considers most honorable to himself. As a teacher of theology, medicine, or law, she is not known.

He has denied her the facilities for obtaining a thorough education—all colleges being closed against her.

He allows her in Church, as well as State, but a subordinate position, claiming Apostolic authority for her exclusion from the ministry, and, with some exceptions, from any public participation in the affairs of the Church.

He has created a false public sentiment, by giving to the world a different code of morals for men and women, by which moral delinquencies which exclude women from society, are not only tolerated but deemed of little account in man.

He has usurped the prerogative of Jehovah himself, claiming it as his right to assign for her a sphere of action, when that belongs to her conscience and to her God.

He has endeavored, in every way that he could, to destroy her confidence in her own powers, to lessen her self-respect, and to make her willing to lead a dependent and abject life.

Now, in view of this entire disfranchisement of one-half the people of this country, their social and religious degradation,--in view of the unjust laws above mentioned, and because women do feel themselves aggrieved, oppressed, and fraudulently deprived of their most sacred rights, we insist that they have immediate admission to all the rights and privileges which belong to them as citizens of the United States.

In entering upon the great work before us, we anticipate no small amount of misconception, misrepresentation, and ridicule; but we shall use every instrumentality within our power to effect our object. We shall employ agents, circulate tracts, petition the State and National legislatures, and endeavor to enlist the pulpit and the press in our behalf. We hope this Convention will be followed by a series of Conventions, embracing every part of the country.

Source: Elizabeth Cady Stanton, Susan B. Anthony, and Matilda Joslyn Gage, eds., *History of Woman Suffrage*, 2 vols. (New York, 1881), 1:70–71.

Charles River Bridge v. Warren Bridge (1837)

John Marshall died July 6, 1835. It had been Marshall's hope that a Whig president would nominate Justice Joseph Story to replace him as chief justice. Had this happened, the chief justice might have continued along lines laid out by Marshall, expanding protection of vested interests in contract cases. President Andrew Jackson, however, selected Roger B. Taney.

In Charles River Bridge v. Warren Bridge, *Taney confronted contract issues similar to those decided by Marshall in* Dartmouth College v. Woodward. *The decision highlights the differences between Taney and Marshall. The bridge case involved a Massachusetts legislative charter enacted in 1785, creating the Charles River Bridge Company. The 1785 charter, extended in 1792, allowed the company to build a bridge and charge tolls. Nothing in the charter explicitly gave the Charles River Bridge Company a monopoly, but its lawyers ar-*

gued that a monopoly was implied. What good did it do to set up a toll bridge if someone could build a free bridge right next to it?

In 1828 the legislature authorized a new bridge not far from the Charles River Bridge. The new bridge company would charge tolls but only until it met construction costs. Taney found in favor of the new bridge, arguing that failing to allow the new construction would discourage enterprise and threaten progress. Taney's decision seemed very Jacksonian: insisting the people's rights must triumph over vested interests. Supreme Court decisions must serve the public, not abstract legal doctrine. Taney urged a strict construction of the contract; there would be nothing implicit in his reading. A corporate charter is not the same as a constitution, but Taney's strict construction did echo Thomas Jefferson's strict construction of the Constitution. And when he claimed to find implied powers in the 1785 charter, Joseph Story sounded like Alexander Hamilton. Venture capital triumphed over vested interests and monopolies. Taney also showed that his Court would not distrust state legislatures as Marshall had.

Taney cleverly disarmed his critics by building his Jacksonian decision on precedent. He made an 1830 Marshall Court decision entitled Providence Bank v. Billings *the pivot point of his opinion. Marshall had rejected the idea that a state bank charter implied exemption from state taxation. Taney extended this reasoning to reject the idea that a state charter implied any powers at all. Time and again Taney disguised his innovation by claiming merely to be following precedent.*

MR. CHIEF JUSTICE TANEY delivered the opinion of the Court.

... [T]he act of the legislature of Massachusetts, of 1785,... incorporated [the plaintiffs] by the name of "The Proprietors of the Charles River Bridge;" and it is here, and in the law of 1792, prolonging their charter, that we must look for the extent and nature of the franchise conferred upon the plaintiffs....

...Can any good reason be assigned for...introducing a new and adverse rule of construction in favour of corporations, while we adopt and adhere to the rules of construction known to the English common law, in every other case, without exception? We think not; and it would be a singular spectacle, if, while the courts in England are restraining, within the strictest limits, the spirit of monopoly, and exclusive privileges in nature of monopolies, and confining corporations to the privileges plainly given to them in their charter; the courts of this country should be found enlarging these privileges by implication; and construing a statute more unfavourably to the public, and to the rights of the community, than would be done in a like case in an English court of justice....

...[T]he charter of 1785, to the proprietors of the Charles River Bridge...is in the usual form, and the privileges such as are commonly given to corporations of that kind. It confers on them the ordinary faculties of a corporation, for the purpose of building the bridge; and establishes certain rates of toll, which the company are authorized to take. This is the whole grant. There is no exclusive privilege given to them over the waters of Charles river, above or below their bridge. No right to erect another bridge themselves, nor to prevent other persons from erecting one. No engagement from the state, that another shall not be erected; and no undertaking not to sanction competition, nor to make improvements that may diminish the amount of its income. Upon all these subjects the charter is silent; and nothing is said in it about a line of travel, so much insisted on in the argument, in which they are to have exclusive privileges. No words are used, from which an intention to grant any of these rights can be inferred. If the plaintiff is entitled to them, it must be implied, simply, from the nature of the grant; and cannot be inferred from the words by which the grant is made.

The relative position of the Warren Bridge has already been described. It does not interrupt the passage over the Charles River Bridge, nor make the way to it or from it less convenient. None of the faculties or franchises granted to that corporation, have been revoked by the legislature; and its right to take the tolls granted by the charter remains unaltered. In short, all the franchises and rights of property enumerated in the charter, and there mentioned to have been granted to it, remain unimpaired. But its income is destroyed by the Warren Bridge; which, being free, draws off the passengers and property which would have gone over it, and renders their franchise of no value. This is the gist of the complaint. For it is not pretended, that the erection of the Warren Bridge would have done them any injury, or in any degree affected their right of property; if it had not diminished the amount of their tolls. In order then to entitle themselves to relief, it is necessary to show, that the legislature contracted not to do the act of which they complain; and that they impaired, or in other words, violated that contract by the erection of the Warren Bridge.

The inquiry then is, does the charter contain such a contract on the part of the state? Is there any such stipulation to be found in that instrument? It must be admitted on all hands, that there is none—no words that even relate to another bridge, or to the diminution of their tolls, or to the line of travel. If a contract on that subject can be gathered from the charter, it must be by implication; and cannot be found in the words used. Can such an agreement be implied? The rule of construction before stated is an answer to the question. In charters of this description, no rights are taken from the public, or given to the corporation, beyond those which the words of the charter, by their natural and proper construction, purport to convey. There are no words which import such a contract as the plaintiffs in error contend for, and none can be implied; and the same answer must be given to them that was given by this Court to the Providence Bank. The whole community are interested in this inquiry, and they have a right to require that the power of promoting their comfort and convenience, and of advancing the public prosperity, by providing safe, convenient, and cheap ways for the transportation of produce, and the purposes of travel, shall not be construed to have been surrendered or diminished by the state; unless it shall appear by plain words, that it was intended to be done.

Indeed, the practice and usage of almost every state in the Union, old enough to have commenced the work of internal improvement, is opposed to the doctrine contended for on the part of the plaintiffs in error. Turnpike roads have been made in succession, on the same line of travel; the later ones interfering materially with the profits of the first. These corporations have, in some instances, been utterly ruined by the introduction of newer and better modes of transportation, and traveling. In some cases, rail roads have rendered the turnpike roads on the same line of travel so entirely useless, that the franchise of the turnpike corporation is not worth preserving. Yet in none of these cases have the corporations supposed that their privileges were invaded, or any contract violated on the part of the state. Amid the multitude of cases which have occurred, and have been daily occurring for the last forty or fifty years, this is the first instance in which such an implied contract has been contended for, and this Court called upon to infer it from an ordinary act of incorporation, containing nothing more than the usual stipulations and provisions to be found in every such law. The absence of any such controversy, when there must have been so many occasions to give rise to it, proves that neither states, nor individuals, nor corporations, ever imagined that such a contract could be implied from such charters. It shows that the men who voted for these laws, never imagined that they were forming such a contract; and if we maintain that they have made it, we must create it by a legal fiction, in opposition to the truth of the fact, and the obvious intention of the party. We cannot deal thus with the rights reserved to the states; and by legal intendments and mere technical reasoning, take away from them any portion of that power over their own internal police and improvement, which is so necessary to their well being and prosperity.

And what would be the fruits of this doctrine of implied contracts on the part of the states...if it should now be sanctioned by this Court? To what results would it lead us? If it is to be found in the charter to this bridge, the same process of reasoning must discover it, in the various acts which have been passed, within the last forty years, for turnpike companies....If this Court should establish the principles now contended for, what is to become of the numerous rail roads established on the same line of travel with turnpike companies; and which have rendered the franchises of the turnpike corporations of no value? Let it once be understood that such charters carry with them these implied contracts, and give this unknown and undefined property in a line of traveling; and you will soon find the old turnpike corporations awakening from their sleep, and calling upon this Court to put down the improvements which have taken their place. The millions of property which have been invested in rail roads and canals, upon lines of travel which had been before occupied by turnpike corporations, will be put in jeopardy. We shall be thrown back to the improvements of the last century, and obliged to stand still, until the claims of the old turnpike corporations shall be satisfied; and they shall consent to permit these states to avail themselves of the lights of modern science, and to partake of the benefit of those improvements which are now adding to the wealth and prosperity, and the convenience and comfort, of every other part of the civilized world.... This Court are not prepared to sanction principles which must lead to such results....

Some questions, also, of a purely technical character, have been made and argued, as to the form of proceeding and the right to relief. But enough appears on the record to bring out the great question in contest; and it is the interest of all parties concerned, that the real controversy should be settled without further delay: and as the opinion of the Court is pronounced on the main question in dispute here, and disposes of the whole case, it is altogether unnecessary to enter upon the examination of the forms of proceeding, in which the parties have brought it before the Court.

The judgment of the supreme judicial court of the commonwealth of Massachusetts, dismissing the plaintiffs' bill, must, therefore, be affirmed, with costs.

Source: 36 U.S. (11 Peters) 420 (1837).

Passenger Cases (1849)

The question of state power came up again in 1849. The Supreme Court, with Taney dissenting, overturned state laws taxing immigrants in a pair of "kindred cases" argued together that came to be called the Passenger Cases. *The justices did not agree on the precise line between the states' police powers and the Congressional power to control commerce. Five justices agreed that state laws taxing immigrants violated the Constitution. Taney insisted the states had a right to protect their populations from foreign paupers and the diseased. Slavery lurked in the background of this case: as some of the justices feared the federal government might try to interfere with the peculiar institution through the commerce clause.*

MR. JUSTICE MCLEAN delivered the opinion of the Court.

...Is the power of Congress to regulate commerce an exclusive power?

...In the eighth section of the first article of the Constitution it is declared that Congress shall have power "to regulate commerce with foreign nations, and among the several States, and with the Indian tribes."...

A concurrent power in the States to regulate commerce is an anomaly not found in the Constitution. If such power exist, it may be exercised independently of the federal authority.

It does not follow, as is often said, with little accuracy, that, when a State law shall conflict with an act of Congress, the former must yield. On the contrary, except in certain cases named in the Federal Constitution, this is never correct when the act of the State is strictly within its powers....

[T]he argument is, that a State acting in a subordinate capacity, wholly inconsistent with its sovereignty, may regulate foreign commerce until Congress shall act on the same subject; and that the State must then yield to the paramount authority. A jealousy of the federal powers has often been expressed, and an apprehension entertained that they would impair the sovereignty of the States. But this argument degrades the States by making their legislation, to the extent stated, subject to the will of Congress. State powers do not rest upon this basis. Congress can in no respect restrict or enlarge State powers, though they may adopt a State law. State powers are at all times and under all circumstances exercised independently of the general government, and are never declared void or inoperative except when they transcend State jurisdiction. And on the same principle, the Federal authority is void when exercised beyond its constitutional limits....

It has been well remarked, that the regulation of commerce consists as much in negative as in positive action. There is not a

Federal power which has been exerted in all its diversified means of operation. And yet it may have been exercised by Congress, influenced by a judicious policy and the instruction of the people. Is a commercial regulation open to State action because the Federal power has not been exhausted? No ingenuity can provide for every contingency; and if it could, it might not be wise to do so. Shall free goods be taxed by a State because Congress have not taxed them? Or shall a State increase the duty, on the ground that it is too low? Shall passengers, admitted by act of Congress without a tax, be taxed by a State? The supposition of such a power in a State is utterly inconsistent with a commercial power, either paramount or exclusive, in Congress.

That it is inconsistent with the exclusive power will be admitted; but the exercise of a subordinate commercial power by a State is contended for. When this power is exercised, how can it be known that the identical thing has not been duly considered by Congress? And how can Congress, by any legislation, prevent this interference? A practical enforcement of this system, if system it may be called, would overthrow the Federal commercial power.

...The power "to regulate commerce with foreign nations, and among the several States," by the Constitution, is exclusively vested in Congress.

Source: 48 U.S. (7 Howard) 283 (1849).

Cooley v. Board of Wardens (1851)

Cooley v. Board of Wardens *followed the* Passenger Cases, *once again testing local regulation of commerce in the nation's seaports. In this case the Pennsylvania legislature had passed a law that required all ships of a certain size to employ a pilot to guide the ship into dock. A state agency called the Board of Wardens enforced this rule. Cooley argued that the law violated his Constitutional rights in that the state tried to regulate commerce, the exclusive job of Congress. As in the* Passenger Cases, *states' rights clashed with the commerce power. States concerned about controlling their slave populations worried that a precedent allowing the federal government to regulate piloting of ships in Pennsylvania might allow federal regulation of their commerce in slaves.*

In Cooley v. Board of Wardens, *the Court compromised. Some aspects of commerce were local, the Court conceded, and the states enjoyed concurrent power with the federal government. Taney silently went along with a rule – "selective exclusiveness" – that posited fairly limited powers for the states in commerce questions.*

MR. JUSTICE CURTIS delivered the opinion of the court.

...That the power to regulate commerce includes the regulation of navigation, we consider settled. And when we look to the nature of the service performed by pilots, to the relations which that service and its compensations bear to navigation between the several States, and between the ports of the United States and foreign countries, we are brought to the conclusion, that the regulation of the qualifications of pilots, of the modes and times of offering and rendering their services, of the responsibilities which shall rest upon them, of the powers they shall possess, of the compensation they may demand, and of the penalties by which their rights and duties may be enforced, do constitute regulations of navigation, and consequently of commerce, within the just meaning of this clause of the Constitution....

Now, a pilot...is the temporary master charged with the safety of the vessel and cargo, and of the lives of those on board, and intrusted with the command of the crew. He is not only one of the persons engaged in navigation, but he occupies a most important and responsible place among those thus engaged. And if Congress has power to regulate the seamen who assist the pilot in the management of the vessel, a power never denied, we can perceive no valid reason why the pilot should be beyond the reach of the same power....

Nor should it be lost sight of, that this subject of the regulation of pilots and pilotage has an intimate connection with...the general subject of commerce with foreign nations and among the several States, over which it was one main object of the Constitution to create a national control....

It becomes necessary, therefore, to consider whether this law of Pennsylvania, being a regulation of commerce, is valid....

If the States were divested of the power to legislate on this subject by the grant of the commercial power to Congress, it is plain this act could not confer upon them power thus to legislate. If the Constitution excluded the States from making any law regulating commerce, certainly Congress cannot regrant, or in any manner reconvey to the States that power.... The grant of commercial power to Congress does not contain any terms which expressly exclude the States from exercising an authority over its subject-matter. If they are excluded it must be because the nature of the power, thus granted to Congress, requires that a similar authority should not exist in the States. If it were conceded on the one side, that the nature of this power, like that to legislate for the District of Columbia, is absolutely and totally repugnant to the existence of similar power in the States, probably no one would deny that the grant of the power to Congress, as effectually and perfectly excludes the States from all future legislation on the subject, as if express words had been used to exclude them. And on the other hand, if it were admitted that the existence of this power in Congress, like the power of taxation, is compatible with the existence of a similar power in the States, then it would be in conformity with the contemporary exposition of the Constitution, (Federalist, No. 32.) and with the judicial construction, given from time to time by this court, after the most deliberate consideration, to hold that the mere grant of such a power to Congress, did not imply a prohibition on the States to exercise the same power; that it is not the mere existence of such a power, but its exercise by Congress, which may be incompatible with the exercise of the same power by the States, and that the States may legislate in the absence of congressional regulations....

How then can we say, that by the mere grant of power to regulate commerce, the States are deprived of all the power to legislate on this subject, because from the nature of the power the legislation of Congress must be exclusive. This would be to affirm that the nature of the power is in any case, something different from the nature of the subject to which, in such case, the power extends, and that the nature of the power necessarily demands, in all cases, exclusive legislation by Congress, while the nature of one of the subjects of that power, not only does not require such exclusive legislation, but may be best provided for by many different systems enacted by the States, in conformity with the circumstances of the ports within their limits. In construing an instrument designed for the formation of a government, and in determining the extent of one of its important grants of power to legislate, we can make no such distinction between the nature of the power and the nature of the subject on which that power was intended practically to operate, nor consider the grant more extensive by affirming of the power, what is not true of its subject now in question.

It is the opinion of a majority of the court that the mere grant to Congress of the power to regulate commerce, did not deprive the States of power to regulate pilots and that although Congress has legislated on this subject, its legislation manifests an intention ...not to regulate on this subject, but to leave its regulation to the States....

We are of opinion that this State law was enacted by virtue of a power, residing in the State to legislate; that it is not in conflict with any law of Congress; that it does not interfere with any system which Congress has established by making regulations, or by intentionally leaving individuals to their own unrestricted action; that this law is therefore valid, and the judgment of the Supreme Court of Pennsylvania in each case must be affirmed....

Source: 53 U.S. (12 Howard) 299 (1851).

2.

Slavery

Slavery did not often enter federal court. The states managed their enslaved populations—or rather, permitted masters to do so outside the law. The United States Congress passed few laws regarding slavery, and federal courts rarely heard cases involving slaves. After the Revolution, Pennsylvania and other northern states used their power to legislate slave questions to abolish slavery within their borders. Mississippi and other southern states used their power to make and enforce laws designed to perpetuate the institution of slavery.

For a federal system to function successfully, the power holders must respect the jurisdiction of others. The respect one jurisdiction accords another is called "comity" and is required by the Constitution. In concrete terms, comity meant that the northern states should respect the southern states' slave laws. The Constitution expected northern judges, lawyers, and police to aid southerners as they retrieved escaped slaves. What few laws Congress did pass respecting slavery, and the few decisions the Supreme Court did hand down regarding slaves, usually involved comity—especially issues arising when slaves traveled from slavery to "free soil" states.

The breakdown of comity signaled the approach of civil war. As Northerners became more hostile to slavery, their legislatures passed "personal liberty laws" designed to trip up southern slave catchers. The collapse of comity can be traced to two sources. First, the slaveowning states and the non-slaveowning states quarreled over slavery in the West. Second, popular sentimental literature along with lectures of figures like Frederick Douglass increasingly presented slaves as human beings rather than property. This rhetoric did not erase northern racism, but it did allow politicians like Abraham Lincoln and journalists like William Lloyd Garrison to appeal for basic rights for all people, regardless of color.

An Act for the Gradual Abolition of Slavery in Pennsylvania (1780)

Although it did not totally abolish slavery until 1847, Pennsylvania began emancipating its slaves in 1780. The nation's first active anti-slavery society made its headquarters in Philadelphia, and the influential Quakers favored abolition. Despite shared borders with slave states, slaves made up only 5 percent of Pennsylvania's population in 1780. In that year legislator George Bryan pushed through the legislature a gradual emancipation statute, designed to eliminate slavery without inhibiting Pennsylvania's economic growth.

SECTION I. When we contemplate our abhorrence of that condition, to which the arms and tyranny of Great Britain were exerted to reduce us, when we look back upon the variety of dangers to which we have been exposed, and how miraculously our wants in many instances have been supplied and our deliverance wrought, when even hope and human fortitude have become unequal to the conflict, we are unavoidably led to a serious and grateful sense of the manifold blessings, which we have undeservedly received from the hand of that Being from whom every good and perfect gift cometh. Impressed with these ideas, we conceive that it is our duty, and we rejoice that it is in our power, to extend a portion of that freedom to others, which hath been extended to us, and release from that state of thraldom, to which we ourselves were tyrannically doomed, and from which we have now every prospect of being delivered. It is not for us to enquire why, in the creation of mankind, the inhabitants of the several parts of the earth were distinguished by a difference in feature or complexion. It is sufficient to know that all are the work of an Almighty Hand. We find, in the distribution of the human species, that the most fertile as well as the most barren parts of the earth are inhabited by men of complexions different from ours, and from each other, from whence we may reasonably, as well as religiously, infer, that He, who placed them in their various situations, hath extended equally His care and protection to all, and that it becometh not us to counteract His mercies.

We esteem it a peculiar blessing granted to us, that we are enabled this day to add one more step to universal civilization, by removing, as much as possible the sorrows of those, who have lived in undeserved bondage, and from which by the assumed authority of the Kings of Great Britain, no effectual, legal relief could be obtained. Weaned, by a long course of experience from those narrow prejudices and partialities we had imbibed, we find our hearts enlarged with kindness and benevolence towards men of all conditions and nations, and we conceive ourselves at this particular period extraordinarily called upon, by the blessings which we have received, to manifest the sincerity of our profession, and to give a substantial proof of our gratitude.

SECTION II. And whereas the condition of those persons, who have heretofore been denominated negro and mulatto slaves, has been attended with circumstances, which not only deprive them of the common blessings that they were by nature entitled to, but has cast them into the deepest afflictions by an unnatural separation and sale of husband and wife from each other, and from their children, an injury the greatness of which can only be conceived by supposing that we were in the same unhappy case. In justice, therefore, to persons so unhappily circumstanced, and who, having no prospect before them whereon they may rest their sorrows and their hopes, have no reasonable inducement to render that service to society which they otherwise might, and also in grateful commemoration of our own happy deliverance from that state of unconditional submission to which we were doomed by the tyranny of Britain.

SECTION III. Be it enacted and it is hereby enacted by the Representatives of the Freemen of the Commonwealth of Pennsylvania in General Assembly met, and by the authority of the same, That all persons, as well negroes and mulattos as others who shall be born within this state, from and after the passing of this act, shall not be deemed and considered as servants for life, or slaves; and that all servitude for life or slavery of children in consequence of the slavery of their mothers, in the case of all children born within this state from and after the passing of this act as aforesaid, shall be and hereby is utterly taken away, extinguished and forever abolished. . . .

Source: James T. Mitchell and Henry Flanders, comp., *The Statutes at Large of Pennsylvania from 1682 to 1801* (Harrisburg, 1904), 10:67–68.

Fugitive Slave Law (1793)

Slaves could get into federal court if they fled slavery across state lines; however, the Constitution guaranteed slaveowners the right to retrieve runaway slaves. To ease southerners' pursuit of their escaped property, Congress enacted a fugitive slave law. This 1793 law depended on comity – the willingness of northern authorities to cooperate with southern slaveowners and their agents. In this case, the 1793 law expected state judges and magistrates to sanction slave catching; it did not envision a federal police force to aid southern slaveowners in their search for runaway slaves.

An Act respecting fugitives from justice, and persons escaping from the service of their masters.

SECT. 3. *And be it also enacted,* That when a person held to labour in any of the United States, or in either of the territories on the northwest or south of the river Ohio, under the laws thereof, shall escape into any other of the said states or territory, the person to whom such labour or service may be due, his agent or attorney, is hereby empowered to seize or arrest such fugitive from labour, and to take him or her before any judge of the circuit or district courts of the United States, residing or being within the state, or before any magistrate of a county, city or town corporate, wherein such seizure or arrest shall be made, and upon proof to the satisfaction of such judge or magistrate, either by oral testimony or affidavit taken before and certified by a magistrate of any such state or territory, that the person so seized or arrested, doth, under the laws of the state or territory from which he or she fled, owe service or labour to the person claiming him or her, it shall be the duty of such judge or magistrate to give a certificate thereof to such claimant, his agent or attorney, which shall be sufficient warrant for removing the said fugitive from labour, to the state or territory from which he or she fled.

SECT. 4. *And be it further enacted,* That any person who shall knowingly and willingly obstruct or hinder such claimant, his agent or attorney in so seizing or arresting such fugitive from labour, or shall rescue such fugitive from such claimant, his agent or attorney when so arrested pursuant to the authority herein given or declared; or shall harbor or conceal such person after notice that he or she was a fugitive from labour, as aforesaid, shall, for either of the said offences, forfeit and pay the sum of five hundred dollars. Which penalty may be recovered by and for the benefit of such claimant, by action of debt, in any court proper to try the same; saving moreover to the person claiming such labour or service, his right of action for or on account of the said injuries or either of them.

Approved, February 12, 1793.

Source: Richard Peters, ed., *Public Statutes at Large of the United States of America* (Boston, 1845), 1:302–305.

Pennsylvania Personal Liberty Law (1826)

Slaves taken into free territory by their masters sometimes sued in court for their freedom, forcing northern judges to confront slavery. Slavery also entered northern courtrooms when escaped slaves fled to the North. Abolitionists accused slave catchers of kidnapping. Both Pennsylvania and Massachusetts passed anti-kidnap laws before 1787. New York passed its anti-kidnap law in 1808. Other states followed. Some of these states made it a crime to remove any African American from their borders. Others specified that free blacks could not be removed, implying that truly enslaved ones could be.

March 25, 1826

An Act to give effect to the provisions of the constitution of the United States, relative to fugitives from labour, for the protection of free people of colour, and to prevent kidnapping.

SECTION 1. *Be it enacted by the Senate and House of representatives of the Commonwealth of Pennsylvania General Assembly met and it is hereby enacted by the authority of the same,* That if any person or persons shall from and after the passing of this act, by force or violence, take and carry away, or cause to be taken or carried away, and shall by fraud or false pretence, seduce, or cause to be seduced, or shall attempt so to take, carry away, or seduce, any negro or mulatto from any part or parts of this commonwealth, to any other place or places, whatsoever, out of this commonwealth, with a design and intention of selling and disposing of, or of causing to be sold, or of keeping and detaining, or of causing to be kept and detained, such negro or mulatto, as a slave or servant for life, or for any term whatsoever, every such person or persons, his or their aiders and abettors, shall on conviction thereof in any court of this commonwealth, having competent jurisdiction, be deemed guilty of a felony, and shall forfeit and pay, at the discretion of the court passing the sentence, any sum not less than five hundred, nor more than two thousand dollars, one half whereof shall be paid to the person or persons who shall prosecute for the same, and the other half to this commonwealth; and, moreover, shall be sentenced to undergo a servitude for any term or time not less than seven years, nor exceeding twenty-one years, and shall be confined, and kept to hard labour, fed and clothed, in the manner as is directed by the penal laws of this commonwealth for persons convicted of robbery.

SECT. 2. *And be it further enacted by the authority aforesaid,* That if any person or persons shall hereafter knowingly sell, transfer, or assign, or shall knowingly purchase, take a transfer or assignment, of any negro or mulatto, for the purpose of fraudulently removing, exporting, or carrying such negro or mulatto out of this state, with the design or intent by fraud or false pretences of making him or her a slave or servant for life, or for any term, whatsoever, every person so offending shall be deemed guilty of a felony, and on conviction thereof, shall forfeit and pay a fine of not less than five hundred dollars, nor more than two thousand dollars, one half whereof shall be paid to the person or persons who shall prosecute for the same, and the other half to the commonwealth; and, moreover, shall be sentenced at the discretion of the court, to undergo a servitude for any term or time not less than seven years, nor exceeding twenty-one years, and shall be confined, kept to hard labour, fed and clothed in the same manner as is directed by the penal laws of this commonwealth for persons convicted of robbery.

SECT. 3. *And be it further enacted by the authority aforesaid,* That when a person held to labor or service in any of the United States, or in either of the territories thereof, under the laws thereof, shall escape into this commonwealth, the person to whom such labor or service is due, his or her duly authorized agent or attorney, constituted in writing, is hereby authorized to apply to any judge, justice of the peace, or alderman, who on such application, supported by the oath or affirmation of such claimant, or authorized agent or attorney, as aforesaid, that the said fugitive hath escaped from his or her service, or from the service of the person for whom he is duly constituted agent or attorney, shall issue his warrant under his hand and seal, and directed to the sheriff or any constable of the proper city or county, authorizing and empowering said sheriff, or constable, to arrest and seize the said fugitive, who shall be named in said warrant, and to bring said fugitive before a judge of the proper county....

SECT. 4. *And be it further enacted by the authority aforesaid,* That no judge, justice of the peace or alderman, shall issue a warrant, on the application of any agent or attorney, as provided in the said third section, unless the said agent or attorney shall, in addition to his own oath or affirmation, produce the affidavit of the claimant of the fugitive, taken before and certified by a justice of the peace or other magistrate authorized to administer oaths, in the state or territory in which such claimant resides, and accompanied by the certificate of the authority of such justice or other magistrate to administer oaths, signed by the clerk or prothonotary, and authenticated by the seal of a court of record, in such state or territory, which affidavit shall state the said claimant's title to the service of such fugitive, and also the name, age and description of the person of such fugitive....

SECT. 6. *And be it further enacted by the authority aforesaid,* That the said fugitive from labor or service, when so arrested, shall be brought before a judge, as aforesaid, and upon proof, to the satisfaction of such judge, that the person so seized or arrested, doth, under the laws of the state or territory from which he or she fled, owe service or labor to the person claiming him or her, it shall be the duty of such judge to give a certificate thereof, to such claimant, or his or her duly authorized agent or attorney, which shall be sufficient warrant for removing the said fugitive to the state or territory from which he or she fled: *Provided,* That the oath of the owner or owners, or other person interested, shall in no case be received in evidence, before the judge, on the hearing of the case....

SECT. 9. *And be it further enacted by the authority aforesaid,* That no alderman or justice of the peace of this commonwealth, shall have jurisdiction, or take cognizance of the case of any fugitive from labor, from any of the United States or territories, under a certain act of congress, passed on the twelfth day of February, one thousand seven hundred and ninety-three, entitled "An act respecting fugitives from justice, and persons escaping from the service of their masters;" nor shall any alderman or justice of the peace of this commonwealth, issue or grant any certificate or warrant of removal, of any such fugitive from labor, as aforesaid, except in the manner and to the effect provided in the third section of this act.

Source: *Acts of the General Assembly of the Commonwealth of Pennsylvania* (Harrisburg, 1826), 150–154.

Commonwealth v. Aves (1836)

One of the most famous cases involving a slave in transit through free territory came from England: Somerset v. Stewart, *1772. James Somerset was a slave brought to England from Jamaica in 1769. England's Lord Mansfield ruled Somerset free, making a Common Law precedent that slaves reaching free soil should be freed.*

In 1836 Lemuel Shaw, chief justice of the Massachusetts state supreme court, had to rule on a similar case. Mrs. Samuel Slater visited her father, Thomas Aves, in Boston with her six-year-old enslaved child named Med. Abolitionist lawyers sued on behalf of Med, claiming the Somerset *precedent could be applied in Massachusetts. Eager to free any slave he could, Shaw found a "loophole"in the fugitive slave clause of the Constitution. Brought to Massachusetts by her owner, the child Med was no fugitive.*

MR. CHIEF JUSTICE SHAW delivered the opinion of the Court.

The question now before the Court arises upon a return to a habeas corpus, originally issued in vacation by Mr. Justice Wilde, for the purpose of bringing up the person of a colored child named Med, and instituting a legal inquiry into the fact of her detention, and the causes for which she was detained....

The precise question presented by the claim of the respondent is, whether a citizen of any one of the United States, where negro slavery is established by law, coming into this State, for any temporary purpose of business or pleasure, staying some time, but not acquiring a domicile here, who brings a slave with him as a personal attendant, may restrain such slave of his liberty during his continuance here, and convey him out of this State on his return, against his consent....

...[W]e may assume that the law of this State is analogous to the law of England, in this respect; that while slavery is considered as unlawful and inadmissible in both, and this because contrary to natural right and to laws designed for the security of personal liberty, yet in both, the existence of slavery in other countries is recognized, and the claims of foreigners, growing out of that condition, are, to a certain extent, respected. Almost the only reason assigned by Lord Mansfield in *Sommerset's case* was, that slavery is of such a nature, that it is incapable, of being introduced on any reasons moral or political, but only by positive law; and, it is so odious, that nothing can be suffered to support it but positive law....

[E]ach independent community, in its intercourse with every other, is bound to act on the principle, that such other country has a full and perfect authority to make such laws for the government of its own subjects, as its own judgment shall dictate and its own conscience approve, provided the same are consistent with the law of nations; and no independent community has any right to interfere with the acts or conduct of another state, within the territories of such state, or on the high seas, which each has an equal right to use and occupy; and that each sovereign state, governed by its own laws, although competent and well authorized to make such laws as it may think most expedient to the extent of its own territorial limits, and for the government of its own subjects, yet beyond those limits, and over those who are not her own subjects, has no authority to enforce her own laws, or to treat the laws of other states as void, although contrary to its own views of morality.

This view seems consistent with most of the leading cases on the subject.

Somerset's case, 20 Howel's State Trials, 1, as already cited, decides that slavery, being odious and against natural right, cannot exist, except by force of positive law. But it clearly admits, that it may exist by force of positive law. And it may be remarked, that by positive law, in this connection, may be as well understood customary law as the enactment of a statute; and the word is used to designate rules established by tacit acquiescence or by the legislative act of any state, and which derive their force and authority from such acquiescence or enactment, and not because they are the dictates of natural justice, and as such of universal obligation....

The conclusion to which we come from this view of the law is this:

That by the general and now well established law of this Commonwealth, bond slavery cannot exist, because it is contrary to natural right, and repugnant to numerous provisions of the constitution and laws, designed to secure the liberty and personal rights of all persons within its limits and entitled to the protection of the laws.

That though by the laws of a foreign state, meaning by "foreign," in this connection, a state governed by its own laws, and between which and our own there is no dependence one upon the other, but which in this respect are as independent as foreign states, a person may acquire a property in a slave, such acquisition, being contrary to natural right, and effected by the local law, is dependent upon such local law for its existence and efficacy, and being contrary to the fundamental laws of this State, such general right of property cannot be exercised or recognized here.

That, as a general rule, all persons coming within the limits of a state, become subject to all its municipal laws, civil and criminal, and entitled to the privileges which those laws confer; that this rule applies as well to blacks as whites, except in the case of fugitives, to be afterwards considered; that if such persons have been slaves, they become free, not so much because any alteration is made in their status, or condition, as because there is no law which will warrant, but there are laws, if they choose to avail themselves of them, which prohibit, their forcible detention or forcible removal.

That the law arising from the comity of nations cannot apply; because if it did, it would follow as a necessary consequence, that all those persons, who, by force of local laws, and within all foreign places where slavery is permitted, have acquired slaves as property, might bring their slaves here, and exercise over them the rights and power which an owner of property might exercise, and for any length of time short of acquiring a domicile; that such an application of the law would be wholly repugnant to our laws, entirely inconsistent with our policy and our fundamental principles, and is therefore inadmissible....

In Art. 4, §2, the constitution declares that no person held to service or labor in one State, under the laws thereof, escaping into another, shall in consequence of any law or regulation therein, be discharged from such service or labor, but shall be delivered up on claim of the party to whom such service or labor may be due.

The law of congress made in pursuance of this article provides, that when any person held to labor in any of the United States, &c. shall escape into any other of the said States or Territories, the person entitled, &c. is empowered to arrest the fugitive, and upon proof made that the person so seized, under the law of the State from which he or she fled, owes service, &c. Act of February 12, 1793, c.7 §3.

In regard to these provisions, the Court are of opinion, that as by the general law of this Commonwealth, slavery cannot exist, and the rights and powers of slave owners cannot be exercised therein; the effect of this provision in the constitution and laws of the United States, is to limit and restrain the operation of this general rule, so far as it is done by the plain meaning and obvious intent and import of the language used, and no further. The constitution and law manifestly refer to the case of a slave escaping from a State where he owes service or labor, into another State or Territory. He is termed a fugitive from labor; the proof to be made is, that he owed service or labor, under the laws of the State or Territory from which he fled, and the authority is given to remove such fugitive to the State from which he fled. This language can, by no reasonable construction, be applied to the case of a slave who has not fled from the State, but who has been brought into the State by his master....

The Constitution and laws of the United States, then, are confined to cases of slaves escaping from other States and coming within the limits of this State without the consent and against the will of their masters, and cannot by any sound construction extend to a case where the slave does not escape and does not come within the limits of this State against the will of the master, but by his own act and permission. The provision is to be construed according to its plain terms and import, and cannot be extended beyond this, and where the case is not that of an escape, the general rule shall have its effect. It is upon these grounds we are of opinion, that an owner of a slave in another State where slavery is warranted by law, voluntarily bringing such slave into this State, has no authority to detain him against his will, or to carry him out of the State against his consent, for the purpose of being held in slavery....

Source: 35 Mass. 193 (1836).

Prigg v. Pennsylvania (1842)

Maryland slaveowner John Ashmore allowed two of his slaves to live in virtual freedom, outside of his supervision. (This was not uncommon – the southern press was filled with complaints about slaveowners who failed to supervise their slave property.) When Ashmore died, he left no will documenting the arrangement he had with his two slaves. One of Ashmore's two slaves, Margaret, continued to live as a free woman of color for years. In 1832, she moved to Pennsylvania, married Jerry Morgan, and began raising a family. Meanwhile, back in Pennsylvania, the heirs of John Ashmore decided to reclaim Margaret.

In 1837, professional slave catcher Edward Prigg seized Margaret Morgan and her children from their Pennsylvania home and transported them to Maryland. Prigg deliberately violated Pennsylvania's personal liberty law. Maryland extradited Prigg to Pennsylvania, where he stood trial for kidnapping. After his conviction, he appealed to the United States Supreme Court, arguing that the Pennsylvania personal liberty law violated the Constitution.

Joseph Story wrote the Court's opinion. Story, born in Massachusetts, had a reputation for his religion, ardent nationalism, and opposition to slavery. Generations of scholars have quarreled over whether this opinion represented a betrayal of Story's abolitionist principles, since it freed Prigg, or a challenge to the institution of slavery, as Taney charged. The effect of Story's decision was to make the 1793 Fugitive Slave Law, which depended on the states' cooperation, virtually unworkable. Slaveowners began to see the need for a new fugitive slave law as urgent. This new fugitive slave law would be the centerpiece of the Compromise of 1850 and one factor in the impending crisis that became the Civil War.

MR. JUSTICE STORY delivered the opinion of the Court.

...The question arising in the case, as to the constitutionality of the statute of Pennsylvania, has been most elaborately argued at the bar. The counsel for the plaintiff in error have contended that the statute of Pennsylvania is unconstitutional; first, because Congress has the exclusive power of legislation upon the subject-matter under the Constitution of the United States, and under the act of the 12th of February, 1793, ch. 51, (7), which was passed in pursuance thereof; secondly, that if this power is not exclusive in Congress, still the concurrent power of the state legislatures is suspended by the actual exercise of the power by Congress; and thirdly, that if not suspended, still the statute of Pennsylvania, in all its provisions applicable to this case, is in direct collision with the act of Congress, and therefore is unconstitutional and void. The counsel for Pennsylvania maintain the negative of all these points.

There are two clauses in the Constitution upon the subject of fugitives, which stand in juxtaposition with each other, and have been thought mutually to illustrate each other. They are both contained in the second section of the fourth article, and are in the following words: "A person charged in any state with treason, felony, or other crime, who shall flee from justice, and be found in another state, shall, on demand of the executive authority of the state from which he fled, be delivered up, to be removed to the state having jurisdiction of the crime."

"No person held to service or labour in one state under the laws thereof, escaping into another, shall in consequence of any law or regulation therein, be discharged from such service or labour; but shall be delivered up, on claim of the party to whom such service or labour may be due."

The last clause is that, the true interpretation whereof is directly in judgment before us. Historically, it is well known, that the object of this clause was to secure to the citizens of the slaveholding states the complete right and title of ownership in their slaves, as property, in every state in the Union into which they might escape from the state where they were held in servitude. The full recognition of this right and title was indispensable to the security of this species of property in all the slaveholding states; and, indeed, was so vital to the preservation of their domestic interests and institutions, that it cannot be doubted that it constituted a fundamental article, without the adoption of which the Union could not have been formed. Its true design was to guard against the doctrines and principles prevalent in the nonslaveholding states, by preventing them from intermeddling with, or obstructing, or abolishing the rights of the owners of slaves.

If, indeed, the Constitution guarantees the right, and if it requires the delivery upon the claim of the owner, (as cannot well be doubted,) the natural inference certainly is, that the national government is clothed with the appropriate authority and functions to enforce it. The fundamental principle applicable to all cases of this sort, would seem to be, that where the end is required, the means are given; and where the duty is enjoined, the ability to perform it is contemplated to exist on the part of the functionaries to whom it is entrusted. The clause is found in the national Constitution, and not in that of any state. It does not point out any state functionaries, or any state action to carry its provisions into effect. The states cannot, therefore, be compelled to enforce them; and it might well be deemed an unconstitutional exercise of the power of interpretation, to insist that the states are bound to provide means to carry into effect the duties of the national government, nowhere delegated or intrusted to them by the Constitution. On the contrary, the natural, if not the necessary conclusion is, that the national government, in the absence of all positive provisions to the contrary, is bound, through its own proper departments, legislative, judicial, or executive, as the case may require, to carry into effect all the rights and duties imposed upon it by the Constitution. The remark of Mr. Madison, in *The Federalist*, (No. 43,) would seem in such cases to apply with peculiar force. "A right (says he) implies a remedy; and where else would the remedy be deposited, than where it is deposited by the Constitution?" meaning, as the context shows, in the government of the United States....

Upon these grounds, we are of opinion that the act of Pennsylvania upon which this indictment is founded, is unconstitutional and void. It purports to punish as a public offence against that state, the very act of seizing and removing a slave by his master, which the Constitution of the United States was designed to justify and uphold. The special verdict finds this fact, and the State Courts have rendered judgment against the plaintiff in error upon that verdict. That judgment must, therefore, be reversed, and the cause remanded to the Supreme Court of Pennsylvania;

with directions to carry into effect the judgment of this Court rendered upon the special verdict in favour of the plaintiff in error....

MR. CHIEF JUSTICE TANEY.

I concur in the opinion pronounced by the Court, that the law of Pennsylvania, under which the plaintiff in error was indicted, is unconstitutional and void; and that the judgment against him must be reversed. But as the questions before us arise upon the construction of the Constitution of the United States, and as I do not assent to all the principles contained in the opinion just delivered, it is proper to state the points on which I differ.

I agree entirely in all that is said in relation to the right of the master, by virtue of the third clause of the second section of the fourth article of the Constitution of the United States, to arrest his fugitive slave in any state wherein he may find him. He has a right, peaceably, to take possession of him and carry him away without any certificate or warrant from a judge of the District or Circuit Court of the United States, or from any magistrate of the state; and whoever resists or obstructs him, is a wrongdoer: and every state law which proposes directly or indirectly to authorize such resistance or obstruction is null and void, and affords no justification to the individual or the officer of the state who acts under it. This right of the master being given by the Constitution of the United States, neither Congress nor a state legislature can by any law or regulation impair it, or restrict it.

I concur also in all that is contained in the opinion concerning the power of Congress to protect the citizens of the slaveholding states, in the enjoyment of this right; and to provide by law an effectual remedy to enforce it, and to inflict penalties upon those who shall violate its provisions; and no state is authorized to pass any law, that comes in conflict in any respect with the remedy provided by Congress....

But, as I understand the opinion of the Court, it goes further, and decides that the power to provide a remedy for this right is vested exclusively in Congress; and that all laws upon the subject passed by a state, since the adoption of the Constitution of the

United States, are null and void; even although they were intended, in good faith, to protect the owner in the exercise of his rights of property, and do not conflict in any degree with the act of Congress.

I do not consider this question as necessarily involved in the case before us; for the law of Pennsylvania, under which the plaintiff in error was prosecuted, is clearly in conflict with the Constitution of the United States, as well as with the law of 1793. But as the question is discussed in the opinion of the Court, and as I do not assent either to the doctrine or the reasoning by which it is maintained, I proceed to state very briefly my objections.

The opinion of the Court maintains that the power over this subject is so exclusively vested in Congress, that no state, since the adoption of the Constitution, can pass any law in relation to it. In other words, according to the opinion just delivered, the state authorities are prohibited from interfering for the purpose of protecting the right of the master and aiding him in the recovery of his property. I think the states are not prohibited; and that, on the contrary, it is enjoined upon them as a duty to protect and support the owner when he is endeavoring to obtain possession of his property found within their respective territories.

The language used in the Constitution does not, in my judgment, justify the construction given to it by the Court. It contains no words prohibiting the several states from passing laws to enforce this right. They are in express terms forbidden to make any regulation that shall impair it. But there the prohibition stops....

Source: 41 U.S. (16 Peters) 539 (1842).

Mississippi Slave Code (1848)

All southern states enacted statutes designed to control their slave populations and regulate the behavior of slaveowners, but these laws intruded very little into daily plantation life. The fundamental fact of life was that law played almost no role in controlling the conduct of whites toward blacks in the antebellum South.

Lawmakers hesitated to insert statute law between slaveowners and their property. Slaveowners punished most crime on their property, giving the slaves no recourse to legal authorities. Slaves charged with theft usually went before a justice of the peace (whites went to circuit court) only when the theft occurred off the plantation and the owner could not work out an agreement with the victim. Justices of the peace did not enforce due process protections as strictly as more formal circuit courts. They administered what the law called "stripes" for the marks made by their whips on their defendants' bare flesh. Slaves charged with capital crimes such as arson, murder, or rape went to circuit court, where they faced the death penalty.

---

1. *What Persons deemed Slaves:* All persons lawfully held to service for life, and the descendants of the females of them, within this state, and such persons and their descendants, as hereafter may be brought into this state, pursuant to law, being held to service for life, by the laws of the state or territory from whence they were removed, and no other person or persons whatsoever, shall henceforth be deemed slaves.
8. *Slaves not to go from Home without Pass:* No slave shall go from the tenements of his master, or other person with whom he lives, without a pass or some letter or token whereby it may appear that he is proceeding by authority from his master, employer or overseer; if he does, it shall be lawful for any person to apprehend and carry him before a Justice of the Peace, to be by his order punished with stripes, or not, at his discretion, not exceeding twenty stripes; and if any slave shall presume to come and be upon the plantation of any person whatsoever, without leave in writing from his or her master, employer or overseer, not being sent upon lawful business, it shall be lawful for the owner or overseer of such plantation, to give, or order such slave ten lashes on his or her bare back, for every such offence: and if any negro or mulatto, bond or free shall furnish a pass or permission, to any slave, without the consent of the master, employer or overseer of such slave, he or she so offending, shall on conviction thereof before any Justice of the Peace, of this state, receive on his or her bare back,

well laid on, any number of lashes not exceeding thirty-nine, at the discretion of the Justice of the Peace.

32. *Punishment of Negro or Mulatto for abusive Language, or Assaulting a White Person:* If any negro, or mulatto, bond or free, shall, at any time use abusive and provoking language to, or lift his or her hand in opposition to any person, not being a negro or mulatto, he or she so offending, shall, for every such offence, proved by the oath of the party, before a justice of the peace, of the county or corporation, where such offence shall be committed, receive such punishment as the justice shall think proper, not exceeding thirty-nine lashes, on his or her bare back, well laid on; except in those cases, where it shall appear to such justice, that such negro or mulatto was wantonly assaulted, and lifted his or her hand in his or her defence.

52. *Punishment of Slave for Assault and Battery on a White Person with Intent to Kill.* If any slave or slaves, shall, at any time, commit an assault and battery, upon any white person, with intent to kill, every such slave or slaves, so committing such assault and battery, with intent to kill, as aforesaid, and being thereof convicted, in manner hereinafter directed, shall suffer death.

55. *Certain Capital Offenses:* If any slave shall maim a free white person, or shall attempt to commit a rape on any free white woman, or female child under the age of twelve years, or shall attempt to commit any capital crime or shall be voluntary accessory before or after the fact, in any capital offence, or shall be guilty of the manslaughter of any free person, or shall be guilty of burning any dwelling-house, store, cotton-house, gin or out-house, barn or stable, or shall be accessory thereto, or shall be guilty of any of the crimes aforesaid, or any other crime made capital by law, or shall be accessory thereto, every such slave shall, on conviction, suffer death.

59. *Punishment of Negro or Mulatto for Perjury; Charge to Negro &c., before sworn.* If any negro or mulatto shall be found, upon due proof made to any county or corporation Court of this State, to have given false testimony, every such offender shall, without further trial, be ordered by the said Court, to have one ear nailed to the pillory, and there to stand for the space of one

hour, and then the said ear to be cut off, and thereafter the other ear nailed in like manner, and cut off at the expiration of one other hour, and moreover to receive thirty-nine lashes on his or her back, well laid on, at the public whipping post, or such other punishment as the Court shall think proper, not extending to life or limb. And whenever it shall be necessary to examine any slave, free negro or mulatto, as a witness in any trial, it shall be the duty of the Court, or Justice sitting on such trial, before such witness shall be examined, to charge him to declare the truth, in the manner following, to wit: "You are brought here as a witness, and, by the direction of the law, I am to tell you before you give your evidence, that you must tell the truth, the whole truth, and nothing but the truth; and if it be found hereafter, that you tell a lie, and give false testimony in this matter, you must, for so doing, have both your ears nailed to the pillory, and cut off, and receive thirty-nine lashes on your bare back, well laid on, at the common whipping post."

Source: A. Hutchinson, comp., *Code of Mississippi; Being an Analytical Compilation of the Public and General Statutes of the Territory and State* (Jackson, 1848), 512, 513–514, 517, 521, 522.

State of North Carolina v. Caesar (1849)

On a summer night in 1848, two drunken white men, one identified in court documents only as Mr. Brickhouse, the other as Kenneth Mizell, stumbled across an open field. As they walked, they encountered two slaves. They lied to the slaves, telling them they were slave patrollers – a government-sanctioned civilian police force charged with patrolling the roads at night, looking for slaves off their plantations. Brickhouse and Mizell hit the two slaves with a board and asked if the slaves could "get some girls for them." The two slaves, Caesar and Dick, refused. At that moment, another slave named Charles approached. Brickhouse and Mizell again identified themselves as slave patrollers and grabbed Charles, ordering Dick to find a whip so they could beat the newcomer. When Dick refused, the two men flew into a rage, beating him with their fists. Watching his friend pummeled unjustly, Caesar cried that he "could not stand" it anymore and grabbed a fence rail. He broke it over the heads of the two white men. Mizell died as a result of the blow. A local trial court convicted Caesar of murder. But, if Caesar had been white, jurors would have convicted him of the lesser crime of manslaughter. Caesar had clearly acted in the heat of passion, without the malice of forethought usually required for murder. The question for the state supreme court was whether slaves could ever be convicted of manslaughter rather than murder. Some whites argued that any killing of a white person by a slave must result in a death penalty. The logic of slavery did not permit slaves to ever lift a hand against a white person, no matter what the provocation.

The Constitution played no role in the North Carolina Supreme Court's review of Caesar's conviction. Normally, state judges relied on the Common Law for guidance. But the Common Law came from England, where there was no slavery. In this case, the North Carolina justices debated how closely they had to adhere to Common Law – which defined manslaughter in a way that covered Caesar – when the defendant was a slave.

MR. JUSTICE PEARSON delivered the opinion of the Court.

The prisoner, a slave, is convicted of murder in killing a *white man*. The case presents the question, whether the rules of law, by which manslaughter is distinguished from murder, as between white men, are applicable, when the party killing is a slave. If not, then to what extent a difference is to be made?

...To present the general question by itself, and prevent confusion, it will be well to ascertain, what would have been the offence, if all the parties had been white men? Two friends are quietly talking together at night – two strangers come up – one strikes each of the friends several blows with a board; the blows are slight, but calculated to irritate – a third friend comes up – one of the strangers seizes him, and orders one of the former to go and get a whip that he might whip him. Upon his refusing thus to become an aider in their unlawful act, the two strangers set upon him – one holds his hands, while the other beats him with his fist upon the head and breast, he not venturing to make resistance and begging for mercy – his friend yielding to a burst of generous indignation, exclaims, "I can't stand this," takes a fence rail, knocks one down, and then knocks the other down, and without a *repetition of the blow*, the three friends make their escape. The blow given to one proves fatal. Is not the bare statement sufficient? Does it require argument, or a reference to adjudged cases to show, that this is not a case of *murder* or, "of a black," diabolical heart, regardless of social duty and fatally bent on mischief? It is clearly a case of manslaughter in its most mitigated form. The provocation was grievous. The blow was inflicted with the first thing that could be laid hold of: it was *not repeated* and must be attributed, *not to malice*, but to a generous impulse, excited by witnessing injury done to a friend ....

As this would have been a case of manslaughter, if the parties had been white men; are the same rules applicable, the party killing being a slave? The lawmaking power has not expressed its will, but has left the law to be declared by the "courts, as it may be deduced from the primary principles of the doctrine of homicide." The task is no easy one, yet it is the duty of the court to ascertain and declare what the law is.

I think the same rules are not applicable; for, from the nature of the institution of slavery, a provocation, which, given by one white man to another, would excite the passions, and "dethrone reason for a time," would not and ought not to produce this effect, when given by a white man to a slave. Hence, although, if a white man, receiving a slight blow, kills with a deadly weapon, it is but manslaughter; if a slave, for such a blow, should kill a white man, it would be *murder*; for accustomed as he is to constant humiliation, it would not be calculated to excite to such a degree as to "dethrone reason," and must be ascribed to a "wicked heart, regardless of social duty."...

The announcement of this proposition, now directly made for the first time, may have somewhat the appearance of a law, *made after the fact*. It is, however, not a *new law*, but merely a new application of a well-settled principle of the common law. The analogy holds in the other relations of life—parent and child, tutor and pupil, master and apprentice, master and slave. A blow given to the child, pupil, apprentice, or slave, is less apt to excite passion, than when the parties are two white men "free and equal;" hence, a blow, given to persons, filling these relations, is not, under ordinary circumstances, a legal provocation. So, a blow given by a white man to a slave, is not, under ordinary circumstances, a legal provocation, because it is less apt to excite passion, than between equals....

Assuming that there is a difference, to what extent is the difference to be carried? In prosecuting this enquiry, it should be borne in mind, that the reason of the difference is, that a blow inflicted upon a white man carries with it a feeling of degradation, as well as bodily pain, and a sense of injustice; all, or either of which, are calculated to excite passion; whereas, a blow inflicted upon a slave is not attended with any feeling of degradation, by reason of his lowly condition, and is only calculated to excite passion from bodily pain and a sense of wrong; for, in the language of Chief Justice TAYLOR, in *Hale's* case, 2 Hawks., 582, "the instinct of a slave may be, and generally is, turned into subserviency to his master's will, and from him he receives chastisement, whether it be merited or not, with perfect submission, for, he knows the extent of the dominion assumed over him, and the law ratifies the claim. But when the same authority is wantonly usurped by a stranger, nature is disposed to assert her rights, and prompt the slave to resistance."

...The general rule is, that whenever force is used upon the person of another, under circumstances amounting to an indictable offence, such force is a legal provocation; otherwise it is not....

I think it clearly deducible from *Hale's* case, and analogies of the common law, that, if a white man wantonly inflicts upon a slave, over whom he has no authority, a severe blow, or repeated blows under unusual circumstances, and the slave *at the instant* strikes and kills, without evincing, by the means used, great wickedness and cruelty, he is only guilty of manslaughter, giving due weight to motives of policy and the necessity for subordination.

The latter consideration, perhaps, requires the killing should be *at the instant*; for, it may not be consistent with due subordination to allow a slave, after he is extricated from his difficulty and is no longer receiving blows or in danger, to return and seek a combat. A wild beast wounded or in danger will turn upon a man, but he seldom so far forgets his sense of inferiority as to seek a combat. Upon this principle, which man has in common with the beast, a slave may, without losing sight of his inferiority, strike a white man, when in danger or suffering wrong; but he will not seek a combat after he is extricated....

We have seen, that had be been a white man, his offense would have been manslaughter; "because of the *passion*, which is *excited*, when one sees his friend assaulted." But he is a slave, and the question is, does that benignant principle of the law, by which allowance is made for the infirmity of our nature, prompting a parent, brother, kinsman, friend, or even a stranger to interfere in a fight and kill, and by which it is held that, under such circumstances, the killing is ascribed to *passion* and not to *malice*, and is manslaughter not *murder*; does this principle apply to a slave? or is he commanded, under *pain of death*, not to yield to these feelings and impulses of human nature, under any circumstances? I think the principle does apply, and am not willing, by excluding it from the case of slaves, to extend the doctrine of constructive murder beyond the limits, now given to it by well-settled principles. The application of this principle will, of course, be restrained and qualified to the same extent and for the same reasons, as the application of the principle of legal provocation, before explained. A slight blow will not extenuate; but, if a white man wantonly inflicts upon a slave, over whom he has no authority, a severe blow, or repeated blows under unusual circumstances, and another, yielding to the impulse, natural to the relations above referred to, strikes at the instant and kills, without evincing, by the means used, great wickedness or cruelty, the offense is extenuated to manslaughter....

The prisoner was the associate or friend of Dick—his general character was shown to be that of an obedient slave, submissive to white men—he had himself received several slight blows, without offence on his part, to which he quietly submitted—he was present from the beginning—saw the wanton injury and suffering inflicted upon his helpless, unoffending and unresisting associate—he must either run away and leave him at the mercy of two drunken ruffians, to suffer, he knew not how much, from their fury and disappointed lust—the hour of the night forbade the hope of aid from white men—or he must yield to a generous impulse and come to the rescue. He used force enough to release his associates and they made their escape, without a *repetition of the blow*. Does this show he has a heart of a murderer? On the contrary, are we not forced, in spite of stern policy, to admire, even in a slave, the generosity, which incurs danger to save a friend? The law requires a slave to tame down his feelings to suit his lowly condition, but would it be savage, to allow him, under no circumstances, to yield to a generous impulse.

I think his Honor erred in charging the jury, that, under the circumstances, the prisoner was guilty of murder, and that there was no legal provocation. For this error the prisoner is entitled to a new trial. He cannot, in my opinion, be convicted of a murder, without overruling *Hale's* case and *Will's* case. It should be borne in mind, that in laying down rules upon this subject, they must apply to white men as a class, and not as individuals; must be suited to the most *degraded*, as well as the most orderly. Hence great caution is required to protect slave property from wanton outrages, while, at the same time, due subordination is preserved.

It should also be borne in mind, that a conviction of manslaughter is far from being an acquittal; it extenuates on account of human infirmity, but does not justify or excuse. Manslaughter is a felony. For the second offense life is forfeited.

I think there ought to be a new trial.

MR. CHIEF JUSTICE RUFFIN dissented.

I am unable to concur in the judgment of the Court, and, upon a point of such general consequence, I conceive it to be a duty to state my dissent, and the grounds of it....

It is very clear, that the question turns on the difference in the condition of the free white man and negro slaves. For, there is no doubt, if all the persons had been white men, that the conduct of the deceased would have palliated the killing by the person assaulted, or by his comrade, to manslaughter. It may also be assumed, that, if all the parties had been slaves, the homicide would have been of the same degree....

...The dissimilarity in the condition of slaves from anything known at the common law cannot be denied; and, therefore, as it appears to me, the rules upon this, as upon all other kinds of intercourse between white men and slaves, must vary from those applied by the common law, between persons so essentially differing in their relations, education, rights, principles of action, habits, and motives for resentment....I am led to the opinion, that the prisoner is guilty of murder....and specifically, that a battery by a white man endangers a slave's life or great bodily harm will amount to a legal provocation; but that clearly an ordinary assault and battery is not such a provocation....

...I believe, this is the very first instance in which a slave has ventured to interpose, either between a white man, or between a white man and a slave, taking part against the white man. Why should he intermeddle upon the plea of resisting the unlawful power, or redressing the wanton wrong, of a white man, when he, to whom the wrong was done, is admitted to have been unresisting? Shall one slave be the arbiter of the quarrels witnessed by him between another slave and the whites? It seems to me to be dangerous to the last degree to hold the doctrine, that negro slaves may assume to themselves the judgment as to the right of propriety of resistance, by one of his own race, to the authority taken over them by the whites, and upon the notion of a generous sympathy with their oppressed fellow servants, may step forward to secure them from the hands of a white man, and much less to avenge their wrongs. First denying their general subordination to the whites, it may be apprehended that they will end in denouncing the injustice of slavery itself, and, upon that pretext, band together to throw off their common bondage entirely. The rule, which extenuates the assistance given by a white man to his friend, in a conflict between him and another white man—all being *in equali jure*—cannot, I think, be safely or fairly extended, so as to allow a slave, upon supposed generous impulses, to do the noble duty of killing a white man because he tyrannizes over a negro man, so far as to give him a rap with a rattan and a few blows with his fists. I have never heard such a position advanced before, either as a doctrine of our law or as an opinion of any portion of our people.

For these reasons, the judgment, I think, ought to be affirmed.

Source: 31 N.C. 391 (1849).

3.

The Impending Crisis

Many threads tied the United States together: a common history, a shared language, political parties that traversed geographic regions, and vital economic connections. A federal system that left the states largely autonomous on racial questions apparently made the nation impervious to divisions over slavery. It seemed that a house divided could stand. Northerners inclined to oppose slavery could live with an institution they saw as immoral so long as it remained confined to other states on the theory that *their* state did not tolerate the peculiar institutions.

This system began to break down in the 1840s when the nation acquired large tracts of western lands from its war with Mexico. Patriotic zealots eager to seize Mexican lands had little notion that they were about to plunge their beloved country into a crisis that would ultimately lead to civil war. Southern planters believed slavery could live and flourish only with the infusion of fresh lands. The sons of Mississippi planters had to push west or south into Cuba just as their fathers had once migrated from Virginia and the Carolinas. Young men needed cheap land to build new plantations.

Those opposed to acquiring new territories so slavery could expand fought back with the Wilmot Proviso, an inflammatory proposal to forbid slavery in lands acquired from Mexico. When southerners demanded a stronger fugitive slave law, one that would use the power of the federal courts to retrieve their escaped property, northerners retaliated with a new wave of personal liberty laws—state laws designed to make it difficult or impossible for slave catchers to take African Americans out of the northern states.

After the 1830s, the federal system's toleration of diversity began to seem grotesquely immoral to those most opposed to slavery. The great abolitionist William Lloyd Garrison burned copies of the Constitution in front of cheering crowds. In the 1850s, the Republican Party emerged, supplanting the old Whig Party. The Whigs had opposed westward expansion and tolerated slavery—many southern cotton barons embraced the Whig Party. The Republicans campaigned against allowing slavery to stain the West. Unlike the old Whigs, the Republicans absorbed Manifest Destiny patriotism; unlike the Democrats, they steadfastly opposed staining the nation's future by allowing the blight of slavery to take hold in the western territories.

While Garrison burned copies of the Constitution, southern planters entrenched themselves behind constitutional parapets. In the great Supreme Court case of *Dred Scott v. Sandford*, Marylander Roger B. Taney insisted that under the Constitution, African Americans could have no citizenship rights. The Fifth Amendment protected the property rights of white southerners, he proclaimed.

In Illinois, an obscure rural Republican named Abraham Lincoln challenged such a view of the Constitution by attacking politically one of the mightiest men in the United States Senate, Stephen A. Douglas. Lincoln charged that the *Dred Scott* case proved a Democratic conspiracy to spread slavery across the nation. If southerners had a constitutional right to take their slaves into the West, Lincoln demanded, what could keep them from bringing slavery into Michigan, Massachusetts, or any other northern state?

The Civil War emerged from this quarrel over slavery in the territories. The one aspect of slavery not clearly decided in the Constitution—whether Congress had the authority to legislate over slavery in the territories—ended up being the spark that set ablaze America's great conflagration.

Manifest Destiny (1846)

In 1846 the United States went to war with Mexico. President James K. Polk dreamed of expanding the territory of the United States all the way to California. Across the South, young men including Jefferson Davis, enthusiastically marched off to war, expecting to add new lands – and new slave territories – to the nation. A journalist named John L. O'Sullivan captured the patriotic fervor of the times when he coined the phrase "Manifest Destiny," meaning that the United States was destined to reach from coast to coast. America would achieve its manifest destiny but, in doing so, would sow the seeds for civil war.

Texas is now ours. Already, before these words are written, her Convention has undoubtedly ratified the acceptance, by her Congress of our proffered invitation into the Union; and made the requisite changes in her already republican form of constitution to adapt it to its future federal relations. Her star and her stripe may already be said to have taken their place in the glorious blazon of our common nationality; and the sweep of our eagle's wing already includes within its circuit the wide extent of her fair and fertile land....

Why, were other reasoning wanting, in favor of now elevating this question of the reception of Texas into the Union, out of the lower region of our past party dissensions, up to its proper level of a high and broad nationality, it surely is to be found, found abundantly, in the manner in which other nations have undertaken to intrude themselves into it, between us and the proper parties to the case, in a spirit of hostile interference against us, for the avowed object of thwarting our policy and hampering our power, limiting our greatness and checking the fulfilment of our manifest destiny to overspread the continent allotted by Providence for the free development of our yearly multiplying millions. This we have seen done by England, our old rival and enemy; and by France, strangely coupled with her against us....

[T]here is [no] just foundation for the charge that Annexation is a great pro-slavery measure—calculated to increase and perpetuate that institution. Slavery had nothing to do with it. Opinions were and are greatly divided, both to the North and South, as to the influence to be exerted by it on Slavery and the Slave States. That it will tend to facilitate and hasten the disappearance of Slavery from all the northern tier of the present Slave States, cannot surely admit of serious question. The greater value in Texas of the slave labor now employed in those States, must soon produce the effect of draining off that labor southwardly....Every new Slave State in Texas will make at least one Free State from among those in which that institution now exists—to say nothing of those portions of Texas on which slavery cannot spring and grow....

In respect to the institution of slavery itself, we have not designed, in what has been said above, to express any judgment of its merits or demerits, *pro* or *con*. National in its character and aims, this Review abstains from the discussion of a topic pregnant with embarrassment and danger....Is the negro race, or is it not, of equal attributes and capabilities with our own? Can they, on a large scale, co-exist side by side in the same country on a footing of civil and social equality with the white race?

To all these, and the similar questions which spring out of any intelligent reflection on the subject, we will attempt no answer. Strong as are our sympathies in behalf of liberty, universal liberty, in all application of the principle not forbidden by great and manifest evils, we confess ourselves not prepared with any satisfactory solution to the great problem of which these questions present various aspects....With no friendship for slavery, though unprepared to excommunicate to eternal damnation...those who are, we see nothing in the bearing of the Annexation of Texas on that institution to awaken a doubt of the wisdom of that measure, or a compunction for the humble part contributed by us towards its consummation.

California will, probably, next fall away from the loose adhesion which, in such a country as Mexico, holds a remote province in a slight equivocal kind of dependence on the metropolis. Imbecile and distracted, Mexico never can exert any real government authority over such a country. The impotence of one and the distance of the other, must make the relation one of virtual independence; unless, by stunting the province of all natural growth, and forbidding the immigration which can alone develop its capability and fulfill the purposes of its creation, tyranny may retain a military dominion, which is no government in the legitimate sense of the term. In the case of California this is now impossible. The Anglo-Saxon foot is already on its borders. Already the advance guard of the irresistible army of Anglo-Saxon emigration has begun to pour down upon it, armed with the plough and the rifle, and marking its trail with schools and colleges, courts and representative halls, mills and meeting-houses. A population will soon be in actual occupation of California, over which it will be idle for Mexico to dream of dominion.

Source: [J.L. O'Sullivan], "Annexation," *The United States Magazine and Democratic Review* 17 (1846): 5–9.

The Wilmot Proviso (1846)

The introduction of the Wilmot Proviso on August 8, 1846, split the Congress along sectional lines. Trouble between the slaveowning South and the free North had been brewing for a long time before David Wilmot introduced his fateful provision, but some historians mark this vote as a turning point, the first step toward war. The sectional crisis overwhelmed party discipline which had helped unite the country across geographic lines. The Wilmot Proviso did not win the vote in 1846, but abolitionists introduced it in every Congress thereafter until the Civil War, aggravating tensions between North and South. Finally, in 1862, Congress did pass a law outlawing slavery in the western territories.

August 8, 1846

Provided, That, as an express and fundamental condition to the acquisition of any territory from the Republic of Mexico by the United States, by virtue of any treaty which may be negotiated between them, and to the use by the Executive of the moneys herein appropriated, neither slavery nor involuntary servitude shall ever exist in any part of said territory, except for crime, whereof the party shall first be duly convicted.

Source: *Congressional Globe*, 29th Congress, 1st session (Washington, 1846), 1217.

Fugitive Slave Law (1850)

The great Compromise of 1850 included a fugitive slave law designed to help southerners retrieve their slaves from the North without the help of northern courts and state officials. While the 1793 law relied on the states to assist slave catchers, the 1850 law made it the business of the federal government to do this job.

Be it enacted by the Senate and House of Representatives of the United States of America in congress assembled, That the persons who have been, or may hereafter be, appointed commissioners, in virtue of any act of Congress, by the Circuit Courts of the United States, and who, in consequence of such appointment, are authorized to exercise the powers that any justice of the peace, or other magistrate of any of the United States, may exercise in respect to offenders for any crime or offence against the United States, by arresting, imprisoning, or bailing the same under and by virtue of the thirty-third section of the act of the twenty-fourth of September seventeen hundred and eighty-nine, entitled "An Act to establish the judicial courts of the United States," shall be, and are hereby, authorized and required to exercise and discharge all the powers and duties conferred by this act.

SECT. 2. *And be it further enacted,* That the Superior Court of each organized Territory of the United States shall have the same power to appoint commissioners to take acknowledgments of bail and affidavits, and to take depositions of witnesses in civil causes, which is now possessed by the Circuit Court of the United States....

SECT. 5. *And be it further enacted,* That it shall be the duty of all marshals and deputy marshals to obey and execute all warrants and precepts issued under the provisions of this act, when to them directed; and should any marshal or deputy marshal refuse to receive such warrant, or other process, when tendered, or to use all proper means diligently to execute the same, he shall, on conviction thereof, be fined in the sum of one thousand dollars, to the use of such claimant, on the motion of such claimant, by the Circuit or District Court for the district of such marshal; and after arrest of such fugitive, by such marshal or his deputy, or whilst at any time in his custody under the provisions of this act, should such fugitive escape, whether with or without the assent of such marshal or his deputy, such marshal shall be liable, on his official bond, to be prosecuted for the benefit of such claimant, for the full value of the service or labor of said fugitive in the State....

SECT. 6. *And be it further enacted,* That when a person held to service or labor in any State or Territory of the United States, has heretofore or shall hereafter escape into another State or Territory of the United States, the person or persons to whom such service or labor may be due, or his, her, or their agent or attorney, duly authorized, by power of attorney, in writing, acknowledged and certified under the seal of some legal officer or court of the State or Territory in which the same may be executed, may pursue and reclaim such fugitive person, either by procuring a warrant from some one of the courts, judges, or commissioners aforesaid, of the proper circuit, district, or county, for the apprehension of such fugitive from service or labor, or by seizing and arresting such fugitive, where the same can be done without process, and by taking, or causing such person to be taken, forthwith before such court, judge, or commissioner, whose duty it shall be to hear and determine the case of such claimant in a summary manner....

SECT. 7. *And be it further enacted,* That any person who shall knowingly and willingly obstruct, hinder, or prevent such claimant, his agent or attorney, or any person or persons lawfully assisting him, her, or them, from arresting such a fugitive from service or labor, either with or without process as aforesaid, or shall rescue, or attempt to rescue, such fugitive from service or labor, from the custody of such claimant, his or her agent or attorney, or other person or persons lawfully assisting as aforesaid, when so arrested, pursuant to the authority herein given and declared; or shall aid, abet, or assist such person so owing service or labor as aforesaid, directly or indirectly, to escape from such claimant, his agent or attorney, or other person or persons legally authorized as aforesaid; or shall harbor or conceal such fugitive, so as to prevent the discovery and arrest of such person, after notice or knowledge of the fact that such person was a fugitive from service or labor as aforesaid, shall, for either of said offences, be subject to a fine not exceeding one thousand dollars, and imprisonment not exceeding six months, by indictment and conviction before the District Court of the United States for the district in which such offence may have been committed, or before the proper court of criminal jurisdiction, if committed within anyone of the organized Territories of the United States; and shall moreover forfeit and pay, by way of civil damages to the party injured by such illegal conduct, the sum of one thousand dollars, for each fugitive so lost as aforesaid, to be recovered by action of debt, in any of the District or Territorial Courts aforesaid, within whose jurisdiction the said offence may have been committed.

Sect. 8. *And be it further enacted,* That the marshals, their deputies, and the clerks of the said District and Territorial Courts, shall be paid, for their service, the like fees as may be allowed to them for similar services in other cases; and where such services are rendered exclusively in the arrest, custody, and delivery of the fugitive to the claimant, his or her agent or attorney, or where such supposed fugitive may be discharged out of custody for the want of sufficient proof as aforesaid, then such fees are to be paid in the whole by such claimant, his agent or attorney, and in all cases where the proceedings are before a commissioner, he shall be entitled to a fee of ten dollars in full for his services in each case, upon delivery of the said certificate to the claimant, his or her agent or attorney; or a fee of five dollars in cases where the proof shall not, in the opinion of such commissioner, warrant such certificate and delivery, inclusive of all services incident to such arrest and examination, to be paid in either case, by the claimant, his or her agent or attorney....

Source: George Minot, ed., *The Statutes at Large and Treaties of the United States of America* (Boston, 1862), 9:462, 463, 464.

Massachusetts Personal Liberty Law (1854)

The commonwealth of Massachusetts had long been the northern state most hostile to slavery. The commonwealth responded to passage of the Fugitive Slave Act with a new personal liberty law. This state law intended to nullify the federal law, making it difficult if not impossible for the national government to enforce its fugitive slave law in Massachusetts. The Massachusetts law used the habeas corpus *writ to frustrate federal authorities – giving every person in Massachusetts the right to demand such a writ, should they be taken prisoner by federal officers. This would force federal officers to produce evidence better than that required by the Fugitive Slave law to justify holding alleged slaves. In other words, Massachusetts legislators wanted state judges to guarantee due process for all persons within the borders of their state, regardless of color and in defiance of federal law.*

An Act to Protect the Rights and Liberties of the People of the Commonwealth of Massachusetts.

Be it enacted by the Senate and House of Representatives, in General Court assembled, and by the authority of the same, as follows:

SECT. 1. All the provisions of the "Act further to protect Personal Liberty," passed the twenty-fourth day of March, in the year one thousand eight hundred and forty-three, shall apply to the act of Congress, approved September eighteen, in the year one thousand eight hundred and fifty, entitled "An Act to amend, and supplementary to, the act entitled 'An Act respecting fugitives from justice and persons escaping from the service of their masters.'"

SECT. 2. The meaning of the one hundred and eleventh chapter of the Revised Statutes is hereby declared to be, that every person imprisoned or restrained of his liberty is entitled, as of right and of course, to the writ of *habeas corpus*, except in the cases mentioned in the second section of that chapter.

SECT. 3. The writ of *habeas corpus* may be issued by the supreme judicial court, the court of common pleas, by any justice's court or police court of any town or city, by any court of record, or by any justice of either of said courts, or by any judge of probate; and it may be issued by any justice of the peace, if no magistrate above named is known to said justice of the peace to be within five miles of the place where the party is imprisoned or restrained, and it shall be returnable before the supreme judicial court, or anyone of the justices thereof, whether the court may be in session or not, and in term time or vacation.

SECT. 4. The supreme judicial court, or any justice of said court before whom the writ of *habeas corpus* shall be made returnable, shall, on the application of any party to the proceeding, order a trial by jury as to any facts stated in the return of the officer, or as to any facts alleged, if it shall appear by the return of the officer or otherwise, that the person whose restraint or imprisonment is in question is claimed to be held to service or labor in another State, and to have escaped from such service or labor, and may admit said person to bail in a sum not exceeding two thousand dollars. In such case, issue may be joined by a general denial of the facts alleged, the plea may be not guilty, and the jury shall have the right to return a general verdict, and the same discretion as juries have in the trial of criminal cases; and the finding of a verdict of not guilty shall be final and conclusive.

SECT. 5. The court or justice before whom the writ of *habeas corpus* is returnable shall, unless a jury is already in attendance, by warrant, command the sheriff of the county, or his deputy, to summon a jury in the manner provided in the twenty-fourth chapter of the Revised Statutes, to attend at the time and place stated in the warrant; at which time and place they shall be impanelled, and having elected a foreman by ballot, the issue so framed shall be put to them for their determination. In case one jury shall disagree, the issue may be submitted to the other jury, or continued to the next term, at the discretion of the court. And in every case of disagreement another jury may be summoned and qualified as above provided, forthwith or at a future day, in the discretion of the court or justice before whom the writ is returned, until a verdict shall finally be rendered upon the issue. If any person summoned as a juror as aforesaid shall fail to attend without sufficient cause, he shall pay a fine of fifty dollars. And if, by reason of challenges or otherwise, there shall not be a full jury of the persons summoned, the officer attending the hearing shall return some suitable person or persons to supply the deficiency.

SECT. 6. If any claimant shall appear to demand the custody or possession of the person for whose benefit said writ is sued out, such claimant shall state in writing the facts on which he relies, with precision and certainty; and neither the claimant of the alleged fugitive, nor any person interested in his alleged obligation to service or labor, nor the alleged fugitive, shall be permitted to testify at the trial of the issue; and no confessions, admissions or declarations of the alleged fugitive against himself shall be given in evidence. Upon every question of fact involved in the issue, the burden of proof shall be on the claimant, and the facts alleged and necessary to be established, must be proved by the testimony of at least two credible witnesses, or other legal evidence equivalent thereto, and by the rules of evidence known and secured by the common law; and no *ex parte* deposition or affidavit shall be received in proof in behalf of the claimant, and no presumption shall arise in favor of the claimant from any proof that the alleged fugitive or any of his ancestors had been actually held as a slave, without proof that such holding was legal.

SECT. 7. If any person shall remove from the limits of this Commonwealth, or shall assist in removing there from, or shall come into the Commonwealth with the intention of removing or of assisting in the removing there from, or shall procure or assist in procuring to be so removed, any person being in the peace thereof who is not "held to service or labor" by the "party" making "claim," or who has not "escaped" from the "party" making "claim," or whose "service or labor" is not "due" to the "party" making "claim," within the meaning of those words in the constitution of the United States, on the pretence that such person is so held or has so escaped, or that his "service or labor" is so "due," or with the intent to subject him to such "service or labor," he shall be punished by a fine not less than one thousand, nor more than five thousand dollars, and by imprisonment in the State Prison not less than one, nor more than five years.

SECT. 8. Any person sustaining wrong or injury by any proceeding punishable by the preceding section, may maintain an action and recover damages therefore in any court competent to try the same.

SECT. 9. No person, while holding any office of honor, trust, or emolument, under the laws of this Commonwealth, shall, in any capacity, issue any warrant or other process, or grant any certificate, under or by virtue of an act of Congress....

SECT. 16. The volunteer militia of this Commonwealth shall not act in any manner in the seizure, detention or rendition of any person for the reason that he is claimed or adjudged to be a fugitive from service or labor. Any member of the same who shall offend against the provisions of this section shall be punished by fine of not less than one thousand, and not exceeding two thousand, dollars, and by imprisonment in the State Prison for not less than one, nor more than two, years.

SECT. 17. The governor, by and with the advice and consent of the council, shall appoint, in every county, one or more commissioners learned in the law, whose duty it shall be, in their respective counties, when any person in this State is arrested or seized, or in danger of being arrested or seized as a fugitive from service or labor, on being informed thereof, diligently and faithfully to use all lawful means to protect, defend and secure to such alleged fugitive a fair and impartial trial by jury and the benefits of the provisions of this act; and any attorney whose services are desired by the alleged fugitive may also act as counsel in the case.

SECT. 18. The commissioners shall defray all expenses of witnesses, clerks' fees, and officers' fees, and other expenses which may be incurred in the protection and defence of any person seized or arrested as a fugitive from service or labor; and the same, together with the reasonable charges of the commissioners for their services as attorneys and counsel in the case, shall be paid by the State treasurer, on a warrant to be issued by the governor.

SECT. 19. No jail, prison, or other place of confinement belonging to, or used by, either the Commonwealth of Massachusetts or any county therein, shall be used for the detention or imprisonment of any person accused or convicted of any offence created by either of the said acts of Congress mentioned in the ninth section of this act, or accused or convicted of obstructing or resisting any process, warrant, or order, issued under either of said acts, or of rescuing, or attempting to rescue, any person arrested or detained under any of the provisions of either of said acts, nor for the imprisonment of any person arrested on *mesne process*, or on execution in any suit for damages or penalties accruing, or being claimed to accrue, in consequence of any aid rendered to any escaping fugitive from service or labor....

Source: *Acts and Resolves Passed by the General Court of Massachusetts in the Year 1855* (Boston, 1855), 924–929.

Dissolution of the Union Essential to the Abolition of Slavery (1855)

William L. Garrison

The most famous abolitionist was William Lloyd Garrison, editor of the fiery newspaper The Liberator. *On the pages of* The Liberator *Garrison excoriated slaveowners, southerners, and their northern sympathizers, making* NO UNION WITH SLAVEHOLDERS *his mantra. Truly radical, Garrison publicly burned copies of the Constitution to show his disdain for a document that protected slaveowner' rights to own human beings.*

September 28, 1855

I do not despair of the triumph of the truth. The slaves in our country are to be set free—that is as certain as that man is man, and God is God. Slavery is doomed, let this country do what it may. But will it go down peaceably? Will the nation relax its grasp willingly? Will it hear the warning voice, and obey the Divine command? Or will it go on, and add iniquity to iniquity, and multiply slaves for the auction block, and extend the slave system, until its doom is irrevocably sealed? That is the question. I know that our success in the anti-slavery cause has been extraordinary, within the last quarter of a century; I know that, having nothing but the simple truth to begin with, with all that is wealthy, and mighty, and powerful, in Church and State combined against us, our march has been right onward. And yet there is such a thing as a nation sinning away its day of grace, so that it is not possible for it to recover itself. There has never yet been made a direct and true issue by the North against slavery. Every thing has been and is in the spirit of compromise. In one-half of the country, we have lost our right of speech; the liberty of conscience is cloven down; editors are driven into exile, and their presses destroyed; the Gospel is fettered, and its mouth-piece gagged; and all the compacts and agreements are perfidiously overturned. All this is the legitimate fruit of the tree; and unless we lay the axe at the root of the tree, and cut it down, and give it to the consuming fire, we shall do nothing—we are lost. I thank God for any kind of opposition to slavery, and am glad that any issue is raised; and I will respect every honest effort in behalf of freedom. But, until we cease to strike hands religiously, politically and governmentally with the South, and declare the Union to be at an end, I believe we can do nothing even against the encroachments of the Slave Power upon our rights. When will the people of the North see that it is not possible for liberty and slavery to commingle, or for a true Union to be formed between freemen and slaveholders? Between those who oppress and the oppressed, no concord is possible. This Union—it is a lie, an imposture, and our first business is, to seek its utter overthrow. In this Union, there are three millions and a half of slaves, clanking their chains in hopeless bondage. Let the Union be accursed! Look at the awful compromises of the Constitution, by which that instrument is saturated with the blood of the slave! But even if every word of it were unexceptionable, the fact would be none the less palpable, that it is not a question of parchment, but of moral possibilities. How can two walk together, except they are agreed? We are against slavery. The slaveholders say to us, "If we catch you south of Mason and Dixon's line, we will lynch you." They declare that no man shall be put into office, who does not go for everlasting and universal slavery. How great the insanity of the North! Like Samson, it has foolishly revealed the secret of its strength, ay, and the source of its weakness; and the Philistines of the South have taken it captive, put out its eyes, and made it grind in the prison-house for them; and if, at last, it shall rise in its returning strength, it will be to feel for the pillars of this heaven-accursed Union, and bring it to the ground. Samson told Delilah that if she should cut off his locks, he would be weak as other men. Then, said the Philistines, we know where the secret of his strength lies; and the deed was done.

O, the folly and infatuation of the people of the North! For sixty-eight years, we have been telling the slaveholders that we consider the preservation of the American Union paramount to all other considerations! "Do what you will for the extension of slavery, or the subversion of our own rights, there is one thing we mean to do, and that is, *always to stand by the Union*!" For that, we will give up everything—conscience, self-respect, manhood, liberty, all! "We ask nothing more," say the slaveholders; "that is a *carte blanc* in our hands to wield against you with omnipotent effect; it is all we want to know. We will have the Fugitive Slave bill. We know you will wince, and remonstrate, and threaten; but we have only to crack the whip of disunion over your heads to bring you down on your knees at once. We will repeal the Missouri Compromise. We expect you to rave and resist but you will yield to the point, like whipped spaniels, when we threaten to dissolve the Union. You have agreed that, to save the Union, you will be submissive to the end." And so, all over the North, there is not a political party that does not say, "We are for the Union." The new "fusion" or "republican" party reiterates the cry of the South, "The Union, it must and shall be preserved." What is this but the betrayal of liberty into the hands of the Philistines? Talk about restoring the Missouri Compromise! As well talk of causing the sun and moon to stand still! Talk of repealing the Fugitive Slave bill! "When the sky falls, we will catch larks." Talk about stopping the progress of slavery, and of saving Nebraska and Kansas!—Why, the fate of Nebraska and Kansas was sealed the first hour Stephen Arnold Douglas consented to play his perfidious part. I hold that any man who talks of a Union with slaveholders, such as they prescribe, has no right to call himself a friend of the slave. In becoming an Abolitionist, I pledged myself to stand by the side of the slave, and make his case my own; and I will not support a Constitution from which he is excluded. I will go in for no Union in which he is doomed to clank his fetters. I will give allegiance to no Government, which does not protect his rights with my own. Therefore, I stand outside of this Government, and, by the help of God, I mean to effect its overthrow. That seems to me to be the only consistent course to be taken. "No Union with Slaveholders!" Why? Because they will have no Union with us, unless we will join in their villainy. I do not know what anti-slavery men mean by saying they are opposed to slavery, and yet for preserving the Union. The colored man who glorifies the Union which makes him an outlaw, is beside himself.—Our first duty is to pronounce the American Union accursed of God—to arraign every man who supports it, and tell him, as Jesus told the rich young man in the Gospel, that whatever else he may have done, one thing he yet lacketh: *he must give up his support of the Union*. Why continue the experiment any longer? It is all madness and delusion; let this slaveholding Union go; and when it goes, slavery will go down with it. What ever stands in the way of freedom, I am for its overthrow. The slaveholders are powerless without us. It is the North, after all, which has done this evil work. Our business is with ourselves. The people of the North hold in their hands the key whereby the dungeon's door may be opened, and the slaves set free. We have little to do with the slaveholders. I do not address myself to them; they are incapable of hearing or understanding our arguments; they are insane men. My appeal is not to them, but to the people of the North, who are the props and the pillars of the slave system. Let our rallying cry be, "No Union with Slaveholders, religiously or politically!" Let us up with the flag of disunion, that we may have a free Northern Republic of our own, by the side of which no slaveholding despotism can exist. And when that hour shall come, God will have made it possible for us to be one people from the Atlantic to the Pacific.

Source: *Boston Liberator*, September 28, 1855.

Republican National Platform (1856)

In the 1850s, the Republican Party emerged as a sectional faction opposed to slavery. The party championed social mobility: the laborer of today could own his own farm or business tomorrow. "Every man holds his fortune in his own right arm." Individual character determined success, the Republicans orated. Unlike the Whigs, the Republicans believed the West should be thrown open to entrepreneurs. But slavery obstructed mobility, threatened to poison the West, and degraded free labor. In a slave society, hard work and personal discipline did not produce success. Introducing slavery to the West, Republicans insisted, would close that region off to the young farmer, ambitious for success based on his own character and capabilities. A planter with slaves and wealth would have such an advantage over competitors that proponents of free labor would be shut out. Slavery also degraded free labor: in a slave society, free people disdained work as they associated labor with slaves. Slavery, Republicans insisted, must be eradicated.

This Convention of Delegates, assembled in pursuance of a call addressed to the people of the United States, without regard to past political differences or divisions, who are opposed to the repeal of the Missouri Compromise; to the policy of the present Administration; to the extension of Slavery into Free Territory; in favor of the admission of Kansas as a Free State; of restoring the action of the Federal Government to the principles of Washington and Jefferson; and for the purpose of presenting candidates for the offices of President and Vice-President, do

Resolved: That the maintenance of the principles promulgated in the Declaration of Independence, and embodied in the Federal Constitution are essential to the preservation of our Republican institutions, and that the Federal Constitution, the rights of the States, and the union of the States, must and shall be preserved.

Resolved: That, with our Republican fathers, we hold it to be self-evident truth, that all men are endowed with the inalienable right to life, liberty, and the pursuit of happiness, and that the primary object and ulterior design of our Federal Government were to secure these rights to all persons under its exclusive jurisdiction; that as our Republican fathers, when they had abolished Slavery in all our National Territory, ordained that no person shall be deprived of life, liberty, or property, without due process of law, it becomes our duty to maintain this provision of the Constitution against all attempts to violate it for the purpose of establishing Slavery in the Territories of the United States by positive legislation, prohibiting its existence or extension therein. That we deny the authority of Congress, of a Territorial Legislature, of any individual, or association of individuals, to give legal existence to Slavery in any Territory of the United States, while the present Constitution shall be maintained.

Resolved: That the Constitution confers upon Congress sovereign powers over the Territories of the United States for their government; and that in the exercise of this power, it is both the right and the imperative duty of Congress to prohibit in the Territories those twin relics of barbarism—Polygamy and Slavery.

Resolved: That while the Constitution of the United States was ordained and established by the people, in order to "form a more perfect union, establish justice, insure domestic tranquility, provide for the common defense, promote the general welfare, and secure the blessings of liberty," and contain ample provision for the protection of the life, liberty, and property of every citizen, the dearest Constitutional rights of the people of Kansas have been fraudulently and violently taken from them;

Their Territory has been invaded by an armed force;

Spurious and pretended legislative, judicial, and executive officers have been set over them, by whose usurped authority, sustained by the military power of the government, tyrannical and unconstitutional laws have been enacted and enforced;

The right of the people to keep and bear arms has been infringed;

Test oaths of an extraordinary and entangling nature have been imposed as a condition of exercising the right of suffrage and holding office.

The right of an accused person to a speedy and public trial by an impartial jury has been denied;

The right of the people to be secure in their persons, houses, papers, and effects, against unreasonable searches and seizures, has been violated;

They have been deprived of life, liberty, and property without due process of law;

The freedom of speech and of the press has been abridged;

The right to choose their representatives has been made of no effect;

Murders, robberies, and arsons have been instigated and encouraged, and the offenders have been allowed to go unpunished;

That all these things have been done with the knowledge, sanction, and procurement of the present National Administration; and that for this high crime against the Constitution, the Union, and humanity, we arraign that Administration, the President, his advisers, agents, supporters, apologists, and accessories, either *before* or *after* the fact, before the country and before the world; and that it is our fixed purpose to bring the actual perpetrators of these atrocious outrages and their accomplices to a sure and condign punishment hereafter.

Resolved, That Kansas should be immediately admitted as a state of this Union, with her present Free Constitution, as at once the most effectual way of securing to her citizens the enjoyment of the rights and privileges to which they are entitled, and of ending the civil strife now raging in her territory.

Resolved, That the highwayman's plea, that "might makes right," embodied in the Ostend Circular, was in every respect unworthy of American diplomacy, and would bring shame and dishonor upon any Government or people that gave it their sanction.

Resolved, That a railroad to the Pacific Ocean by the most central and practicable route is imperatively demanded by the interests of the whole country, and that the Federal Government ought to render immediate and efficient aid in its construction, and as an auxiliary thereto, to the immediate construction of an emigrant road on the line of the railroad.

Resolved, That appropriations by Congress for the improvement of rivers and harbors, of a national character, required for the accommodation and security of our existing commerce, are authorized by the Constitution, and justified by the obligation of the Government to protect the lives and property of its citizens.

Resolved, That we invite the affiliation and co-operation of the men of all parties, however differing from us in other respects, in support of the principles herein declared; and believing that the spirit of our institutions as well as the Constitution of our country, guarantees liberty of conscience and equality of rights among citizens, we oppose all legislation impairing their security.

Source: Proceedings of the First Three Republican National Conventions of 1856, 1860, and 1864 (Minneapolis, 1893), 43–44.

Dred Scott v. John Sandford (1857)

Dred Scott is one of the most famous plaintiffs in constitutional history. Yet, little is known about him. He may have been born in 1800. A doctor named John Emerson bought him in 1832. As an army surgeon, Emerson served at Fort Armstrong in Illinois from December 1, 1833, until May 4, 1836. He kept Scott with him as a slave during this time even though Illinois was a free state. Under the law of Missouri and other states, taking a slave to free soil freed the slave. For reasons unknown, Scott did not file a lawsuit for his freedom until 1846, when he was living in St. Louis. In his first bid for freedom, Scott lost on a procedural technicality. But the law was on his side. He filed a motion for a new trial, which was granted. In 1850, Dred Scott won the case of Dred Scott v. Emerson. *Two years later, however, the Missouri Supreme Court broke with precedent and ruled that Scott was still a slave. In 1853, Scott and his wife filed suit in federal court. They did so under the Constitution's diversity of citizenship clause, the part of Article* III *that allows citizens of different states to sue each other in federal court. The easiest way to get into federal court is through such a "diversity of citizenship." Of course, the parties to such a lawsuit have to actually be citizens in order to proceed. This suit became the infamous* Dred Scott *case.*

The justices vigorously disagreed, but Chief Justice Roger B. Taney wrote what is usually considered to be the Court's opinion in the case. Taney argued that Dred Scott did not even have standing to be in federal court – he was not a citizen. That was enough to decide the case against Scott, but Taney went on to attack the Missouri Compromise. Most scholars agree that he did so to forestall the Civil War: if Americans accepted his decision, the crisis over slavery in the western territories was at an end. The Supreme Court had ruled that no one could constitutionally prevent slavery in the West.

MR. CHIEF JUSTICE TANEY delivered the opinion of the court.

...The question is simply this: Can a negro, whose ancestors were imported into this country, and sold as slaves, become a member of the political community formed and brought into existence by the Constitution of the United States, and as such become entitled to all the rights, and privileges, and immunities, guarantied by that instrument to the citizen? One of which rights is the privilege of suing in a court of the United States in the cases specified in the Constitution....

The question then arises, whether the provisions of the Constitution, in relation to the personal rights and privileges to which the citizen of a State should be entitled, embraced the negro African race, at that time in this country, or who might afterwards be imported, who had then or should afterwards be made free in any State; and to put it in the power of a single State to make him a citizen of the United States, and endue him with the full rights of citizenship in every other State without their consent? Does the Constitution of the United States act upon him whenever he shall be made free under the laws of a State, and raised there to the rank of a citizen, and immediately clothe him with all the privileges of a citizen in every other State, and in its own courts?...

It becomes necessary, therefore, to determine who were citizens of the several States when the Constitution was adopted. And in order to do this, we must recur to the Governments and institutions of the thirteen colonies, when they separated from Great Britain and formed new sovereignties, and took their places in the family of independent nations. We must inquire who, at that time, were recognised as the people or citizens of a State, whose rights and liberties had been outraged by the English Government; and who declared their independence, and assumed the powers of Government to defend their rights by force of arms.

In the opinion of the court, the legislation and histories of the times, and the language used in the Declaration of Independence, show, that neither the class of persons who had been imported as slaves, nor their descendants, whether they had become free or not, were then acknowledged as a part of the people, nor intended to be included in the general words used in that memorable instrument....

They had for more than a century before been regarded as beings of an inferior order, and altogether unfit to associate with the white race, either in social or political relations; and so far inferior, that they had no rights which the white man was bound to respect; and that the negro might justly and lawfully be reduced to slavery for his benefit. He was bought and sold, and treated as an ordinary article of merchandise and traffic, whenever a profit could be made by it. This opinion was at that time fixed and universal in the civilized portion of the white race. It was regarded as an axiom in morals as well as in politics, which no one thought of disputing, or supposed to be open to dispute; and men in every grade and position in society daily and habitually acted upon it in their private pursuits, as well as in matters of public concern, without doubting for a moment the correctness of this opinion....

And upon a full and careful consideration of the subject, the court is of opinion, that, upon the facts stated in the plea in abatement, Dred Scott was not a citizen of Missouri within the meaning of the Constitution of the United States, and not entitled as such to sue in its courts; and, consequently, that the Circuit Court had no jurisdiction of the case, and that the judgment on the plea in abatement is erroneous....

The principle of law is too well settled to be disputed, that a court can give no judgment for either party, where it has no jurisdiction; and if, upon the showing of Scott himself, it appeared that he was still a slave, the case ought to have been dismissed, and the judgment against him and in favor of the defendant for costs, is, like that on the plea in abatement, erroneous, and the suit ought to have been dismissed by the Circuit Court for want of jurisdiction in that court....

The correction of one error in the court below does not deprive the appellate court of the power of examining further into the record, and correcting any other material errors which may have been committed by the inferior court. There is certainly no rule of law—nor any practice—nor any decision of a court—which even questions this power in the appellate tribunal. On the contrary, it is the daily practice of this court, and of all appellate courts where they reverse the judgment of an inferior court for error, to correct by its opinions whatever errors may appear on the record material to the case; and they have always held it to be their duty to do so where the silence of the court might lead to misconstruction or future controversy, and the point has been relied on by either side, and argued before the court.

In the case before us, we have already decided that the Circuit Court erred in deciding that it had jurisdiction upon the facts admitted by the pleadings. And it appears that, in the further progress of the case, it acted upon the erroneous principle it had decided on the pleadings, and gave judgment for the defendant, where, upon the facts admitted in the exception, it had no jurisdiction.

We proceed, therefore, to inquire whether the facts relied on by the plaintiff entitled him to his freedom....

In considering this part of the controversy, two questions arise: 1. Was he, together with his family, free in Missouri by reason of the stay in the territory of the United States hereinbefore mentioned? And 2. If they were not, is Scott himself free by reason of his removal to Rock Island, in the State of Illinois, as stated in the above admissions?

We proceed to examine the first question.

The act of Congress, upon which the plaintiff relies, declares that slavery and involuntary servitude, except as a punishment for crime, shall be forever prohibited in all that part of the territory ceded by France, under the name of Louisiana, which lies north of thirty-six degrees thirty minutes north latitude, and not included within the limits of Missouri. And the difficulty which meets us at the threshold of this part of the inquiry is, whether Congress was authorized to pass this law under any of the powers granted to it by the Constitution; for if the authority is not given by that instrument, it is the duty of this court to declare it void and inoperative, and incapable of conferring freedom upon any one who is held as a slave under the laws of any one of the States.

The counsel for the plaintiff has laid much stress upon that article in the Constitution which confers on Congress the power 'to dispose of and make all needful rules and regulations respecting the territory or other property belonging to the United States;' but, in the judgment of the court, that provision has no bearing on the present controversy, and the power there given, whatever it may be, is confined, and was intended to be confined, to the territory which at that time belonged to, or was claimed by, the United States, and was within their boundaries as settled by the treaty with Great Britain, and can have no influence upon a territory afterwards acquired from a foreign Government. It was a special provision for a known and particular territory, and to meet a present emergency, and nothing more.

This brings us to examine by what provision of the Constitution the present Federal Government, under its delegated and restricted powers, is authorized to acquire territory outside of the original limits of the United States, and what powers it may exercise therein over the person or property of a citizen of the United States, while it remains a Territory, and until it shall be admitted as one of the States of the Union.

There is certainly no power given by the Constitution to the Federal Government to establish or maintain colonies bordering on the United States or at a distance, to be ruled and governed at its own pleasure; nor to enlarge its territorial limits in any way, except by the admission of new States. That power is plainly given; and if a new State is admitted, it needs no further legislation by Congress, because the Constitution itself defines the relative rights and powers, and duties of the State, and the citizens of the State, and the Federal Government. But no power is given to acquire a Territory to be held and governed permanently in that character.

...It may be safely assumed that citizens of the United States who migrate to a Territory belonging to the people of the United States, cannot be ruled as mere colonists, dependent upon the will of the General Government, and to be governed by any laws it may think proper to impose. The principle upon which our Governments rest, and upon which alone they continue to exist, is the union of States, sovereign and independent within their own limits in their internal and domestic concerns, and bound together as one people by a General Government, possessing certain enumerated and restricted powers, delegated to it by the people of the several States, and exercising supreme authority within the scope of the powers granted to it, throughout the dominion of the United States. A power, therefore, in the General Government to obtain and hold colonies and dependent territories, over which they might legislate without restriction, would be inconsistent with its own existence in its present form. Whatever it acquires, it acquires for the benefit of the people of the several states who created it. It is their trustee acting for them, and charged with the duty of promoting the interests of the whole people of the Union in the exercise of the powers specifically granted.

At the time when the Territory in question was obtained by cession from France, it contained no population fit to be associated together and admitted as a State; and it therefore was absolutely necessary to hold possession of it, as a Territory belonging to the United States, until it was settled and inhabited by a civilized community capable of self-government, and in a condition to be admitted to equal terms with the other States as a member of the Union. But, as we have before said, it was acquired by the General Government, as the representative and trustee of the people of the United States, and it must therefore be held in that character for their common and equal benefit; for it was the people of the several States, acting through their agent and representative, the Federal Government, who in fact acquired the Territory in question, and the Government holds it for their common use until it shall be associated with the other States as a member of the Union.

But until that time arrives, it is undoubtedly necessary that some Government should be established, in order to organize society, and to protect the inhabitants in their persons and property; and as the people of the United States could act in this matter only through the Government which represented them, and through which they spoke and acted when the Territory was obtained, it was not only within the scope of its powers, but it was its duty to pass such laws and establish such a Government as would enable those by whose authority they acted to reap the advantages anticipated from its acquisition, and to gather there a population which would enable it to assume the position to which it was destined among the States of the Union. The power to acquire necessarily carries with it the power to preserve and apply to the purposes for which it was acquired. The form of government to be established necessarily rested in the discretion of Congress. It was their duty to establish the one that would be best suited for the protection and security of the citizens of the United States, and other inhabitants who might be authorized to take up their abode there, and that must always depend upon the existing condition of the Territory, as to the number and character of its inhabitants, and their situation in the Territory. In some cases a Government, consisting of persons appointed by the Federal Government, would best subserve the interests of the Territory, when the inhabitants were few and scattered, and new to one another. In other instances, it would be more advisable to commit the powers of self-government to the people who had settled in the Territory, as being the most competent to determine what was best for their own interests. But some form of civil authority would be absolutely necessary to organize and preserve civilized society, and prepare it to become a State; and what is the best form must always depend on the condition of the Territory at the time, and the choice of the mode must depend upon the exercise of a discretionary power by Congress, acting within the scope of its constitutional authority, and not infringing upon the rights of person or rights of property of the citizen who might go there to reside, or for any other lawful purpose. It was acquired by the exercise of this discretion, and it must be held and governed in like manner, until it is fitted to be a State.

But the power of Congress over the person or property of a citizen can never be a mere discretionary power under our Constitution and form of Government. The powers of the Government and the rights and privileges of the citizen are regulated and plainly defined by the Constitution itself. And when the Territory becomes a part of the United States, the Federal Government enters into possession in the character impressed upon it by those who created it. It enters upon it with its powers over the citizen strictly defined, and limited by the Constitution, from which it derives its own existence, and by virtue of which alone it continues to exist and act as a Government and sovereignty. It has no power of any kind beyond it; and it cannot, when it enters a Territory of the United States, put off its character, and assume discretionary or despotic powers which the Constitution has denied to it. It cannot create for itself a new character separated from the citizens of the United States, and the duties it owes them under of the United States, the Government and the citizen both enter it under the authority of the Constitution, with their respective rights defined and marked out; and the Federal Government can exercise no power over his person or property, beyond what that instrument confers, nor lawfully deny any right which it has reserved.

A reference to a few of the provisions of the Constitution will illustrate this proposition.

For example, no one, we presume, will contend that Congress can make any law in a Territory respecting that establishment of religion, or the free exercise thereof, or abridging the freedom of speech or of the press, or the right of the people of the Territory peaceably to assemble, and to petition the Government for the redress of grievances.

Nor can Congress deny to the people the right to keep and bear arms, nor the right to trial by jury, nor compel any one to be a witness against himself in a criminal proceeding.

These powers, and others, in relation to rights of person, which it is not necessary here to enumerate, are, in express and positive terms, denied to the General Government; and the rights of private property have been guarded with equal care. Thus the rights of property are united with the rights of person, and placed on the same ground by the fifth amendment to the Constitution, which provides that no person shall be deprived of life, liberty, and property, without due process of law. And an act of Congress which deprives a citizen of the United States of his liberty or property, merely because he came himself or brought his property into a particular Territory of the United States, and who had committed no offence against the laws, could hardly be dignified with the name of due process of law.

Upon the whole, therefore, it is the judgment of this court, that it appears by the record before us that the plaintiff in error is not a citizen of Missouri, in the sense in which that word is used in the Constitution; and that the Circuit Court of the United States, for that reason, had no jurisdiction in the case, and could give no judgment in it. Its judgment for the defendant must, consequently, be reversed, and a mandate issued, directing the suit to be dismissed for want of jurisdiction.

Source: 60 U.S. (19 Howard) 393 (1857).

The Lincoln–Douglas Debates (1858)

Abraham Lincoln had been elected to Congress as a Whig in 1846; he opposed the Mexican War and left after one term to practice law in Illinois. The Kansas-Nebraska Act reawakened Lincoln's interest in politics. Outraged at the role played by his own senator, Stephen A. Douglas, in pushing the measure through Congress, Lincoln insisted, for the first time, that "a house divided against itself cannot stand." When Douglas returned to Illinois to mend his political fences, Lincoln shadowed him, making speeches attacking Douglas and criticizing popular sovereignty. In 1858 Illinois Republicans picked Lincoln to challenge Douglas. "I shall have my hands full," Douglas confided to friends, "He is the strong man of the party—full of wit, facts, dates--and the best stump speaker." Lincoln asked for fifty debates; Douglas agreed to seven. In the debates Douglas tried to intimidate Lincoln with his loud voice and scowling gestures, cross-examining Lincoln with interrogatories. Douglas also played the race card, charging that Republicans wanted to make blacks the social equals of whites. "Never!" someone in the audience yelled. For his part, Lincoln accused the Democrats of conspiring to spread slavery into the North. Each candidate tried to force his opponent into taking a position that would hurt him with some segment of the electorate. By that standard, Lincoln won the debates though he lost the election.

The Chicago Press and Tribune, *a Republican paper, and the* Chicago Times, *a Democratic paper, both sent stenographers to each debate, printing a full transcript of the proceedings. The first excerpt comes from the Freeport debate. According to the highly partisan Press and Tribune, fifteen thousand attended, and Lincoln "tumbled" Douglas, "The Dred Scott Champion." One of Lincoln's questions for Douglas involved a bill proposed by Indiana Congressman William English. English wanted to resubmit the controversial Lecompton Constitution to Kansas voters by offering it as land-grant legislation. The English bill passed over Douglas' opposition. Three weeks before this debate, Kansas decisively rejected the Lecompton Constitution.*

*The second excerpt comes from the Charleston debate, where Lincoln made his most racist comments. A huge crowd turned out, jamming the hotels. Flags and bunting covered the town; one eighty-foot banner proclaimed "*COLES COUNTY, FOUR HUNDRED MAJORITY FOR LINCOLN.*" Perhaps the friendly crowd encouraged Lincoln to speak more frankly about race. Or, perhaps, he simply knew what he had to say for this audience. Lincoln's father lived outside Charleston, and Lincoln himself had practiced law in the town. Lincoln's mention of "Egypt" refers to a common nickname for southern Illinois. Lincoln's attack on Douglas included a teasing jab at Colonel Richard M. Johnston, a Kentucky Democrat who had served as vice president and had maintained an affair with an African American mistress. Predictably, the* Press *and* Tribune *again thought Lincoln won, writing that Lincoln "tomahawked" his opponent.*

The Second Joint Debate at Freeport

Friday, August 27, 1858

Mr. Lincoln's Opening Speech

...As to the first one, in regard to the fugitive slave law, I have never hesitated to say, and I do not now hesitate to say, that I think, under the Constitution of the United States the people of the southern states are entitled to a Congressional Fugitive Slave Law. Having said that, I have had nothing to say in regard to the existing Fugitive Slave Law further than this, that I think it might have been framed to have been free from some of the objections that pertain to it, without at all lessening its efficiency. And inasmuch as we are not in an agitation in regard to alteration or modification of that law, I would not be the man to introduce it as a new subject of a new agitation upon the general question of slavery.

In regard to the other question of whether I am pledged to the admission of any more slave States in the Union, I state to you very frankly that I would be exceedingly sorry ever to be put in a position of having to pass upon that question. I should be exceedingly glad to know that there would never be another slave State admitted into the Union; [applause]; but I must add, that if slavery shall be kept out of the Territories during the territorial existence of any one given territory, and then the people shall, having a fair chance and clear field, when they come to adopt the Constitution, do such an extraordinary thing as to adopt a Slave Constitution, uninfluenced by the actual presence of the institution among them, I see no alternative, if we own the country, but we must admit them into the Union. [Applause.]...

The fourth one is in regard to the abolition of slavery in the District of Columbia. In relation to that, I have my mind very distinctly made up. I should be exceedingly glad to see slavery abolished in the District of Columbia. [Cries of "good, good."] I believe that Congress possesses the constitutional power to abolish it. Yet as a member of Congress, I should not with my present views, be in favor of *endeavoring* to abolish slavery in the District of Columbia, unless it should be upon these conditions. *First,* that it should be gradual; *second,* it should be on a vote of the majority of the qualified voters within the district, and *third,* that compensation should be made to unwilling owners. With these three conditions, I confess that I would be exceedingly glad to see Congress abolish slavery in the District of Columbia, and, in the language of Henry Clay, "sweep from the national capital that foul blot upon our nation." [Loud applause.]

In regard to the fifth interrogatory, I must say here, that as to the question of the abolition of the Slave Trade between the different States, I can truly answer, as I have, that I am *pledged* to nothing about it. It is a subject to which I have not given that mature consideration that would make me feel authorized to state a position so as to hold myself entirely bound by it. In other words, that question has never been prominently enough before me to induce me to investigate whether we really have the Constitutional power to do it. I could investigate it if I had sufficient time, to bring myself to a conclusion upon that subject, but I have not done so and I say so frankly to you here, and to Judge Douglas. I must say, however, that if I should be of opinion that Congress does possess the Constitutional power to abolish slavery among the different states, I should not be in favor of the exercise of that power unless upon some conservative principle as I conceive it, akin to what I have said in relation to the abolition of slavery in the District of Columbia....

Now in all this the judge has me and he has me on the record. I suppose he had flattered himself, that I was really entertaining one set of opinions in one place and another set for in another place—that I was afraid to say at one place what I uttered at another. What I am saying here I suppose I say to a vast audience as strongly tending to abolitionism as any audience in the State of Illinois, and I believe I am saying that which, if it would be affirmed to any persons and render them enemies to myself, would be offensive to persons in this audience.

I now proceed, to propound to the Judge the interrogatories, so far as I have framed them. I will bring forward a new installment when I get them ready. [Laughter.] I will bring them forward now, only reaching to number four.

The first one is—

Question 1. If the people of Kansas shall, by means entirely unobjectionable in all other respects, adopt a State Constitution, and ask admission into the Union under it *before* they have the requisite number of inhabitants according to the English bill—some ninety-three thousand—will you vote to admit them? [Applause.]

Q. 2. Can the people of a United States Territory in any lawful way, against the wish of any citizen of the United States, exclude slavery from their limits prior to the formation of a State Constitution? [Renewed applause.]

Q. 3. If the Supreme Court of the United States shall decree that States can not exclude slavery from their limits, are you in favor of acquiescing in adopting and following such decision as a rule of political action? [Loud applause.]

Q. 4. Are you in favor of acquiring additional territory, in disregard of how such acquisition may affect that nation on the slavery question? [Cries of "good," "good."]...

But to draw your attention to one of the points I made in this case, beginning at the beginning. When the Nebraska bill was introduced, or a short while afterwards by an amendment, I believe, it was provided that it must be considered "the true intent and meaning of this act not to legislate slavery into any State or Territory, nor to exclude it therefrom, but to leave the people thereof perfectly free to form and regulate their domestic institutions in their own way, subject only to the Constitution of the United States." I have called his attention to the fact, that when he and some others began arguing, that they were giving an increased degree of liberty to the people in the Territories over and above what they formerly had on the question of slavery, a question was raised whether the law was enacted to give such conditional liberty to the people, and to test the sincerity of this mode of argument. Mr. Chase, of Ohio, introduced an amendment, in which he made the law—if the amendment were adopted—expressly declare that the people of the Territory should have the power to exclude slavery if they saw fit. I have asked attention also to the fact that Judge Douglas and those who acted with him, voted that amendment down, notwithstanding it expressed exactly the thing that they said was the true intent and meaning of the law. I have called attention to the fact that in subsequent times, a decision of the Supreme Court has been made in which it has been declared that a Territorial Legislature has no constitutional right to exclude slavery. And I have argued and said that for men who did intend that the people of the territory should have the right to exclude slavery absolutely and unconditionally, the voting down of Chase's amendment is wholly inexplicable. It is a puzzle—a riddle....

Go on, Judge Douglas.

Mr. Douglas' Reply to Lincoln

...I will proceed in a few moments to review the answers which he has given to these interrogatories; but in order to relieve his anxiety, I will first respond to those which he has presented to me. Mark you, he has not presented interrogatories which are or ever have received the sanction of the party with which I am, and hence he has no other foundation for them than that they are merely his interrogatories.

First: He desires to know whether, if the people of Kansas shall form a Constitution by means entirely proper and unobjectionable, and ask for admission as a State before they have the requisite population for a member of Congress, whether I will vote for the admission. Well, even I regret exceedingly that when he put that interrogatory to me that he did not first answer it himself, instead of leaving us to infer which side he was on. Gentlemen, Mr. Trumbull, during the last session of Congress, voted, from beginning to end, against the admission of Oregon into the Union, although a free State, because she had not the requisite population. Mr. Trumbull is in the field fighting for Mr. Lincoln. I would like to have Mr. Lincoln answer his own question, and tell me whether he is fighting Trumbull on that issue or not, but I will answer his questions. In my opinion, whenever Kansas has people enough to constitute a slave State, she has people enough for a free State. I will not make any exception of Kansas to the other States of this Union....

The next question Mr. Lincoln propounded to me is, "Can the people of a Territory exclude slavery from their limits by any fair means, before it comes into the Union as a State." I answer emphatically, as Mr. Lincoln has heard me answer a hundred times, on every stump in Illinois, that in my opinion the people of a Territory can by lawful means exclude slavery before it comes in as a State. [Cheers.] Mr. Lincoln knew that I had given that answer over and over again. He heard me argue the Nebraska Bill on that principle, all over the State in 1854, '5 and '6, and he has now no excuse to pretend to have any doubt upon that subject. Whatever the Supreme Court may hereafter decide as to the abstract question of whether slavery may go in under the Constitution or not, the people of a Territory have the lawful means to admit it or exclude it as they please, for the reason that slavery cannot exist a day or an hour anywhere unless supported by local police regulations, furnishing remedies and means of enforcing the right to hold slaves. Those local and police regulations can only be furnished by the local legislature. If the people of the Territory are opposed to slavery they will elect members to the legislature who will adopt unfriendly legislation to it. If they are for it they will adopt the legislative measures friendly to slavery. Hence, no matter what may be the decision of the Supreme Court on that abstract question, still the right of the people to make it a slave Territory or a free Territory is perfect and complete under the Nebraska Bill. I hope Mr. Lincoln will deem my answer satisfactory on this point....

The third question Mr. Lincoln presents is this: If the Supreme Court of the United States shall decide that a State of this Union cannot exclude slavery from its own limits, will I submit to it. Now I am amused that Mr. Lincoln should ask such a question....

...Mr. Lincoln knows that that reply was made on the subject a year ago, and now he wants to put the question, suppose the Supreme Court of the United States shall decide that the States can't exclude slavery from their limits, would I sanction it? He might as well ask you, Suppose Mr. Lincoln should steal a horse, would I sanction it? It would be as gentlemanly in me to ask him what, in the event of his stealing a horse, ought to be done, as for him to ask me such a question. He throws an imputation upon the Supreme Court of the United States, that they would violate the Constitution of the country. I tell him that such a proposition as that is not possible, but it would be an act of moral treason—an act that no man on the bench could ever descend to. Why, Mr. Lincoln himself would never so forget himself in his partisan feelings as to be guilty of an act of that kind.

The fourth question is, Are you in favor of acquiring more territory, without regard to how it may affect the country on the slavery question? That question is very ingeniously and cunningly put. The Black Republican party, in their creed, laid down the proposition that under no circumstances would we acquire any more territory, unless slavery be first prohibited in the country. I ask Mr. Lincoln whether he is in favor of the proposition. Are you against any further acquisition of territory under any circumstances, unless slavery is prohibited? That he didn't like to answer. I ask him if he stands up to that article in the platform, and he turns around, Yankee fashion, and, without answering it himself, asks me: Are you opposed to admitting a slave Territory? I answer him that, whenever it becomes necessary for our growth and progress to acquire more territory, I am for it without reference to the question of slavery, and when we have got it, that we leave the people in the Territory free to do as they please—either to make a slave Territory or a free Territory, just as they choose [Applause.]....

The Fourth Joint Debate at Charleston

Saturday, September 18, 1858

Mr. Lincoln's Opening Speech

Mr. Lincoln took the stand at a quarter before three, and was greeted with vociferous and protracted applause; after which, he said:

LADIES AND GENTLEMEN:—It will be very difficult for an audience of the size of this to hear what is said, and consequently, it is very important that as profound silence be observed as is possible.

While I was up at the hotel today, an elderly gentleman called upon me to know whether I was really in favor of producing a perfect equality between the negroes and the white people. [Great laughter.] While I had not proposed to myself upon this occasion to say much upon that subject, as that question was asked me, I thought I would occupy, perhaps, five minutes, in saying something in regard to it. I will say then, that I am not nor ever have been in favor of bringing about in any way, the social and political equality of the white and black races [applause]—that I am not, nor ever have been in favor of making voters or jurors of the negroes, or of qualifying them to hold office, nor to intermarry with white people; and I will say in addition to this that there is a physical difference between the white and black races, which I believe will for ever forbid the two races living together on terms of social and political equality. And inasmuch, as they cannot so live, while they do remain together, there must be the position of superior and inferior, I as much as any other man am in favor of the superior position assigned to the white race. I say upon this occasion, I do not perceive that because the white man is to have the superior position, the negro should be denied everything. I do not understand because I do not want a negro woman for a slave, that I must necessarily want her for a wife. [Cheers and laughter.] My understanding is that I can just leave her alone. I am now in my fiftieth year, and I certainly never have had a black woman for either a slave or wife. So that it seems to me quite possible for us to get along without making either slaves or wives of negroes. I will add to this that I have never seen to my knowledge a man, woman, or child that was in favor of producing a perfect equality, social and political, between negroes and white men. I recollect of but one distinguished instance that I ever heard of so frequently as to be entirely satisfied of its correctness—and that is the case of my friend Douglas' old friend, Col. Richard M. Johnston. [Laughter and cheers.] I will also add to the few remarks that I have made (for I am not going to enter at large upon this subject) that I have never had the least apprehension that I or my friends would marry negroes if there was no law to keep them from it [Laughter.], but as my friend Douglas and his friends seem to be under great apprehension that maybe they might if there was no law to keep them from it, [Roars of laughter.] I give him the most solemn pledge that I will to the very last stand by the law in this State that forbids the marriage of white folks with Negroes. [Continued laughter and applause.] I will add one further word, which is this, that I do not understand there is any place where any alteration of the social and political relations of the negro and white man would be changed except in the State legislature—not in the Congress of the United States—and as I do not really apprehend the approach of any such thing myself, and as Judge Douglas seems to be in constant horror that some such danger is rapidly approaching, *I propose as the best means to prevent it, that the Judge be kept at home, and be placed in the State Legislature to fight the measure.* [Uproarious laughter and applause.] I do not propose dwelling longer at this time on this subject....

Mr. Douglas' Reply

...Mr. Lincoln simply contented himself in the outset by saying that he was not in favor of social and political equality between the white and the negro; nor did he desire to have the law changed so as to make them voters or eligible to office. I am glad to have got an answer from him on that proposition, to wit: the right of suffrage and holding office by negroes, for I have been trying to get him to answer that point during the whole time that the canvass has been going on....

Why, sir, if you will go to Waukegan, fifteen miles north of Chicago, you will find a paper with Lincoln's name at the head, and you will find it said at the head of it, this paper is devoted to the cause of Black Republicanism. [Applause.] I had a copy of it to carry with me down here into Egypt to let you see by what name they went up there. And their principles vary as much up there as they vary from the name down here. Their principles up there are jet black; when you get down into the centre they are a decent colored mulatto; when you get down into lower Egypt they are almost white. [Laughter.] There were many white sentiments contained in Lincoln's speech down in Jonesboro, and I could not help contrasting them with the speeches of the same distinguished orator in the northern parts of the State. [Hit him again.] Up there his party say they are for no more slave States under any circumstances; down here they pretend that they are willing to allow the people of each State, when they come into the Union, to do just as they please on the subject of slavery. Up there, you will find Lovejoy, their candidate for Congress in the Bloomington district, and Farnsworth, their candidate for Congress in the district of Chicago, and Washburne, the candidate in the Galena district, all pledged; never under any circumstances will they consent to admit another slave State in this Union, even if the people want it. Thus while they there have one set of principles, down here they have another.

Here let me remind Mr. Lincoln of his scriptural quotations which he has applied to the Federal Government, that a house divided against itself cannot stand. Does he expect this Abolition party to stand, when in one half of the State they advocate one set of principles, and in the other half repudiate them and advocate another? [Laughter.]

I am told I have but eight minutes more. I want to talk about one hour more, but I will make the best that I can of that eight minutes.

Mr. Lincoln has said in his first speech that he was not in favor of the social and political equality of the negro and the white man; but I will now tell you what he has said everywhere at the north. He there said he was not in favor of the political and social equality of the negro, but he would not say up there that he was opposed to negro voting and negro citizenship. He declared his utter opposition to the Dred Scott decision, and advanced as a reason that the Court decided that it was not possible that a negro shall be a citizen under the Constitution of the United States.

Now, if he is opposed to the Dred Scott decision for that reason, he must be in favor of conferring the rights and privileges of citizenship upon the negro. I have been trying to get an answer from him on this point, but I have never yet obtained it, and I will show you why. In nearly every speech he made in the North, he quoted the Declaration of Independence to prove that all men were born free and equal, and that meant the negro as well as the white man; that their equality rested on the Divine law. I will read what he said upon this point.

"I should like," Mr. Lincoln said, "to know if you take this old Declaration which declares that all men are created equal and make exception to it, where will it stop? If one man says it don't mean a negro, why not another say it doesn't mean a white man?"

Hence, Mr. Lincoln asserted that the Declaration of Independence declared that the negro was the equal of the white man, and that too by divine law, being endowed by his creator with certain inalienable rights. Now if he believes that by the divine law he was our equal, it was certain he should advocate negro citizenship. And when you grant negro citizenship, then you have put them on an equality under the law. I say to you, gentlemen, in all frankness, that in my opinion a negro is not a citizen, cannot and ought not to be under the Constitution of the United States, I would not even qualify my opinion, although the Supreme Court in the Dred Scott case say that a negro descended of African parents and imported in this country as a slave is not, cannot and ought not to be a citizen. I say that this Government was created on the white basis by white men for white men and their posterity forever, and should never be administered by any but white men. I declare that a negro ought not to be a citizen whether imported into this country or born here, whether his parents were slave or not. It don't depend upon the question where he was born, or where his parents were placed, but it depends on the fact that the negro belongs to a race incapable of self-government, and for that reason ought not to be put on an equality with the white man....

Source: Chicago Press and Tribune, August 30, September 21, 1858.

4.

The Civil War

The Civil War began with a cannon shot in Charleston Harbor. We still hear the echo of that artillery in our debates over the competing powers and authorities of the national government and the states.

In the Civil War, very little of the work of shaping the Constitution occurred at the Supreme Court level. In his speeches, writings, and actions, Abraham Lincoln expanded the powers of his own office and the national government while claiming to guard values promoted by the founders. And he made protecting liberty the business of the federal government in new ways. Lincoln's policies mattered more constitutionally than any wartime Supreme Court decision; perhaps no president has had more constitutional impact.

Lincoln jousted with Jefferson Davis, who saw the war as an assault on the states' sovereignty, an assault on the notion that the Constitution is a compact of sovereign states. Lincoln countered that secession meant anarchy. He also described the war as a "people's contest," which amounted to a bid to make the national government responsible for all the people and not simply a coordinator of sovereign states. Lincoln's phrase, a people's contest, captured the essence of the argument made by the most ardent nationalists. The federal government in Washington should be more powerful than the states, they held, because it alone represents all the people.

The Civil War also raised questions about presidential power. Does the president have the power to arrest and jail American citizens he considers dangerous without making formal charges against them or producing evidence? Such questions came up when Lincoln arrested a Maryland militia lieutenant named John Merryman; they came up again after the September 11, 2001, attack on New York and Washington, D.C., when President George W. Bush arrested American citizens like Jose Padillo, remanding some to a military brig.

During the Civil War, Republicans in power strengthened the national government, expanding its powers. Congress drafted young men into the army for the first time in American history, passed an income tax law that took money directly from citizens' paychecks, and seized citizens' property. These were all unprecedented actions by a national government that, before the war, had little or no impact on the lives of ordinary Americans.

Ultimately, the war suggested to some a new meaning for liberty. In the Jacksonian era, Americans defined their liberty as freedom *from* government. A *liberal* sought to live his or her life free of government supervision. By the end of the Civil War, some understood liberty in a new fashion. Sometimes there could only be freedom when fostered and protected *by* government. In the twentieth century, new meanings for the word liberal would reflect this change in thinking.

Jefferson Davis's Farewell Address (1861)

On November 6, 1860, 1,866,452 Americans voted to make Abraham Lincoln president, less than 40 percent of the total voting. Lincoln did better in the electoral college, though, winning 180 votes, enough to cinch the prize without throwing the election into the House of Representatives. White southerners took the election of a "Black Republican" hard, seeing Lincoln as an intolerable threat to slavery. On November 10, the South Carolina legislature authorized a state convention to consider secession. Before the year was out, every state in the lower South had begun to move toward seceding from the Union.

When Mississippi seceded, Jefferson Davis still served as its United States senator in Washington. Davis, like the members of almost all the southern Congressional delegations, left Washington when he learned that his state had left the Union. Before heading to Mississippi, Davis gave a farewell speech to his fellow senators, explaining the rationale for southern secession.

Senate Chamber, U.S. Capitol, January 21, 1861

MR. DAVIS. I rise,...for the purpose of announcing to the Senate that I have satisfactory evidence that the State of Mississippi, by a solemn ordinance of her people in convention assembled, has declared her separation from the United States. Under these circumstances, of course my functions are terminated here. It has seemed to me proper, however, that I should appear in the Senate to announce that fact to my associates, and I will say but very little more. The occasion does not invite me to go into argument; and my physical condition would not permit me to do so if it were otherwise; and yet it seems to become me to say something on the part of the State I here represent, on an occasion so solemn as this.

It is known to Senators who have served with me here, that I have for many years advocated, as an essential attribute of State sovereignty, the right of a State to secede from the Union. Therefore, if I had not believed there was justifiable cause; if I had thought that Mississippi was acting without sufficient provocation, or without an existing necessity, I should still, under my theory of the Government, because of my allegiance to the State of which I am a citizen, have been bound by her action. I, however, may be permitted to say that I do think she has justifiable cause, and I approve of her act. I conferred with her people before that act was taken, counseled them then that if the state of things which they apprehended should exist when the convention met, they should take the action which they have now adopted.

I hope none who hear me will confound this expression of mine with the advocacy of the right of a State to remain in the Union, and to disregard its constitutional obligations by the nullification of the law. Such is not my theory. Nullification and secession, so often confounded, are indeed antagonistic principles. Nullification is a remedy which it is sought to apply within the Union, and against the agent of the States. It is only to be justified when the agent has violated his constitutional obligation, and a State, assuming to judge for itself, denies the right of the agent thus to act, and appeals to the other States of the Union for a decision; but when the States themselves, and when the people of the States, have so acted as to convince us that they will not regard our constitutional rights, then, and then for the first time, arises the doctrine of secession in its practical application.

A great man who now reposes with his fathers, and who has been often arraigned for a want of fealty to the Union, advocated the doctrine of nullification, because it preserved the Union. It was because of his deep-seated attachment to the Union, his determination to find some remedy for existing ills short of a severance of the ties which bound South Carolina to the other States, that Mr. Calhoun advocated the doctrine of nullification, which he proclaimed to be peaceful, to be within the limits of State power, not to disturb the Union, but only to be a means of bringing the agent before the tribunal of the States for their judgment.

Secession belongs to a different class of remedies. It is to be justified upon the basis that the States are sovereign. There was a time when none denied it. I hope the time may come again, when a better comprehension of the theory of our Government, and the inalienable rights of the people of the States, will prevent any one from denying that each State is a sovereign, and thus may reclaim the grants which it has made to any agent whomsoever.

I therefore say I concur in the action of the people of Mississippi, believing it to be necessary and proper, and should have been bound by their action if my belief had been otherwise; and this brings me to the important point which I wish on this last occasion to present to the Senate. It is by this confounding of nullification and secession that the name of a great man, whose ashes now mingle with his mother earth, has been invoked to justify coercion against a seceded State. The phrase "to execute the laws," was an expression which General Jackson applied to the case of a State refusing to obey the laws while yet a member of the Union. That is not the case which is now presented. The laws are to be executed over the United States, and upon the people of the United States. They have no relation to any foreign country. It is a perversion of terms, at least it is a great misapprehension of the case, which cites that expression for application to a State which has withdrawn from the Union. You may make war on a foreign State. If it be the purpose of gentlemen, they may make war against a State which has withdrawn from the Union; but there are no laws of the United States to be executed within the limits of a seceded State. A State finding herself in the condition in which Mississippi has judged she is, in which her safety requires that she should provide for the maintenance of her rights out of the Union, surrenders all the benefits, (and they are known to be many,) deprives herself of the advantages, (they are known to be great,) severs all the ties of affection, (and they are close and enduring,) which have bound her to the Union; and thus divesting herself of every benefit, taking upon herself every burden, she claims to be exempt from any power to execute the laws of the United States within her limits.

I well remember an occasion when Massachusetts was arraigned before the bar of the Senate, and when then the doctrine of coercion was rife and to be applied against her because of the rescue of a fugitive slave in Boston. My opinion then was the same that it is now. Not in a spirit of egotism, but to show that I am not influenced in my opinion because the case is my own, I refer to that time and that occasion as containing the opinion which I then entertained, and on which my present conduct is based. I then said, if Massachusetts, following her through a stated line of conduct, chooses to take the last step which separates her from the Union, it is her right to go, and I will neither vote one dollar nor one man to coerce her back; but will say to her, God speed, in memory of the kind associations which once existed between her and the other States.

It has been a conviction of pressing necessity, it has been a belief that we are to be deprived in the Union of the rights which our fathers bequeathed to us, which has brought Mississippi into her present decision. She has heard proclaimed the theory that all men are created free and equal, and this made the basis of an attack upon her social institutions; and the sacred Declaration of Independence has been invoked to maintain the position of the equality of the races. That Declaration of Independence is to be construed by the circumstances and purposes for which it was made. The communities were declaring their independence; the people of those communities were asserting that no man was born—to use the language of Mr. Jefferson—booted and spurred to ride over the rest of mankind; that men were created equal—meaning the men of the political community; that there was no divine right to rule; that no man inherited the right to govern; that there were no classes by which power and place descended to families, but that all stations were equally within the grasp of each member of the body-politic. These were the great principles they announced; these were the purposes for which they made their declaration; these were the ends to which their enunciation was directed. They have no reference to the slave; else, how happened it that among the items of arraignment made against George III was that he endeavored to do just what the North has been endeavoring of late to do—to stir up insurrection among our slaves? Had the Declaration announced that the negroes were free and equal, how was the Prince to be arraigned for stirring up insurrection among them? And how was this to be enumerated among the high crimes which caused the colonies to sever their connection with the mother country? When our Constitution was formed, the same idea was rendered more palpable, for there we find provision made for that very class of persons as property; they were not put upon the footing of equality with white men—not even upon that of paupers and convicts; but, so far as representation was concerned, were discriminated against as a lower caste, only to be represented in the numerical proportion of three fifths.

Then, Senators, we recur to the compact which binds us together; we recur to the principles upon which our Government was founded; and when you deny them, and when you deny to us the right to withdraw from a Government which thus perverted threatens to be destructive of our rights, we but tread in the path of our fathers when we proclaim our independence, and take the hazard. This is done not in hostility to others, not to injure any section of the country, not even for our own pecuniary benefit; but from the high and solemn motive of defending and protecting the rights we inherited, and which it is our sacred duty to transmit unshorn to our children.

I find in myself, perhaps, a type of the general feeling of my constituents towards yours. I am sure I feel no hostility to you, Senators from the North. I am sure there is not one of you, whatever sharp discussion there may have been between us, to whom I cannot now say, in the presence of my God, I wish you well; and such, I am sure, is the feeling of the people whom I represent towards those whom you represent. I therefore feel that I but express their desire when I say I hope, and they hope, for peaceful relations with you, though we must part. They may be mutually beneficial to us in the future, as they have been in the past, if you so will it. The reverse may bring disaster on every portion of the country; and if you will have it thus, we will invoke the God of our fathers, who delivered them from the power of the lion, to protect us from the ravages of the bear; and thus, putting our trust in God and in our own firm hearts and strong arms, we will vindicate the right as best we may.

In the course of my service here, associated at different times with a great variety of Senators, I see now around me some with whom I have served long; there have been points of collision; but whatever of offense there has been to me, I leave here; I carry with me no hostile remembrance. Whatever offense I have given which has not been redressed, or for which satisfaction has not been demanded, I have, Senators, in this hour of our parting, to offer you my apology for any pain which, in heat of discussion, I have inflicted. I go hence unencumbered of the remembrance of any injury received, and having discharged the duty of making the only reparation in my power for any injury offered.

Mr. President, and Senators, having made the announcement which the occasion seemed to me to require, it only remains to me to bid you a final adieu.

Source: Congressional Globe, 36th Congress, 2nd session, part 1, (Washington, 1861), 487.

Abraham Lincoln's First Inaugural Address (1861)

Lincoln's election seemed illegitimate to many white southerners. His name had not even appeared on the ballot in many southern states, and few chose to vote for him when it did. Once elected, Lincoln hoped a violent confrontation could be avoided. In his inaugural, Lincoln offered a conciliatory message, reassuring southerners that he did not intend to interfere with slavery. Instead, he skillfully framed the crisis in terms of law and order. He vowed to follow the Constitution; southern secessionists threatened anarchy.

March 4, 1861

Apprehension seems to exist among the people of the Southern States, that by the accession of a Republican Administration, their property and their peace and personal security are to be endangered. There has never been any reasonable cause for such apprehension. Indeed, the most ample evidence to the contrary has all the while existed, and been open to their inspection. It is found in nearly all the published speeches of him who now addresses you. I do but quote from one of those speeches when I declare that

"I have no purpose, directly or indirectly, to interfere with the institution of slavery in the States where it exists. I believe I have no lawful right to do so, and I have no inclination to do so."

Those who nominated and elected me did so with full knowledge that I had made this and many similar declarations and had never recanted them; and more than this, they placed in the platform for my acceptance, and as a law to themselves and to me, the clear and emphatic resolution which I now read:

"*Resolved,* That the maintenance inviolate of the rights of the States, and especially the right of each State to order and control its own domestic institutions according to its own judgment exclusively, is essential to that balance of power on which the perfection and endurance of our political fabric depend; and we denounce the lawless invasion by armed force of the soil of any State or Territory, no matter under what pretext, as among the gravest of crimes."

I now reiterate these sentiments, and in doing so, I only press upon the public attention the most conclusive evidence of which the case is susceptible, that the property, peace, and security of no section are to be in anywise endangered by the now incoming Administration. I add, too, that all the protection which, consistently with the Constitution and the laws, can be given will be cheerfully given to all the States when lawfully demanded, for whatever cause—as cheerfully to one section, as to another.

There is much controversy about the delivering up of fugitives from service or labor. The clause I now read is as plainly written in the Constitution as any other of its provisions:

"No person held to service or labor in one State, under the laws thereof, escaping into another, shall in consequence of any law or regulation therein be discharged from such service or labor, but shall be delivered up on claim of the party to whom such service or labor may be due."

It is scarcely questioned that this provision was intended by those who made it for the reclaiming of what we call fugitive slaves; and the intention of the lawgiver is the law. All members of Congress swear their support to the whole Constitution—to this provision as much as to any other. To the proposition, then, that slaves whose cases come within the terms of this clause, "shall be delivered up," their oaths are unanimous. Now, if they would make the effort in good temper, could they not with nearly equal unanimity frame and pass a law by means of which to keep good that unanimous oath?...

I hold, that in contemplation of universal law, and of the Constitution, the Union of these States is perpetual. Perpetuity is implied, if not expressed, in the fundamental law of all national governments. It is safe to assert that no government proper, ever had a provision in its organic law for its own termination. Continue to execute all the express provisions of our National Constitution, and the Union will endure forever, it being impossible to destroy it, except by some action not provided for in the instrument itself.

Again: if the United States be not a government proper, but an association of the States in the nature of contract merely, can it, as a contract, be peaceably unmade, by less than all the parties who made it? One party to a contract may violate it—break it, so to speak—but does it not require all to lawfully rescind it?

Descending from these general principles, we find the proposition that, in legal contemplation, the Union is perpetual confirmed by the history of the Union itself. The Union is much older than the Constitution. It was formed in fact, by the Articles of Association in 1774. It was matured, and continued by the Declaration of Independence in 1776. It was further matured and the faith of all the then thirteen States expressly plighted and engaged that it should be perpetual, by the Articles of Confederation in 1778. And finally, in 1787, one of the declared objects for ordaining and establishing the Constitution, was "*to form a more perfect union.*"

But if destruction of the Union by one or by a part only, of the States, be lawfully possible, the Union is *less* perfect than before the Constitution, having lost the vital element of perpetuity.

It follows from these views that no State, upon its own mere motion, can lawfully get out of the Union; that *resolves* and *ordinances* to that effect are legally void and that acts of violence, within any State or States, against the authority of the United

States are insurrectionary or revolutionary, according to circumstances.

I therefore consider that in view of the Constitution and the laws the Union is unbroken, and to the extent of my ability, I shall take care, as the Constitution itself expressly enjoins upon me, that the laws of the Union be faithfully executed in all the States. Doing this I deem to be only a simple duty on my part, and I shall perform it, so far as practicable, unless my rightful masters, the American people, shall withhold the requisite means or in some authoritative manner direct the contrary. I trust this will not be regarded as a menace, but only as the declared purpose of the Union that it *will* constitutionally defend and maintain itself.

Plainly, the central idea of secession, is the essence of anarchy. A majority, held in restraint by constitutional checks and limitations and always changing easily with deliberate changes of popular opinions and sentiments, is the only true sovereign of a free people. Whoever rejects it does of necessity fly to anarchy or to despotism. Unanimity is impossible. The rule of a minority, as a permanent arrangement, is wholly inadmissible; so that, rejecting the majority principle, anarchy, or despotism in some form is all that is left.

Source: James D. Richardson, ed., *A Compilation of the Messages and Papers of the Presidents* (New York, 1897), 7:3206–3207, 3209, 3210.

Lincoln and the Writ of Habeas Corpus (1861)

The writ of habeas corpus allows prisoners to ask a judge to make their jailers show that they are imprisoned for good reason. The Constitution allows Congress to suspend the writ of habeas corpus – that is, permit persons to be arrested with no charges or evidence presented in court. When Lincoln suspended the great writ, Congress was not in session, but as critics pointed out, he could have called it back into session. Secession and Civil War threatened the United States with its deepest crisis ever – Lincoln may have saved the Union by acting decisively. In some cases local officials in border states refused to prosecute southern sympathizers guilty of arson and rioting in the first weeks of the war. One Maryland secessionist arrested by the Army was John Merryman. The Chief Justice of the Supreme Court, Roger Brooke Taney, arrived in Baltimore on May 26, 1861. Taney ruled that only Congress could suspend the writ of habeas corpus and chastised Lincoln. According to Taney, Lincoln should "perform his constitutional duty" and release Merryman. Lincoln replied to Taney in several speeches. His July message to Congress eloquently defended his actions. Congress did not authorize suspension of the writ until March 1863. Lincoln ignored Taney's ruling.

The Supreme Court ultimately ratified Lincoln's actions. In Ex parte Vallandigham, *the justices refused to hear the case of a prisoner appealing his conviction by a military court – in essence, the Court endorsed Lincoln's policy of arresting troublesome civilians in wartime. The Court decided* Ex parte Vallandigham *in 1864. Two years later, after the war had ended, the Court decided in* Ex parte Milligan *that neither the president nor Congress could try civilians by military commissions when civilian courts functioned.*

Ex parte Merryman

MR. JUSTICE TANEY, Circuit Justice, delivered the opinion of the court.

The case, then, is simply this: a military officer, residing in Pennsylvania, issues an order to arrest a citizen of Maryland, upon vague and indefinite charges, without any proof, so far as appears; under this order, his house is entered in the night, he is seized as a prisoner, and conveyed to Fort McHenry, and there kept in close confinement; and when a habeas corpus is served on the commanding officer, requiring him to produce the prisoner before a justice of the supreme court, in order that he may examine into the legality of the imprisonment, the answer of the officer, is that he is authorized by the president to suspend the writ of habeas corpus at his discretion, and in the exercise of that discretion, suspends it in this case, and on that ground refuses obedience to the writ.

As the case comes before me, therefore, I understand that the president not only claims the right to suspend the writ of habeas corpus himself, at his discretion, but to delegate that discretionary power to a military officer, and to leave it to him to determine whether he will or will not obey judicial process that may be served upon him. No official notice has been given to the courts of justice, or to the public, by proclamation or otherwise, that the president claimed this power, and had exercised it in the manner stated in the return. And I certainly listened to it with some surprise, for I had supposed it to be one of those points of constitutional law upon which there was no difference of opinion, and that it was admitted on all hands, that the privilege of the writ could not be suspended, except by act of congress....

The clause of the constitution, which authorizes the suspension of the privilege of the writ of habeas corpus, is in the 9th section of the first article. This article is devoted to the legislative department of the United States, and has not the slightest reference to the executive department. It begins by providing 'that all legislative powers therein granted, shall be vested in a congress of the United States, which shall consist of a senate and house of representatives.' And after prescribing the manner in which these two branches of the legislative department shall be chosen, it proceeds to enumerate specifically the legislative powers which it thereby grants [and legislative powers which it expressly prohibits]; and at the conclusion of this specification, a clause is inserted giving congress 'the power to make all laws which shall be necessary and proper for carrying into execution the foregoing powers, and all other powers vested by this constitution in the government of the United States, or in any department or officer thereof.'

It is the second article of the constitution that provides for the organization of the executive department, enumerates the powers conferred on it, and prescribes its duties. And if the high power over the liberty of the citizen now claimed, was intended to be conferred on the president, it would undoubtedly be found in plain words in this article; but there is not a word in it that can furnish the slightest ground to justify the exercise of the power....

...I can see no ground whatever for supposing that the president, in any emergency, or in any state of things, can authorize the suspension of the privileges of the writ of habeas corpus, or the arrest of a citizen, except in aid of the judicial power. He certainly does not faithfully execute the laws, if he takes upon himself legislative power, by suspending the writ of habeas corpus, and the judicial power also, by arresting and imprisoning a person without due process of law....

...The documents before me show, that the military authority in this case has gone far beyond the mere suspension of the privilege of the writ of habeas corpus. It has, by force of arms, thrust aside the judicial authorities and officers to whom the constitution has confided the power and duty of interpreting and administering the laws, and substituted a military government in its place, to be administered and executed by military officers. For, at the time these proceedings were had against John Merryman, the district judge of Maryland, the commissioner appointed under the act of congress, the district attorney and the marshal, all resided in the city of Baltimore, a few miles only from the home of the prisoner. Up to that time, there had never been the slightest resistance or obstruction to the process of any court or judicial officer of the United States, in Maryland, except by the military authority. And if a military officer, or any other person, had reason to believe that the prisoner had committed any offence against the laws of the United States, it was his duty to give information of the fact and the evidence to support it, to the district attorney; it would then have become the duty of that officer to bring the matter before the district judge or commissioner, and if there was sufficient legal evidence to justify his arrest, the judge or commissioner would have issued his warrant to the marshal to arrest him; and upon the hearing of the case, would have held him to bail, or committed him for trial, according to the character of the offence, as it appeared in the testimony, or would have discharged him immediately, if there was not sufficient evidence to support the accusation. There was no danger of any obstruction or resistance to the action of the civil authorities, and therefore no reason whatever for the interposition of the military.

Yet, under these circumstances, a military officer, stationed in Pennsylvania, without giving any information to the district attorney, and without any application to the judicial authorities, assumes to himself the judicial power in the district of Maryland; undertakes to decide what constitutes the crime of treason or rebellion; what evidence (if indeed he required any) is sufficient to support the accusation and justify the commitment; and commits the party, without a hearing, even before himself, to close custody, in a strongly garrisoned fort, to be there held, it would seem, during the pleasure of those who committed him.

The constitution provides, as I have before said, that 'no person shall be deprived of life, liberty or property, without due process of law.' It declares that 'the right of the people to be secure in their persons, houses, papers and effects, against unreasonable searches and seizures, shall not be violated; and no warrant shall issue, but upon probable cause, supported by oath or affirmation, and particularly describing the place to be searched, and the persons or things to be seized.' It provides that the party accused shall be entitled to a speedy trial in a court of justice.

These great and fundamental laws, which congress itself could not suspend, have been disregarded and suspended, like the writ of habeas corpus, by a military order, supported by force of arms. Such is the case now before me, and I can only say that if the authority which the constitution has confided to the judiciary department and judicial officers, may thus, upon any pretext or under any circumstances, be usurped by the military power, at its discretion, the people of the United States are no longer living under a government of laws, but every citizen holds life, liberty and property at the will and pleasure of the army officer in whose military district he may happen to be found.

In such a case, my duty was too plain to be mistaken. I have exercised all the power which the constitution and laws confer upon me, but that power has been resisted by a force too strong for me to overcome. It is possible that the officer who has incurred this grave responsibility may have misunderstood his instructions, and exceeded the authority intended to be given him; I shall, therefore, order all the proceedings in this case, with my opinion, to be filed and recorded in the circuit court of the United States for the district of Maryland, and direct the clerk to transmit a copy, under seal, to the president of the United States. It will then remain for that high officer, in fulfillment of his constitutional obligation to 'take care that the laws be faithfully executed,' to determine what measures he will take to cause the civil process of the United States to be respected and enforced.

Source: 17 Federal Cases 144 (Circuit Court Md, 1861) (No. 9487).

Lincoln's Message to Congress (1861)

July 4, 1861

Soon after the first call for militia it was considered a duty to authorize the Commanding General in proper cases, according to his discretion, to suspend privilege of the writ of *habeas corpus*, or, in other words, to arrest and detain without resort to the ordinary processes and forms this law such individuals as he might deem dangerous to the public safety. This authority has purposely been exercised but very sparingly. Nevertheless, the legality and propriety of what has been done under it are questioned, and the attention of the country has been called to the proposition that one who is sworn to "take care that the laws be faithfully executed" should not himself violate them. Of course some consideration was given to the questions of power and propriety before this matter was acted upon. The whole of the laws which were required to be faithfully executed were being resisted and failing of execution in nearly one third of the States. Must they be allowed to finally fail of execution, even had it been perfectly clear that by the use of the means necessary to their execution some single law, made in such extreme tenderness of the citizen's liberty that practically it relieves more of the guilty than of the innocent, should to a very limited extent be violated? To state the question more directly, Are all the laws *but one* to go unexecuted, and the Government itself go to pieces lest that one be violated? Even in such a case, would not the official oath be broken if the Government should be overthrown when it was believed that disregarding the single law would tend to preserve it? But it was not believed that this question would be presented. It was not believed that any law was violated. The provision of the

Constitution that "the privilege of the writ of *habeas corpus* shall not be suspended unless when, in cases of rebellion or invasion, the public safety may require it" is equivalent to a provision—is a provision—that such privilege may be suspended when, in case of rebellion or invasion, the public safety *does* require it....Now it is insisted that Congress, and not the Executive, is vested with this power; but the Constitution itself is silent as to which or who is to exercise the power; and as the provision was plainly made for a dangerous emergency, it can not be believed the framers of the instrument intended that in every case the danger should run its course until Congress could be called together, the very assembling of which might be prevented, as was intended in this case, by the rebellion.

This is essentially a people's contest. On the side of the Union is a struggle for maintaining in the world that form and substance of government whose leading object is to elevate the condition of men; to lift artificial weights from all shoulders; to clear the paths of laudable pursuit for all; to afford all an unfettered start and a fair chance in the race of life. Yielding to partial and temporary departures, from necessity, this is the leading object of the Government for whose existence we contend.

I am most happy to believe that the plain people understand and appreciate this. It is worthy of note that while in this the Government's hour of trial large numbers of those in the Army and Navy who have been favored with the offices have resigned and proved false to the hand which had pampered them, no one common soldier or common sailor is known to have deserted his flag.

Source: James D. Richardson, ed., *A Compilation of the Messages and Papers of the Presidents* (New York, 1897), 7:3225–3226, 3231.

Confiscation Act (1862)

The national government scarcely touched the lives of most Americans before the Civil War. Now Congress intervened on behalf of Americans deprived of their liberty. Congress passed this Confiscation Act after hearing reports that some

Army officers opened their camps to southern slaveowners pursuing escaped slaves. Congress wanted to make sure that black Americans resourceful enough to escape to freedom would not be returned to slavery.

An Act to suppress Insurrection, to punish Treason and Rebellion, to seize and confiscate the Property of Rebels, and for other Purposes.

Be it enacted by the Senate and House of Representatives of the United States of America in Congress assembled, That every person who shall hereafter commit the crime of treason against the United States, and shall be adjudged guilty thereof, shall suffer death, and all his slaves, if any, shall be declared and made free; or, at the discretion of the court, he shall be imprisoned for not less than five years and fined not less than ten thousand dollars, and all his slaves, if any, shall be declared and made free; said fine shall be levied and collected on any or all of the property, real and personal, excluding slaves, of which the said person so convicted was the owner at the time of committing the said crime, any sale or conveyance to the contrary notwithstanding....

SECT. 5. *And be it further enacted,* That, to insure the speedy termination of the present rebellion, it shall be the duty of the President of the United States to cause the seizure of all the estate and property, money, stocks, credits, and effects of the persons hereinafter named in this section, and to apply and use the same and the proceeds thereof for the support of the army of the United States, that is to say:

First. Of any person hereafter acting as an officer of the army or navy of the rebels in arms against the government of the United States.

Secondly. Of any person hereafter acting as President, Vice-President, member of Congress, judge of any court, cabinet officer, foreign minister, commissioner or consul of the so-called confederate states of America.

Thirdly. Of any person acting as governor of a state, member of a convention or legislature, or judge of any court of any of the so-called confederate states of America.

Fourthly. Of any person who, having held an office of honor, trust, or profit in the United States, shall hereafter hold an office in the so-called confederate states of America.

Fifthly. Of any person hereafter holding any office or agency under the government of the so-called confederate states of America, or under any of the several states of the said confederacy, or the laws thereof, whether such office or agency be national, state, or municipal in its name or character: *Provided,* That the persons, thirdly, fourthly, and fifthly above described shall have accepted their appointment or election since the date of the pretended ordinance of secession of the state, or shall have taken an oath of allegiance to, or to support the constitution of the so-called confederate states.

Sixthly. Of any person who, owning property in any loyal State or Territory of the United States, or in the District of Columbia, shall hereafter assist and give aid and comfort to such rebellion; and all sales, transfers, or conveyances of any such property shall be null and void; and it shall be a sufficient bar to any suit brought by such person for the possession or the use of such property, or any of it, to allege and prove that he is one of the persons described in this section.

SECT. 6. *And be it further enacted,* That if any person within any State or Territory of the United States, other than those named as aforesaid, after the passage of this act, being engaged in armed rebellion against the government of the United States, or aiding or abetting such rebellion, shall not, within sixty days after public warning and proclamation duly given and made by the President of the United States, cease to aid, countenance, and abet such rebellion, and return to his allegiance to the United States, all the estate and property, moneys, stocks, and credits of such person shall be liable to seizure as aforesaid, and it shall be the duty of the President to seize and use them as aforesaid or the proceeds thereof. And all sales, transfers, or conveyances, of any such property after the expiration of the said sixty days from the date of such warning and proclamation shall be null and void; and it shall be a sufficient bar to any suit brought by such person for the possession or the use of such property, or any of it, to allege and prove that he is one of the persons described in this section....

Source: George P. Sanger, ed., *Statutes at Large, Treaties, and Proclamations of the United States of America* (Boston, 1863), 12:589–591.

Income Tax Statute (1862)

Like all wars, the Civil War cost not only blood but money. Shrinking financial reserves forced Congress to tax the wages of ordinary Americans. Once again, the Congress flexed new muscle, building the power of the federal government.

July 1, 1862

An Act to provide Internal Revenue to support the Government and to pay Interest on the Public Debt.

Be it enacted by the Senate and House of Representatives of the United States of America in Congress assembled, That, for the purpose of superintending the collection of internal duties, stamp duties, licenses, or taxes imposed by this act, or which may be hereafter imposed, and of assessing the same, an office is hereby created in the Treasury Department to be called the office of the Commissioner of Internal Revenue; and the President of the United States is hereby authorized to nominate, and, with the advice and consent of the Senate, to appoint, a Commissioner of Internal Revenue, with an annual salary of four thousand dollars, who shall be charged, and hereby is charged, under the direction of the Secretary of Treasury, with preparing all the instructions, regulations, directions, forms, blanks, stamps, and licenses, and distributing the same, or any part thereof, and all other matters pertaining to the assessment and collection of the duties, stamp duties, licenses, and taxes, which may be necessary to carry this act into effect, and with the general superintendence of his office, as aforesaid, and shall have authority, and hereby is authorized and required, to provide proper and sufficient stamps or dies for expressing and denoting the several stamp duties, or the amount thereof in the case of percentage duties, imposed by this act, and to alter and renew or replace such stamps from time to time, as occasion shall require; and the Secretary of the Treasury may assign to the office of the Commissioner of Internal Revenue such number of clerks as he may deem necessary, or the exigencies of the public service may require, and the privilege of franking all letters and documents pertaining to the duties of his office, and of receiving free of postage all such letters and documents, is hereby extended to said commissioner....

Sect. 90. *And be it further enacted,* That there shall be levied, collected, and paid annually, upon the annual gains, profits, or income of every person residing in the United States, whether derived from any kind of property, rents, interest, dividends, salaries, or from any profession, trade, employment, or vocation carried on in the United States or elsewhere, or from any other source whatever, except as hereinafter mentioned, if such annual gains, profits, or income exceed the sum of six hundred dollars, and do not exceed the sum of ten thousand dollars, a duty of three per centum on the amount of such annual gains, profits, or income over and above the said sum of six hundred dollars; if said income exceeds the sum of ten thousand dollars, a duty of five per centum upon the amount thereof exceeding six hundred dollars....

Source: George P. Sanger, ed., *The Statutes at Large, Treaties, and Proclamations of the United States of America* (Boston, 1863), 12:432–433, 473.

The War Powers of the President (1863)

William Whiting

A book by William Whiting entitled The War Powers of the President *influenced Lincoln's thinking. Whiting argued that Lincoln possessed far more powers than even he understood. In his book, Whiting made a Hamilton-like argument for a loose construction of the Constitution, allowing for many implied powers. The Constitution, Whiting insisted, was adequate to meet the crisis white southerners posed to the Union because it gave enormous powers to the president in times of war. In part because he found Whiting persuasive, Lincoln signed the Confiscation bill into law and then issued an executive order authorizing military officers to seize secessionists' property, including their human property. Lincoln expected his officers would put freed slaves to work, paying them a wage for their labors. Also after reading Whiting, Lincoln used his presidential war powers to issue the Emancipation Proclamation.*

Constitution
OF THE
United States of America

THE PURPOSE FOR WHICH IT WAS FOUNDED

The Constitution of the United States, as declared in the preamble, was ordained and established by the people, "in order to form a more perfect union, establish justice, insure domestic tranquility, provide for the common defense, promote the general welfare, and secure the blessings of liberty to themselves and their posterity."

HOW IT HAS BEEN VIOLATED

A handful of slave-masters have broken up that Union, have overthrown justice, and have destroyed domestic tranquility. Instead of contributing to the common defense and public welfare, or securing the blessings of liberty to themselves and their posterity, they have waged war upon their country, and have attempted to establish, over the ruins of the Republic, an aristocratic government founded upon Slavery.

"THE INSTITUTION" *vs.* THE CONSTITUTION

It is the conviction of many thoughtful persons, that slavery has now become practically irreconcilable with republican institutions, and that it constitutes, at the present time, the chief obstacle to the restoration of the Union. They know that slavery can triumph only by overthrowing the republic; they believe that the republic can triumph only by overthrowing slavery.

"THE PRIVILEGED CLASS"

Slaveholding communities constitute the only *"privileged class"* of persons who have been admitted into the Union. They alone have the right to vote for their *property* as well as for themselves. In the free States citizens vote only for themselves. The former are allowed to count, as part of their representative numbers, three fifths of all slaves. If this privilege, which was accorded only to the original States, had not been extended (contrary, as many jurists contend, to the true intent and meaning of the constitution) so as to include other States subsequently formed, the stability of government would not have been seriously endangered by the temporary toleration of this "institution," although it was inconsistent with the principles which that instrument embodied, and revolting to the sentiments cherished by a people who had issued to the world the Declaration of Independence, and had fought through the revolutionary war to vindicate and maintain the rights of man....

LIBERAL AND STRICT CONSTRUCTIONISTS

The friends and defenders of the constitution of the United States of America, ever since its ratification, have expressed widely different opinions regarding the limitation of the powers of government in time of peace, no less than in time of war. Those who have contended for the most narrow and technical construction, having stuck to the letter of the text, and not appreciating the spirit in which it was framed, are opposed to all who view it as only a *frame* of government, a *plan-in-outline*, for regulating the affairs of an enterprising and progressive nation.

Some treat that frame of government as though it were a cast-iron mould, incapable of adaptation or alteration—as one which a blow would break in pieces. Others think it a hoop placed around the trunk of a living tree, whose growth must girdle the tree, or burst the hoop. But sounder judges believe that it more resembles the tree itself,—native to the soil that bore it,—waxing strong in sunshine and in storm, putting forth branches, leaves, and roots, according to the laws of its own growth, and flourishing with eternal verdure. Our constitution, like that of England, contains all that is required to adapt itself to the present and future changes and wants of a free and advancing people. This great nation, like a distant planet in the solar system, may sweep round a wide orbit; but in its revolutions it never gets beyond the reach of the central light. The sunshine of constitutional law illumines its pathway in all its changing positions. We have not yet arrived at the "dead point" where the hoop must burst—the mould be shattered—the tree girdled—or the sun shed darkness rather than light. By a liberal construction of the constitution, our government has passed through many storms unharmed. Slaveholding States, other than those whose inhabitants originally formed it, have found their way into the Union, notwithstanding the guarantee of equal rights to all. The territories of Florida and Louisiana have been purchased from European powers. Conquest has added a nation to our borders. The purchased and the conquered regions are now legally a part of the United States. The admission of new States containing a privileged class, the incorporation into our Union of a foreign people, are held to be lawful and valid by all the courts of the country. Thus far from the old anchorage have we sailed under the flag of "public necessity," "general welfare," or "common defence." Yet the great charter of our political rights "still lives;" and the question of to-day is, whether that instrument, which has not prevented America from acquiring one country by purchase, and another by conquest, will permit her to *save herself?*

POWERS WE SHOULD EXPECT TO FIND

If the ground-plan of our government was intended to be more than a temporary expedient,—if it was designed, according to the declaration of its authors, for a *perpetual* Union,—then it will doubtless be found, upon fair examination, to contain whatever is essential to carry that design into effect. Accordingly, in addition to provisions for adapting it to great changes in the situation and circumstances of the people by *amendments*, we find that powers essential to its own perpetuity are vested in the executive and legislative departments, to be exercised *according to their discretion*, for the good of the country—powers which, however dangerous, must be intrusted to every government, to enable it to maintain its own existence, and to protect the rights of the people. Those who founded a government for themselves intended that it should never be overthrown; nor even altered, except by those under whose authority it was established. Therefore they gave to the President, and to Congress, the means essential to the preservation of the republic, but none for its dissolution.

LAWS FOR PEACE, AND LAWS FOR WAR

Times of peace have required the passage of numerous statutes for the protection and development of agricultural, manufacturing, and commercial industry, and for the suppression and punishment of ordinary crimes and offenses. A state of general civil war in the United States is, happily, new and unfamiliar. These times have demanded new an unusual legislation to call into action those powers which the constitution provides for times of war.

Leaving behind us the body of laws regulating the rights, liabilities, and duties of citizens, in time of public tranquility, we must now turn our attention to the RESERVED and HITHERTO UNUSED powers contained in the constitution, which enable Congress to pass a body of laws to regulate the rights, liabilities, and duties of citizens in time of war. We must enter and explore the arsenal and armory, with all their engines of defence, enclosed, by our wise forefathers for the safety of the republic, within the old castle walls of that constitution; for now the garrison is summoned to surrender; and if there be any cannon, it is time to unlimber and run them out the port-holes, to fetch up the hot shot, to light the match, and hang out our banner on the *outer* walls.

THE UNION IS GONE FOREVER IF THE CONSTITUTION DENIES THE POWER TO SAVE IT

The question whether republican constitutional government shall now cease in America, must depend upon the construction to these *hitherto unused powers.* Those who desire to see an end of this government will deny that it has the ability to save itself. Many new inquiries have arisen in relation to the existence and limitation of its powers. Must the successful prosecution of war against rebels, the preservation of national honor, and securing of permanent peace,—if attainable only by rooting out the evil which caused and maintains the rebellion,—be effected by destroying rights solemnly guaranteed by the constitution we are defending? If so, the next question will be, whether the law of self-defense and overwhelming necessity will not justify the country in denying to rebels and traitors in arms whatever rights they or their friends may claim under a charter which they have repudiated, and have armed themselves to overthrow and destroy? Can one party break the contract, and justly hold the other party bound by it? Is the constitution to be so interpreted that rebels and traitors cannot be put down? Are we so hampered, as some have asserted, that even if war end in reëstablishing the Union, and enforcing the laws over all the land, the results of victory will be turned against us, and the conquered enemy may then treat us as though they had been victors? Will vanquished criminals be able to resume their rights to the same political superiority over the citizens of Free States, which, as the only "privileged class," they have hitherto enjoyed?

Have they who alone have made this rebellion, while committing treason and other high crimes against the republic, a protection, an immunity against punishment for these crimes, whether by forfeiture of life or property, by reason of any clause in the constitution? Can government, the people's agent, wage genuine and effectual war against their enemy? or must the soldier of the Union, when in action, keep one eye upon his rifle, and the other upon the constitution? Is the power to make war, when once lawfully brought into action, to be controlled, baffled, and emasculated by any obligation to guard or respect rights set up by or for belligerent traitors?

Source: William Whiting, *The War Powers of the President and the Legislative Powers of Congress in Relation to Rebellion, Treason and Slavery* (Boston, 1863), 3–4, 10–15.

Lincoln's Emancipation Proclamation (1863)

Congress passed the Second Confiscation Act on July 17, 1862. In September, a little more than a year after he insisted he would not interfere with slavery, Lincoln declared that slavery would be over in that part of the South behind Confederate lines on January 1, 1863. Some have criticized Lincoln's proclamation for not freeing a single slave, but the document is useful for understanding the development of Lincoln's thinking. As the Civil War progressed, Lincoln's prewar ideas about African Americans softened. For their part, African Americans often walked off plantations, freeing themselves more effectively than could any government official.

January 1, 1863

WHEREAS, on the twenty-second day of September, in the year of Lord one thousand eight hundred and sixty-two, a proclamation was issued by the President of the United States, containing, among other things, the following, to wit:

"That on the 1st day of January, in the year of our Lord one thousand eight hundred sixty-three, all persons held as slaves within any state or designated part of a state, the people whereof shall then be in rebellion against the United States, shall be then, thenceforward, and forever free; and the Executive Government of the United States, including the military and naval authority thereof, will recognize and maintain the freedom of such persons, and will do no act or acts to repress such persons and will do no act or acts to repress such persons, or any of them, in any efforts they may make for their actual freedom.

"That the Executive will, on the 1st day of January aforesaid, by proclamation, designate the states and parts of states, if any, in which the people thereof, respectively, shall then be in rebellion against the United States; and the fact that any state, or the people thereof, shall on that day be in good faith represented in the Congress of the United States by members chosen thereto at elections wherein a majority of the qualified voters of such States shall have participated, shall, in the absence of strong countervailing testimony, be deemed conclusive evidence that such state, and the people thereof, are not then in rebellion against the United States."

Now, therefore, I, ABRAHAM LINCOLN, President of the United States, by virtue of the power in me vested as Commander-in-Chief of the army and navy of the United States, in time of actual armed rebellion against authority and Government of the United States, and as a fit and necessary war measure for suppressing said rebellion, do, on this first day of January, in the year of our Lord one thousand eight hundred and sixty-three, and in accordance with my purpose so to do, publicly proclaimed for the full period of one hundred days from the day first above mentioned, order and designate as the States and parts of States wherein the people thereof, respectively, are this day in rebellion against the United States, the following, to wit:

Arkansas, Texas, Louisiana (except the parishes of St. Bernard, Plaquemines, Jefferson, St. John, St. Charles, St. James, Ascension, Assumption, Terre Bonne, Lafourche, St. Mary, St. Martin, and Orleans, including the city of New Orleans), Mississippi, Alabama, Florida, Georgia, South Carolina, North Carolina, and Virginia (except the forty-eight counties designated as West Virginia, and also the counties of Berkeley, Accomac, Northampton, Elizabeth City, York, Princess Anne, and Norfolk, including the cities of Norfolk and Portsmouth), and which excepted parts are for the present left precisely as if this proclamation were not issued.

And by virtue of the power and for the purpose aforesaid, I do order and declare that all persons held as slaves within said designated States and parts of States are, and henceforward shall be, free; and that the Executive Government of the United States, including the military and naval authorities thereof, will recognize and maintain the freedom of said persons.

And I hereby enjoin upon the people so declared to be free to abstain from all violence, unless in necessary self-defence; and I recommend to them that, in all cases when allowed, they labor faithfully for reasonable wages.

And I further declare and make known that such persons, of suitable condition, will be received into the armed service of the United States to garrison forts, positions, stations, and other places and to man vessels of all sorts in said service.

And upon this act, sincerely believed to be an act of justice, warranted by the Constitution upon military necessity, I invoke the considerate judgment of mankind and gracious favor of Almighty God.

In witness whereof, I have hereunto set my hand and caused the seal of the United States to be affixed.

Done at the city of Washington, this 1st day of January, A.D. 1863, and of the Independence of the United States of America the eighty-seventh.

Abraham Lincoln

By the President:
WILLIAM H. SEWARD, *Secretary of State*

Source: George P. Sanger, ed., *The Statutes at Large, Treaties, Proclamations of the United States of America* (Boston, 1863), 12:1268–1269.

Draft Statute (1863)

As the war dragged on, the numbers of white volunteers willing to serve in the Union Army dwindled. This legislation pressed the unwilling into service and sparked resistance to the war and to the draft. Many young white men, once skeptical that blacks could ever be made into soldiers, now faced the prospect that they would themselves be forced into the army. Some took a second look at the idea of allowing blacks to enlist. The draft law helped build support for allowing African American men into the army.

March 3, 1863

An Act for enrolling and calling out the national Forces, and for other Purposes.

Whereas there now exist in the United States an insurrection and rebellion against the authority thereof, and it is, under the Constitution of the United States, the duty of the government to suppress insurrection and rebellion, to guarantee to each State a republican form of government, and to preserve the public tranquility; and whereas, for these high purposes, a military force is indispensable, to raise and support which all persons ought willingly to contribute; and whereas no service can be more praiseworthy and honorable than that which is rendered for the maintenance of the Constitution and Union, and the consequent preservation of free government: Therefore—

Be it enacted by the Senate and House of Representatives of the United States of America in Congress assembled, That all able-bodied male citizens of the United States, and persons of foreign birth who shall have declared an oath their intention to become citizens under and in pursuance of the laws thereof, between the ages of twenty and forty-five years, except as hereinafter excepted, are hereby declared to constitute the national forces, and shall be liable to perform military duty in the service of the United States when called out by the President for that purpose....

SECT. 5. *And be it further enacted,* That for each of said districts there shall be appointed by the President a provost-marshal, with the rank, pay, and emoluments of a captain of cavalry, or an officer of said rank shall be detailed by the President, who shall be under the direction and subject to the orders of the provost-marshal-general, appointed or detailed by the President of the United States, whose office shall be at the seat of government, forming a separate bureau of the War Department, and whose rank, pay, and emoluments shall be these of the colonel of cavalry....

SECT. 8. *And be it further enacted,* That in each of said districts there shall be a board of enrolment....

SECT. 9. *And be it further enacted,* That is shall be the duty of the said board...to appoint...an enrolling officer...and he shall immediately proceed to enroll all persons subject to military duty, noting their respective places of residence....

SECT. 11. *And be it further enacted,* That all persons thus enrolled shall be subject...to be called into the military service of the United States....

Sect. 12. *And be it further enacted,* That whenever it may be necessary to call out the national forces for military service, the President is hereby authorized to assign to each district the number of men to be furnished by said district; and thereupon the enrolling board shall, under direction of the President, make a draft of the required number....

Source: George P. Sanger, ed., *The States at Large, Treaties, and Proclamations of the United States of America* (Boston, 1863), 12:731, 732, 733.

The Gettysburg Address (1863)

Shortly after the 1863 election, Lincoln journeyed to Gettysburg, Pennsylvania, to help dedicate a new national cemetery for the thousands who fell fighting there. Lincoln worked long and hard on his speech, crafting an address that spoke in plain but poetic language. Lincoln anticipated that the principal speaker, Edward Everett, would speak for the Union as it was, with a restoration of state sovereignty and states' rights. (In fact, Everett's two-hour speech made no such appeal but rather brought many in the audience to tears with his unvarnished account of the battle.)

Lincoln's speech was so brief many seemed surprised when he sat down. In just 272 words Lincoln painted his nationalist argument in bold strokes. He cited the Declaration of Independence as proof that the nation had been "conceived in liberty." In other words, it was the job of the newly powerful national government to displace the states as defender of freedom and protector of citizens' rights. It always had been, he implied.

November 19, 1863

Four score and seven years ago our fathers brought forth on this continent, a new nation, conceived in Liberty, and dedicated to the proposition that all men are created equal.

Now we are engaged in a great civil war, testing whether that nation, or any nation, so conceived and so dedicated, can long endure.

We are met here on a great battle-field of that war. We have come to dedicate a portion of it as a final resting place for those who gave their lives that the nation might live. It is altogether fitting and proper that we should do this.

But, in a larger sense, we can not dedicate—we can not consecrate—we can not hallow—this ground. The brave men, living and dead, who struggled here, have consecrated it, far above our poor power to add or detract. The world will little note, nor long remember what we say here, but it can never forget what they did here. It is for us the living, rather to be dedicated here to the unfinished work which they who fought here have, thus far, so nobly carried on. It is rather for us to be here dedicated to the great task remaining before us—that from these honored dead we take increased devotion to that cause for which they gave the last full measure of devotion—that we here highly resolve that these dead shall not have died in vain; that this nation shall have a new birth of freedom; and that government of the people, by the people, for the people, shall not perish from the earth.

Source: Roy P. Basler, ed., Marion Delores Pratt and Lloyd A. Dunlap, asst. eds., *The Collected Works of Abraham Lincoln*, 9 vols. (New Brunswick, 1953 and 1955), 7:18–19. Courtesy Abraham Lincoln Association.

Abraham Lincoln's Address at the Sanitary Fair (1864)

By 1864 Lincoln had begun to understand liberty *in new ways. The Civil War had taught him that not all Americans understood the term in the same way. Lincoln had also learned that Confederate troops could be brutal toward black Union Army soldiers. Southern troops under the command of Nathan Bedford Forrest attacked and massacred surrendering African Americans at a place called Fort Pillow.*

April 18, 1864

The world has never had a good definition of the word liberty, and the American people, just now, are much in want of one. We all declare for liberty; but in using the same *word* we do not all mean the same *thing*. With some the word liberty may mean for each man to do as he pleases with himself, and the product of his labor; while with others the same word may mean for some men to do as they please with other men, and the product of other men's labor. Here are two, not only different, but incompatible things, called by the same name—liberty. And it follows that each of the things is, by the respective parties, called by two different and incompatible names—liberty and tyranny.

The shepherd drives the wolf from the sheep's throat, for which the sheep thanks the shepherd as a *liberator*, while the wolf denounces him for the same act as the destroyer of liberty, especially as the sheep was a black one. Plainly the sheep and the wolf are not agreed upon a definition of the word liberty; and precisely the same difference prevails to-day among us human creatures, even in the North, and all professing to love liberty. Hence we behold the processes by which thousands are daily passing from under the yoke of bondage, hailed by some as the advance of liberty, and bewailed by others as the destruction of all liberty….

It is not very becoming for one in my position to make speeches at great length; but there is another subject upon which I feel that I ought to say a word. A painful rumor, true I fear, had reached us of the massacre, by the rebel forces, at Fort Pillow, in the West end of Tennessee, on the Mississippi river, of some three hundred colored soldiers and white officers, who had just been overpowered by their assailants. There seems to be some anxiety in the public mind whether the government is doing its duty to the colored soldier, and to the service, at this point. At the beginning of the war, and for some time, the use of colored troops was not contemplated; and how the change of purpose was wrought, I will not now take time to explain. Upon a clear conviction of duty I resolved to turn that element of strength to account; and I am responsible for it to the American people, to the christian world, to history, and on my final account to God. Having determined to use the negro as a soldier, there is no way but to give him all the protection given to any other soldier. The difficulty is not in stating the principle, but in practically applying it. It is a mistake to suppose the government is indiffe[re]nt to this matter, or is not doing the best it can in regard to it. We do not to-day *know* that a colored soldier, or white officer commanding colored soldiers, has been massacred by the rebels when made a prisoner. We fear it, believe it, I may say, but we do not *know* it. To take the life of one of their prisoners, on the assumption that they murder ours, when it is short of certainty that they do murder ours, might be too serious, too cruel a mistake. We are having the Fort-Pillow affair thoroughly investigated; and such investigation will probably show conclusively how the truth is. If, after all that has been said, it shall turn out that there has been none, and will be none elsewhere. If there has been the massacre of three hundred there, or even the tenth part of three hundred, it will be conclusively proved; and being so proved, the retribution shall as surely come. It will be matter of grave consideration in what exact course to apply the retribution; but in the supposed case, it must come.

Source: Roy P. Basler, ed., Marion Dolores Pratt and Lloyd A. Dunlap, asst. eds., *The Collected Works of Abraham Lincoln*, 9 vols. (New Brunswick, 1953 and 1955), 7:301–303. Courtesy Abraham Lincoln Association.

Lincoln's Second Inaugural Address (1865)

Lincoln's second inaugural address explained the origins of the Civil War and stated its significance. Slavery was "somehow" the cause of the war. The South was willing to "rend the Union even by war" to protect slavery. Lincoln made no predictions as to when the war might end, he predicted only that it might necessarily continue until "all the wealth piled by the bondsman's two hundred and fifty years of unrequited toil shall be sunk, and until every drop of blood drawn with the lash shall be paid by another drawn with the sword."

March 4, 1865

Fellow-Countrymen: At this second appearing to take the oath of the Presidential office there is less occasion for an extended address than there was at the first. Then a statement somewhat in detail of a course to be pursued seemed fitting and proper. Now, at the expiration of four years, during which public declarations have been constantly called forth on every point and phase of the great contest which still absorbs the attention and engrosses the energies of the nation, little that is new could be presented. The progress of our arms, upon which all else chiefly depends, is as well known to the public as to myself, and it is, I trust, reasonably satisfactory and encouraging to all. With high hope for the future, no prediction in regard to it is ventured.

On the occasion corresponding to this four years ago all thoughts were anxiously directed to an impending civil war. All dreaded it, all sought to avert it. While the inaugural address was being delivered from this place, devoted altogether to *saving* the Union without war, insurgent agents were in the city seeking to *destroy* it without war—seeking to dissolve the Union and divide effects by negotiation. Both parties deprecated war, but one of them would *make* war rather than let the nation survive, and the other would *accept* war rather than let it perish, and the war came.

One-eighth of the whole population were colored slaves, not distributed generally over the Union, but localized in the southern part of it. These slaves constituted a peculiar and powerful interest. All knew that this interest was somehow the cause of the war. To strengthen, perpetuate, and extend this interest was the object for which the insurgents would rend the Union even by war, while the Government claimed no right to do more than to restrict the territorial enlargement of it. Neither party expected for the war the magnitude or the duration which it has already attained. Neither anticipated that the *cause* of the conflict might cease with or even before the conflict itself should cease. Each looked for an easier triumph, and a result less fundamental and astounding. Both read the same Bible and pray to the same God, and each invokes His aid against the other. It may seem strange that any men should dare to ask a just God's assistance in wringing their bread from the sweat of other men's faces, but let us judge not, that we be not judged. The prayers of both could not be answered. That of neither has been answered fully. The Almighty has His own purposes. "Woe unto the world because of offenses; for it must needs be that offenses come, but woe to that man by whom the offense cometh." If we shall suppose that American slavery is one of those offenses which, in the providence of God, must needs come, but which, having continued through His appointed time, He now wills to remove, and that He gives to both North and South this terrible war as the woe due to those by whom the offense came, shall we discern therein any departure from those divine attributes which the believers in a living God always ascribe to Him? Fondly do we hope, fervently do we pray, that this mighty scourge of war may speedily pass away. Yet, if God wills that it continue until all the wealth piled by the bondsman's two hundred and fifty years of unrequited toil shall be sunk, and until every drop of blood drawn with the lash shall be paid by another drawn with the sword, as was said three thousand years ago, so still it must be said "the judgments of the Lord are true and righteous altogether."

With malice toward none, with charity for all, with firmness in the right as God gives us to see the right, let us strive on to finish the work we are in, to bind up the nation's wounds, to care for him who shall have borne the battle and for his widow and his orphan, to do all which may achieve and cherish a just and lasting peace among ourselves and with all nations.

Source: James D. Richardson, ed., *A Compilation of the Messages and Papers of the Presidents* (New York, 1897), 7:3477, 3478.

The Thirteenth Amendment (1865)

Proposed in Congress in January 1865, the necessary three-fourths of the states ratified the Thirteenth Amendment by December. The national government gave the southern states little choice, making ratification of the Thirteenth Amendment a condition for their resuming representation in Congress. Congress, however, demanded even more concessions from the states and refused to seat the southern congressmen when they appeared to take their seats.

Some Republicans argued that the Thirteenth Amendment articulated the new national protections of citizens' rights achieved on Civil War battlefields. Ending slavery transformed the former slaves into citizens, they thought. And emancipation meant ending discrimination – the effects of slavery – as well. White southerners challenged that thinking, seeking to limit its impact. Just because African Americans were no longer slaves, *they insisted, did not make them citizens. Ending slavery, they continued, did not give Congress plenary power over citizens' rights.*

SECT. 1. Neither slavery nor involuntary servitude, except as a punishment for crime whereof the party shall have been duly convicted, shall exist within the United States, or any place subject to their jurisdiction.

SECT. 2. Congress shall have power to enforce this article by appropriate legislation.

Source: Francis Newton Thorpe, ed., *The Federal and State Constitutions, Colonial Charters and other Organic Laws* (Washington, 1909), 1:31.

5.

Reconstructing Citizenship

The Civil War and Reconstruction changed the basis of Americans' liberty. Thomas Jefferson's ideology of agrarian independence, modified by Andrew Jackson, had dominated American thinking before the war. Citizens possessed, or expected to possess, sufficient land to guarantee economic independence. A reservoir of frontier land insured each citizen a measure of autonomy. Denied access to land, black Americans had no choice but to seek a source other than land for their freedoms. They found it in national citizenship. They argued that the United States Constitution protected their personal rights, including the right to testify, vote, and own property, but also the right to live. Today this is a truism, but in Reconstruction it amounted to a highly controversial claim unprecedented in American history.

Ultimately, this new source of citizens' rights revolutionized the distribution of power in the United States. Through Reconstruction, however, courts and lawmakers sharply disputed the power of Congress to protect individual rights through the federal courts. In 1865 this new Congressional role likely seemed plausible because the relationship of American citizens to their national government must have been permanently and profoundly changed by the Civil War. Fought by massive armies in the name of national unity against states' rights, the war killed 600,000 people and freed four million African Americans. Perhaps because they understood that such a consequential event promised great change, some whites demanded a return to the old ways. One Mississippi planter explained to a skeptical audience of blacks that the Civil War had indeed freed them. But, he went on, now that the war was over he expected them to return to work—as slaves! More realistically, many Americans understood that the war had destroyed slavery but still expected states to retain the robust powers they had once enjoyed.

"Reconstruction" is the name given to efforts to make sure that the war really did change things and that black freedom would continue even after Appomattox. It could be argued that Reconstruction began in 1863 when Abraham Lincoln proposed the first Reconstruction program. More often, scholars argue that Reconstruction began when the Union Army seized control of significant portions of the Mississippi Valley the same year.

Lincoln's scheme, followed by the policies of his successor, Andrew Johnson, form what has been called "Presidential Reconstruction." Lincoln proposed only slight federal interference in states' rights, allowing southern states back into the Union just as soon as 10 percent of the qualified voters in 1860 took a loyalty oath. Lincoln's plan abolished slavery but made no promises regarding black voting. When Johnson became president, he began the wholesale pardoning of Confederates and restoration of ex-Confederates to power. By protecting the rights of the defeated southern states and vetoing Congressional Reconstruction measures, Johnson rallied the flagging spirits of defeated rebels, encouraging resistance to national power.

Reconstruction worked dramatic changes in the South, but northerners saw a spectacular transformation as well. American industrial production increased by 75 percent between 1865 and 1873. During that same time, powerful railroad corporations laid 35,000 miles of track. By 1873, the United States had the second-largest industrial capacity in the world. More Americans worked off the farm than in agricultural occupations. Whites subjugated Indians as settlers raced to the West by the millions, putting vast tracts of land into agricultural cultivation for the first time. These farmers' production fed eastern manufacturing centers as did the ore stripped from the earth by western miners. All this generated vast wealth and power. State and federal governments eagerly solicited the good will of powerful new corporations and reckless promoters alike. Such concentrated power worked against the egalitarianism inherent in Reconstruction's reform impulse.

Northern states did make some, very limited, progress. Pennsylvania and New York enacted important civil rights laws in 1867 and 1873. Chicago, Cleveland, and Milwaukee ended school segregation. But most northern blacks lived in urban poverty and suffered ubiquitous prejudice. Women found the limits of Reconstruction reformism when they petitioned for the right to vote. Lydia Maria Child warned Charles Sumner that if she vented her anger over the subordination of women, "I might frighten you." She added that women either had the right to vote or else the whole theory of American constitutionalism was false. Wyoming territory gave women the vote but only in hopes of swelling the population with "an immigration of ladies." Utah Mormons also allowed women the vote but only in hopes of countering the political strength of largely unmarried and non-Mormon miners.

Continued prejudice shows the limitations of Reconstruction benevolence. Even this weak reform effort faded over time. Historians argue about when Reconstruction ended, with Eric Foner now insisting it continues even today as our racial problems remain unresolved. Traditionally it is said to have ended in 1877, when Rutherford B. Hayes became president, though Republican efforts to protect the rights of black citizens lingered into the twentieth century.

As a reform movement, Reconstruction withered. Yet the most important legacy of the Civil War and its aftermath may well have been the permanent changes Reconstruction made to the United States Constitution. In the midst of the Civil War and in the Reconstruction era that followed, Congress wrote three new amendments to the Constitution. These amendments ultimately transformed the Constitution from a protector of slavery to a guardian of civil rights. Notice they *ultimately* made the national government a protector of rights. Most of the Republicans who proposed these new amendments and piloted them through Congress and the state ratifying process did not want to upset the balance of power between the states and the national government.

They expected the states to continue to protect the rights of their citizens. The new amendments meant they did so under the supervision of the United States government.

Attorney General Edward Bates on the Meaning of Citizenship (1862)

In the first eight decades of American history, the meaning of citizenship did not often seem a pressing issue. Although it came up in the Dred Scott case, when Chief Justice Roger Taney insisted that African Americans could never be a part of whites' "political community," important questions remained unresolved.

In the Civil War four million African Americans forced whites to confront their claims to citizenship. Blacks demanded full citizenship rights; they wanted to vote, hold office, and debate public issues. These demands came early in the war. In 1862 Secretary of the Treasury Salmon Chase asked Attorney General Edward Bates for an opinion on black citizenship. No abolitionist, Bates stalled, only reluctantly answering the question. When he did, Bates did not deny that blacks could be citizens. He did insist that citizenship carried with it few benefits.

November 29, 1862

Who is a citizen? What constitutes a citizen of the United States? I have often been pained by the fruitless search in our law books and the records of our courts, for a clear and satisfactory definition of the phrase *citizen of the United States*. I find no such definition, no authoritative establishment of the meaning of the phrase, neither by a course of judicial decisions in our courts, nor by the continued and consentaneous action of the different branches of our political government. For aught I see to the contrary, the subject is now as little understood in its details and elements, and the question as open to argument and to speculative criticism, as it was at the beginning of the Government. Eighty years of practical enjoyment of citizenship, under the Constitution, have not sufficed to teach us either the exact meaning of the word, or the constituent elements of the thing we prize so highly....

[W]ith regard to the right of suffrage, that is, the right to choose officers of government, there is a very common error to the effect that the right to vote for public officers is one of the constituent elements of American citizenship, the leading faculty indeed of the citizen, the test at once of his legal right, and the sufficient proof of his membership of the body politic. No error can be greater than this, and few more injurious to the right understanding of our constitutions and the actual working of political governments....the reverse is conspicuously true...there is no district in the nation in which a majority of the known and recognized citizens are not excluded by law from the right of suffrage. Besides those who are excluded specially on account of some personal defect, such as paupers, idiots, lunatics, and men convicted of infamous crimes, and, in some States, soldiers, all females and all minor males are also excluded. And these, in every community, make the majority; and yet, I think, no one will venture to deny that women and children, and lunatics, and even convict felons, may be citizens of the United States....

In my opinion, the Constitution uses the word citizen only to express the political quality of the individual in his relations to the nation; to declare that he is a member of the body politic, and bound to it by the reciprocal obligation of allegiance on the one side and protection on the other....

Source: J. Hubley Ashton, ed., *Official Opinions of the Attorneys General of the United States, Advising the President and Heads of Departments* (Washington, 1868), 10:382–418.

Lincoln's Last Speech (1865)

The Civil War launched President Abraham Lincoln on an intellectual journey. In 1858 Lincoln had insisted that under no circumstances could African Americans enjoy full citizenship rights. By 1865 he had begun to change his mind. We will never know how far he might have gone, his so-called "last" speech provides a clue. Lincoln delivered this address after dark from a second-story window of the White House when cheering crowds celebrating the Confederate surrender called for him to speak. Lincoln had carefully prepared a speech for the occasion and read it, holding a candle in one hand and his manuscript in the other, so as to get his words on a sensitive subject exactly right.

The speech dealt with the fruits of Lincoln's Ten Percent Plan. Under this plan seceded southern states could return to the Union if only 10 percent of the number of persons voting in 1860 took a loyalty oath. Lincoln's policies allowed Tennessee, Louisiana, and Arkansas to propose constitutions and elect governments. Louisiana's constitution dared broach the most controversial and explosive issue of the day: black voting. While it would be too much to say that Lincoln's speech on this question caused his assassination (John Wilkes Booth had been plotting to kill the president, vice president, and secretary of state for some time), Lincoln's limited and conditional endorsement of black suffrage spurred Booth into action.

...[T]he question is not whether the Louisiana government, as it stands, is quite all that is desirable. The question is "Will it be wiser to take it as it is, and help to improve it; or to reject, and disperse it?" "Can Louisiana be brought into proper practical relation with the Union *sooner* by *sustaining*, or by *discarding* her new State Government?"

Some twelve thousand voters in the heretofore slave-state of Louisiana have sworn allegiance to the Union, assumed to be the rightful political power of the State, held elections, organized a State government, adopted a free-state constitution, giving the benefit of public schools equally to black and white, and empowering the Legislature to confer the elective franchise upon the colored man. Their Legislature has already voted to ratify the constitutional amendment recently passed by Congress, abolishing slavery throughout the nation. These twelve thousand persons are thus fully committed to the Union and to perpetual freedom in the State—committed to the very things, and nearly all the things, the nation wants—and they ask the nation's recognition and its assistance to make good their committal. Now, if we reject, and spurn them, we do our utmost to disorganize and disperse them. We in effect say to the white men "You are worthless or worse—we will neither help you, nor be helped by you." To the blacks we say: "This cup of liberty which these, your old masters, hold to your lips, we will dash from you, and leave you to the chances of gathering the spilled and scattered contents in some vague and undefined when, where, and how." If this course, discouraging and paralyzing both white and black, has any tendency to bring Louisiana into proper practical relations with the Union, I have, so far, been unable to perceive it. If, on the contrary, we recognize and sustain the new government of Louisiana, the converse of all this is made true. We encourage the hearts and nerve the arms of the twelve thousand to adhere to their work, and argue for it, and proselyte for it, and fight for it, and feed it, and grow it, and ripen it to a complete success. The colored man, too, in seeing all united for him, is inspired with vigilance, and energy, and daring, to the same end. Grant that he desires the elective franchise, will he not attain it sooner by saving the already advanced steps toward it than by running backward over them? Concede that the new government of Louisiana is only what it should be as the egg is to the fowl, we shall sooner have the fowl by hatching the egg than by smashing it.

...What has been said of Louisiana will apply generally to other States.

Source: Roy P. Basler, ed., Marion Dolores Pratt and Lloyd A. Dunlap, asst. eds., *The Collected Works of Abraham Lincoln*, 9 vols. (New Brunswick, 1953 and 1955), 8:403–404. Courtesy Abraham Lincoln Association.

Black Code of Mississippi (1865)

Lincoln's assassination made his vice president, Tennessean Andrew Johnson, president. Under President Andrew Johnson's leadership, southern states tried to bar blacks from the rights of citizenship. Many southern states wrote statutes after the Civil War designed to substitute law for the slaveholders' lash. Johnson had returned to power old Whigs, white southern politicians opposed to secession but otherwise not much different from the South's antebellum rulers. The Chicago Tribune *named the statutes these old Whigs wrote "black codes." The codes backfired badly for Johnson and the southerners, proving very effective in mobilizing northern public opinion against Johnson and his policies.*

An act to confer Civil Rights on Freedmen, and for other purposes.

SECT. 1. *Be it enacted by the Legislature of the State of Mississippi* . . . Provided that the provisions of this section shall not be so construed, as to allow any freedman, free negro or mulatto, to rent or lease any lands or tenements, except in incorporated towns or cities in which places the corporate authorities shall control the same....

SECT. 3. *Be it further enacted,* That all freedmen, free negroes and mulattoes, who do now and have heretofore lived and cohabited together as husband and wife shall be taken and held in law as legally married, and the issue shall be taken and held as legitimate for all purposes. That it shall not be lawful for any freeman, free negro or mulatto to intermarry with any white person; nor for any white person to intermarry with any freedman, free negro or mulatto; and any person who shall so intermarry shall be deemed guilty of felony, and on conviction thereof, shall be confined in the State Penitentiary for life; and those shall be deemed freemen, free negroes and mulattoes, who are of pure negro blood, and those descended from a negro to the third generation inclusive, though one ancestor of each generation may have been a white person.

SECT. 5. *Be it further enacted,* That every freedman, free negro and mulatto, shall, on the second Monday of January, one thousand eight hundred and sixty-six, and annually thereafter, have a lawful home or employment, and shall have written evidence thereof....

SECT. 7. *Be it further enacted,* That every civil officer shall, and every person may arrest and carry back to his or her legal employer any freedman, free negro or mulatto, who shall have quit the service of his or her employer before the expiration of his or her term of service without good cause....

SECT. 8. *Be it further enacted,* That upon affidavit made by the employer of any freedman, free negro or mulatto, or other credible person, before any justice of the peace or member of the board of police, that any freedman, free negro or mulatto, legally employed by said employer, has illegally deserted said employment, such justice of the peace or member of the board or police, shall issue his warrant or warrants, returnable before himself, or other such officer, directed to any sheriff, constable or special deputy, commanding him to arrest said deserter and return him or her to said employer, and the like proceedings shall be had as provided in the preceding section; and it shall be lawful for any officer to whom such warrant shall be directed, to execute said warrant in any county of this State, and that said warrant may be transmitted without endorsement to any like officer of another county, to be executed and returned as aforesaid, and the said employer shall pay the cost of said warrants and arrest and return, which shall be set off for so much against the wages of said deserter.

Source: *Laws of the State of Mississippi* (Jackson, 1866), 82–84.

State v. Wash Lowe (1866)

Even in the South white conservatives recognized that the Civil War had changed the meaning of citizenship. This case from the circuit court in Adams County, Mississippi, shows the reaction of one Mississippi judge to emancipation. Mississippi judges and lawyers had to decide whether emancipation made their former slaves into citizens. Not surprisingly, they resisted that idea. But they did concede that things had changed. This circuit court judge ruled that the right to carry arms amounted to a natural right that could not be denied African Americans. Distinguishing natural rights from political rights, this judge decided that freed slaves could carry guns but not vote.

The information in these cases charges the accused with carrying arms,...an...act was passed prohibiting freedmen, free negroes and mulattoes, unless licensed by the Board of Police, from keeping or carrying fire-arms of any kind, or any ammunition, dirk or bowie knife, under penalty of $10 fine and forfeiture of arms and ammunition. When this act was passed our State was overrun by thieves, robbers and murderers. *It was not safe for white or black to travel, or even to stay at home.* Without having artificial means of defence at home, negroes who had received pay and discharge from the United States service, were special subjects for attack by these merciless brigands. The citizen has the right to bear arms in defence of himself, secured by the constitution. So too, the citizens of other States, including thieves and robbers, have the right to bear arms. *Should not then, the freedmen have and enjoy the same constitutional right to bear arms in defence of themselves, that is enjoyed by the citizen? It is a natural and personal right – the right of self-preservation.* It is not a political right. The emancipation of the slaves restored them to their natural rights. It did not restore them to political rights, for they never had any. They were never members of our social and political compact. The act, therefore, prohibiting them from keeping or carrying firearms, *was a violation of that article in the Constitution which provides for and makes it incumbent upon the Legislature to pass laws for the protection of person and property of the freedmen....*

Source: *New York Times*, October 2, 1866.

Redistribution of Property (1866)

John H. Rice

Some Republicans associated citizenship with ownership of land. John H. Rice of Maine favored breaking up southern plantations and distributing the land amongst the slaves. The idea that citizens must own land comes from Thomas Jefferson, who envisioned America as a republic of independent and self-sufficient farmers. Rice's speech in the House of Representatives reveals a Jeffersonian "conservatism" behind his "radicalism."

...The lands of the leading rebels of the South should have been confiscated and given out in homesteads to the loyal men of the South and to our gallant soldiers who, by their prowess, have saved them from the control of the most accursed despotism and aristocracy that can be imagined....

I have said that we must strike to the very foundation of the difficulties existing in the South. We must educate the people in the rights and duties of freemen. This can be done in no other way than by planting them upon the soil and protecting them there. Why, sir, what is the use of giving liberty and the right of suffrage to men, if you say that they shall not have the right to live and support themselves by honest labor? Unless you grant them this, you give them a stone when they ask you for bread. Wherever there are small farms, there you find liberty and independence. Give the lands of any country into the control and ownership of great monopolies, and there the masses of the people will be oppressed, ignorant, and miserable. The greatest and most difficult problem to solve in this century is a political and social one combined; and that is to protect the poor and the ignorant against the wrongs and oppression of capital and aristocracy. This is a labor which needs to be done everywhere, in the North as well as in the South, in the East and the West; and most abundantly in the monarchies and oligarchies of the Old World. May its solution be wrought out to its greatest perfection in our own favored country....

I admit that more of the black race will be able to avail themselves of [my proposal] than the white race of the South, for the reason that they are mostly loyal, and the whites are mostly disloyal; and the blacks, too, are more anxious to take up farms and labor upon them than the whites. The evidence comes up to us from every source that the great desire of the freedman is to have a small farm for the support of himself and family, and very soon release the Government from all expense on their account....

Source: *Congressional Globe*, 39th Congress, 1st session, part 1 (Washington, 1866), 717.

Civil Rights Act of 1866

The South's Black Codes galvanized northern support for civil rights legislation. After the Civil War, the Republican party split into factions. Radicals like John Rice favored a dramatic overhaul of the federal system, shifting power to the national government along the lines Alexander Hamilton had favored in the early years of the nation's development. But Rice and his allies never commanded a majority in Congress. Moderate Republicans favored a more circumspect approach. They expected the states to retain the duty to protect citizens' health and well-being, but they wanted the national government to force them to do so without discrimination, according black citizens the same protections enjoyed by whites. The Civil Rights Act of 1866 became the basis for the Fourteenth Amendment to the Constitution.

Be it enacted by the Senate and House of Representatives of the United States of America in Congress assembled, That all persons born in the United States and not subject to any foreign power, excluding Indians not taxed, are hereby declared to be citizens of the United States; and such citizens, of every race and color, without regard to any previous condition of slavery or involuntary servitude, except as a punishment for crime whereof the party shall have been duly convicted, shall have the same right, in every State and Territory in the United States, to make and enforce contracts, to sue, be parties, and give evidence, to inherit, to purchase, lease, sell, hold, and convey real and personal property, and to full and equal benefit of all laws and proceedings for the security of person and property, as is enjoyed by white citizens, and shall be subject to like punishment, pains, and penalties, and to none other, any law, statute, ordinance, regulation, or custom, to the contrary notwithstanding....

SECT. 3. *And be it further enacted,* That the district courts of the United States, within their respective districts, shall have, exclusively of the courts of the several States, cognizance of all crimes and offences committed against the provisions of this act, and also, concurrently with the circuit courts of the United States, of all causes, civil and criminal, affecting persons who are denied or cannot enforce in the courts or judicial tribunals of the State or locality where they may be any of the rights secured to them by the first section of this act....

Source: George P. Sanger, ed., *The Statutes at Large, Treaties, and Proclamations of the United States of America* (Boston, 1868), 14:27.

Andrew Johnson's Veto of the Civil Rights Act of 1866

Johnson vetoed the Civil Rights Act. Like Abraham Lincoln, Johnson professed to speak for the common man, attacking the "slavocracy" as a "pampered, bloated, corrupted aristocracy." In this role, Johnson had supported public education and homestead legislation. But while Lincoln's administration turned away from states' rights, Johnson could not imagine upsetting the old balance of power between the states and the national government. Johnson did not have Lincoln's openness to new ideas.

By the time Congress passed the Civil Rights Act, Johnson had become deeply unpopular. Congress swiftly overturned his veto.

WASHINGTON, D.C., *March 27, 1866*

To the Senate of the United States:

I regret that the bill, which has passed both Houses of Congress, entitled "An act to protect all persons in the United States in their civil rights and furnish the means of their vindication," contains provisions which I can not approve consistently with my sense of duty to the whole people and my obligations to the Constitution of the United States. I am therefore constrained to return it to the Senate, the House in which it originated, with my objections to its becoming law.

By the first section of the bill all persons born in the United States and not subject to any foreign power, excluding Indians not taxed, are declared to be citizens of the United States....

The grave question presents itself whether, when eleven of the thirty-six States are unrepresented in Congress at the present time, it is sound policy to make our entire colored population and all other excepted classes citizens of the United States. Four millions of them have just emerged from slavery into freedom. Can it be reasonably supposed that they possess the requisite qualifications to entitle them to all the privileges and immunities of citizens of the United States? Have the people of the several States expressed such a conviction?...The bill in effect proposes a discrimination against large numbers of intelligent, worthy, and patriotic foreigners, and in favor of the negro, to whom, after long years of bondage, the avenues to freedom and intelligence have just now been suddenly opened....

The legislation...proposed invades the judicial power of the State. It says to every State court or judge, If you decide that this act is unconstitutional; if you refuse, under the prohibition of a State law, to allow a negro to testify; if you hold that over such a subject-matter the State law is paramount, and "under color" of a State law refuse the exercise of the right to the negro, your error of judgment, however conscientious, shall subject you to fine and imprisonment....

The Constitution expressly declares that the judicial power of the United States "shall extend to all cases, in law and equity, arising under this Constitution, the laws of the United States, and treaties made or which shall be made under their authority; to all cases affecting ambassadors, other public ministers, and consuls; to all cases of admiralty and maritime jurisdiction; to controversies to which the United States, between a State and citizens of another State, between citizens of different States, between citizens of the same State claiming lands under grants of different States, and between a State, or the citizens thereof, and foreign states, citizens, or subjects." Here the judicial power of the United States is expressly set forth and defined; and the act of September 24, 1789, establishing the judicial courts of the United States, in conferring upon the Federal courts jurisdiction over cases originating in State tribunals, is careful to confine them to the classes enumerated in the above-recited clause of the Constitution. This section of the bill undoubtedly comprehends cases and authorizes the exercise of powers that are not, by the

Constitution, within the jurisdiction of the courts of the United States. To transfer them to those courts would be an exercise of authority well calculated to excite distrust and alarm on the part of all the States, for the bill applies alike to all of them—as well to those that have as to those that have not been engaged in rebellion....

In all our history, in all our experience as a people living under Federal and State law, no such system as that contemplated by the details of this bill has ever before been proposed or adopted. They establish for the security of the colored race safeguards which go infinitely beyond any that the General Government has ever provided for the white race. In fact, the distinction of race and color is by the bill made to operate in favor of the colored and against the white race. They interfere with the municipal legislation of the States, with the relations existing exclusively between a State and its citizens, of between inhabitants of the same State—an absorption and assumption of power by the General Government which, if acquiesced in, must sap and destroy our federative system of limited powers and break down the barriers which preserve the rights of the States. It is another step, or rather stride, toward centralization and the concentration of all legislative powers in the National Government.

Source: James D. Richardson, comp., *A Compilation of the Messages and Papers of the Presidents* (New York, 1897), 8:3603, 3604, 3607, 3608–3609, 3610–3611.

Radicalism (1866)

George Julian

During Reconstruction, Democrats very effectively labeled all Republicans "radicals," charging they wanted to fundamentally change American society. This sobriquet proved so effective that for years many history books referred to Congressional Reconstruction (1867–1877) as "Radical Reconstruction." In fact, few Republicans espoused truly radical proposals in the Reconstruction era. Almost all Republicans were themselves infested with conservative views on race, opposed a dramatic shift of power away from the states, and did not want to break up antebellum plantations. But some Republicans were "radical." Indiana Republican George W. Julian favored distributing southern plantation land to the freed slaves. Even before the end of the Civil War he favored allowing blacks to vote, a radical notion at that time. In this speech before the House of Representatives, Julian discusses the meaning of radicalism.

June 16, 1866

...The conflict going on to-day between Conservatism and Radicalism is not a new one. It only presents new phases, and more decided characteristics in its progress toward a final settlement. These elements in our political life were at war long years prior to the late rebellion. After the old questions concerning trade, currency, and the public lands had ceased to be the pivots on which our national policy turned, and were only nominally in dispute, Conservatism put them on its banner, and shouted for them as the living issues of the times, while intelligent men everywhere saw that the real and sole controversy was that very question of slavery which the leaders of parties were striving so anxiously to keep out of sight. Conservatism stubbornly closed its eyes to this truth. It believed in conciliation, and concession. It preached the gospel of compromise. Professing hostility to slavery, it paraded its readiness to yield up its convictions as a virtue. Resistance to aggression and wrong, it branded as fanaticism or wickedness, while it was ever ready to purchase peace at the cost of principle....

But Radicalism assumed a directly antagonistic position. It did not believe in conciliation and compromise. It did not believe that a powerful and steadily advancing evil was to be mastered by submission to its behests, but by timely and resolute resistance....[F]or had [Radicals] been seconded in their earnest efforts to rouse the people and to lay hold of the aggressions of slavery in their incipient stages, the black tide of southern domination which has since inundated the land might have been rolled back, and the Republic saved without the frightful surgery of war....

But the war at length came....Conservatism, in its unexampled stupidity, denied that rebels in arms against the Government were its enemies, and declared them to be only misguided friends. The counsel it perpetually volunteered was that of great moderation and forbearance on our part in the conduct of the war....It insisted that slavery and freedom were...equally sacred in its sight....

But here, again, Radicalism squarely met the issue tendered by the Conservatives. That slavery caused the war and was necessarily involved in its fortunes it accepted as a simple truism....In the very beginning of the conflict Radicalism...demanded the employment of all the powers of war in the accomplishment of its purpose. It understood the conflict not as simply a struggle to save the Union, but a grand and final battle for the rights of man....

But...the war is over....Conservatism...now demands the indiscriminate pardon of all the rebel leaders. It recognizes the revolted States as still in the Union, in precisely the same sense as are the loyal States, and restored to all their rights as completely as if no rebellion had happened. It opposes any constitutional amendment which shall deprive the rebels of the representation of the freedmen in Congress, who have no voice as citizens, and thus sanctions this most flagrant outrage upon justice and democratic equality, in the interest of unrepentant traitors. It opposes the protection of the millions of loyal colored people of the South through the agency of a Freedman's Bureau, and thus hands them over to starvation, and scourgings, and torture, by their former masters. It opposes, likewise, the civil rights bill, which seeks to protect these people in their right to sue, to testify in the courts, to make contracts, and to own property. It opposes, of course, with all bitterness, the policy of giving the freedmen the ballot, which "is as just a demand as governed men ever made of governing," and should be accorded at once, both on the score of policy and justice. In short, it seeks to make void and of non-effect, for any good purpose, the sacrifice of more than three hundred thousand lives and three thousand millions of money, by its eager service of the heaven-defying villains who causelessly brought this sacrifice upon the nation.

But on all these points Radicalism takes issue. It holds that treason is a crime, and that it ought to be punished. While it does not ask for vengeance, it demands public justice against some at least of the rebel leaders. It deals with the revolted States as outside of their constitutional relations to the Union, and as incapable of restoring themselves to it except on conditions to be prescribed by Congress. It demands the immediate reduction of representation in the States of the South to the basis of actual voters, and the amendment of the Constitution for that purpose. It favors the protection of the colored people of the South, through the Freedmen's Bureau and civil rights bills, as necessary to make effective the constitutional amendment abolishing slavery. And for the same reason, Radicalism, when not smitten by unnatural fear or afflicted by policy, demands the ballot as the right of every colored citizen of the rebellious States....

Source: *Congressional Globe*, 39th Congress, 1st session, part 4, (Washington, 1866), 3208, 3209.

Reconstruction Act of 1867

As president, Andrew Johnson gave the South political victories it could not win on the battlefield. Although Johnson did not intend to persuade northern veterans of the Civil War and the sisters, widows, brothers, mothers, and fathers of those who had died, that Union soldiers had fought for nothing, his actions nevertheless had that effect. Johnson's political ineptitude contributed to his eventual political irrelevance. Public opinion shifted decisively against Johnson and in favor of his opponents in Congress. As a result, Congress in 1867 moved to take control of Reconstruction. The era of Presidential Reconstruction came to an end with the passage of the Reconstruction Act of 1867. The law divided the South into military districts, placing a general in charge of each district. The law threw out the state governments established by Lincoln and Johnson, setting up a procedure for new elections and new state constitutions, with blacks participating in the voting. Congressional Reconstruction had begun.

Whereas no legal State governments or adequate protection for life or property now exists in the rebel States of Virginia, North Carolina, South Carolina, Georgia, Mississippi, Alabama, Louisiana, Florida, Texas, and Arkansas; and whereas it is necessary that peace and good order should be enforced in said States until loyal and republican State governments can be legally established: Therefore,

Be it enacted by the Senate and House of Representatives of the United States of America in Congress assembled, That said rebel States shall be divided into military districts and made subject to the military authority of the United States as hereinafter prescribed, and for that purpose Virginia shall constitute the first district; North Carolina and South Carolina the second district; Georgia, Alabama, and Florida the third district; Mississippi and Arkansas the fourth district; and Louisiana and Texas the fifth district.

SECT. 2. *And be it further enacted,* That it shall be the duty of the President to assign to the command of each of said districts and officer of the army, not below the rank of brigadier-general, and to detail a sufficient military force to enable such officer to perform his duties and enforce his military force within the district to which he is assigned.

SECT. 3. *And be if further enacted,* That it shall be the duty of each officer assigned as aforesaid, to protect all persons in their rights of person and property, to suppress insurrection, disorder, and violence, and to punish, or cause to be punished, all disturbers of the public peace and criminals; and to this end he may allow local civil tribunals to take jurisdiction of and to try offenders, or, when in his judgment it may be necessary for the trial of offenders, he shall have power to organize military commissions or tribunals for that purpose, and all interference under color of State authority with the exercise of military authority under this act, shall be null and void.

SECT. 4. *And be it further enacted,* That all persons put under military arrest by virtue of this act shall be tried without unnecessary delay, and no cruel or unusual punishment shall be inflicted, and no sentence of any military commission or tribunal hereby authorized, affecting the life or liberty of any person, shall be executed until it is approved by the officer in command of the district, and the laws and regulations for the government of the army shall not be affected by this act, except in so far as they conflict with its provisions: *Provided,* That no sentence of death under the provisions of this act shall be carried into effect without the approval of the President.

SECT. 5. *And be it further enacted,* That when the people of any one of said rebel States shall have formed a constitution of government in conformity with the Constitution of the United States in all respects, framed by a convention of delegates elected by the male citizens of said State, twenty-one years old and upward, of whatever race, color, or previous condition, who have been resident in said State for one year previous to the day of such election, except such as may be disfranchised for participation in the rebellion or for felony at common law, and when such constitution shall provide that the elective franchise shall be enjoyed by all such persons as have the qualifications herein stated for electors of delegates, and when such constitution shall have been submitted to Congress for examination and approval, and Congress shall have approved the same, and when said State, by a vote of its legislature elected under said constitution, shall have adopted the amendment to the Constitution of the United States, proposed by the Thirty-ninth Congress, and known as article fourteen, and when said article shall have become a part of the Constitution of the United States, said State shall be declared entitled to representation in Congress, and senators and representatives shall be admitted therefrom on their taking the oath prescribed by law, and then and thereafter the preceding sections of this act shall be inoperative in said State: *Provided,* That no person excluded from the privilege of holding office by said proposed amendment to the Constitution of the United States, shall be eligible to election as a member of the convention to frame a constitution for any of said rebel States, nor shall any such person vote for members of such convention.

SECT. 6. *And be it further enacted,* That, until the people of said rebel States shall be by law admitted to representation in the

Congress of the United States, any civil governments which may exist therein shall be deemed provisional only, and in all respects subject to the paramount authority of the United States at any time to abolish, modify, control, or supersede the same; and in all elections to any office under such provisional governments all persons shall be entitled to vote, and none others, who are entitled to vote, under the provisions of the fifth section of this act; and no person shall be eligible to any office under any such provisional governments who would be disqualified from holding office under the provisions of the third *article* of said constitutional amendment.

Source: George P. Sanger, ed., *The Statutes at Large, Treaties and Proclamations of the United States of America* (Boston, 1868), 14:428.

Articles of Impeachment (1868)

Impeachment is essentially a political process: it is a method by which federal officials who have lost the confidence of the people can be removed from office. At least in part, Ronald Reagan's successful deflection of calls for his impeachment in the Iran-Contra scandal can be traced to his immense popularity. Richard Nixon resigned to avoid impeachment not only because he committed a crime, but because he decisively lost public support. Republicans pursued Bill Clinton in defiance of his popularity. Northern public opinion turned against Andrew Johnson when it perceived him as winning for the South what it had lost in war. He restored Confederates to power. He obstructed Congress as it tried to manage Reconstruction – and after the 1866 elections Congress clearly acted for most voters. In 1867, Congress required that all orders to subordinate military commanders pass through Ulysses Grant, commander of the Army. Congress also enacted the Tenure in Office Act. Under this law, officials appointed with the Senate's consent could not be removed until the Senate approved a successor. Johnson removed Secretary of War Edwin M. Stanton from office on February 21, 1868.

The House voted to impeach; Johnson went on trial in the Senate. Because this was a political process, it must be remembered that senators considered not just whether Johnson should be removed from office but whether the president pro tem of the Senate should become president. Johnson had no vice president, leaving the president pro tem next in line. In 1868 Ben Wade, a radical Republican proponent of high tariffs, inflationary monetary policies, and pro-

labor sympathies, served as president pro tem. By a one-vote margin, the Senate voted not to remove Johnson from office. The vote may have been as much against Wade as for Johnson.

ARTICLE I. That said Andrew Johnson, President of the United States, on the 21st day of February, A.D. 1868, at Washington, in the District of Columbia, unmindful of the high duties of his office, of his oath of office, and of the requirement of the Constitution that he should take care that the laws be faithfully executed, did unlawfully and in violation of the Constitution and laws of the United States issue an order in writing for the removal of Edwin M. Stanton from the office of Secretary for the Department of War, said Edwin M. Stanton having been theretofore duly appointed and commissioned, by and with the advice and consent of the Senate of the United States, as such Secretary; and said Andrew Johnson, President of the United States, on the 12th day of August, A.D. 1867, and during the recess of said Senate, having suspended by his order Edwin M. Stanton from said office, and within twenty days after the first day of the next meeting of said Senate—that is to say, on the 12th day of December in the year last aforesaid—having reported to said Senate such suspension, with the evidence and reasons for his action in the case and the name of the person designated to perform the duties of such office temporarily until the next morning of the Senate; and said Senate thereafterwards, on the 13th day of January, A.D. 1868, having duly considered the evidence and reasons reported by said Andrew Johnson for said suspension, and having refused to concur in said suspension, whereby and by force of the provisions of an act entitled "An act regulating the tenure of certain civil offices," passed March 2, 1867, said Edwin M. Stanton did forthwith resume the functions of his office, whereof the said Andrew Johnson had then and there due notice; and said Edwin M. Stanton, by reason of the premises, on said 21st day of February, being lawfully entitled to hold said office of Secretary for the Department of War:

EXECUTIVE MANSION,
Washington, D.C., February 21, 1868

HON. EDWIN M. STANTON,
Washington, D.C.

SIR: By virtue of the power and authority vested in me as President by the Constitution and laws of the United States, you are hereby removed from office as Secretary for the Department of War, and your functions as such will terminate upon the receipt of this communication.

You will transfer to Brevet Major-General Lorenzo Thomas, Adjutant-General of the Army, who has this day been authorized and empowered to act as Secretary of War *ad interim,* all records, books, papers, and other public property now in your custody and charge.

Respectfully, yours,

ANDREW JOHNSON

which order was unlawfully issued with intent then and there to violate the act entitled "An act regulating the tenure of certain civil offices," passed March 2, 1867, and with the further intent, contrary to the provisions of said act, in violation thereof, and contrary to the provisions of the Constitution of the United States, and without the advice and consent of the Senate of the United States, the said Senate then and there being in session, to remove said Edwin M. Stanton from the office of Secretary for the Department of War, the said Edwin M. Stanton being then and there in the due and lawful execution and discharge of the duties of said office; whereby said Andrew Johnson, President of the United States, did then and there commit and was guilty of a high misdemeanor in office....

ARTICLE IX. That said Andrew Johnson, President of the United States, on the 22d day of February, A.D. 1868, at Washington, in the District of Columbia, in disregard of the Constitution and the laws of the United States duly enacted, as Commander in Chief of the Army of the United States, did bring before himself then and there William H. Emory, a major-general by brevet in the Army of the United States, actually in command of the Department of Washington and the military forces thereof, and did then and there, as such Commander in Chief, declare to and instruct said Emory that part of a law of the United States, passed March 2, 1867, entitled "An act making appropriations for the support of the Army for the year ending June 30, 1868, and for other purposes," especially the second section thereof, which provides, among other things, that "all orders and instructions relating to military operations issued by the President or Secretary of War shall be issued through the General of the Army, and in case of his inability through the next rank," was unconstitutional and in contravention of the commission of said Emory, and which said provision of law had been theretofore duly and legally promulgated by general order for the government and direction of the Army of the United States, as the said Andrew Johnson then and there well knew, with intent thereby to induce said Emory, in his official capacity as commander of the Department of Washington, to violate the provisions of said act and to take and receive, act upon, and obey such orders as he, the said Andrew Johnson, might make and give, and which should not be issued through the General of the Army of the United States, according to the provisions of the said act, and with the further intent thereby to enable him, the said Andrew Johnson, to prevent the execution of the act entitled, "An act regulating the tenure of certain civil offices," passed March 2, 1867, and to unlawfully prevent Edwin M. Stanton, then being Secretary for the Department of the War, from holding said office and discharging the duties thereof; whereby said Andrew Johnson, President of the United States, did then and there commit and was guilty of a high misdemeanor in office....

ARTICLE X. That said Andrew Johnson, President of the United States,...did, on the 18th day of August, A.D. 1866, and on divers other days and times, as well before as afterwards, make and deliver with a loud voice certain intemperate, inflammatory, and scandalous harangues, and did therein utter loud threats and bitter menaces, as well against Congress as the laws of the United

States, duly enacted thereby, amid the cries, jeers, and laughter of the multitudes then assembled and in hearing....

Source: James D. Richardson, ed., *A Compilation of the Messages and Papers of the Presidents* (New York, 1897), 8:3907-3908, 3911-3912, 3913.

Texas v. White (1868)

In 1868 the Supreme Court heard a case that required the justices to decide some of the most important issues of the day. Had the southern states really left the Union when they purported to secede? In other words, can states leave the Union? Should Congress or the president decide Reconstruction policies? Did that clause of the Constitution guaranteeing a republican form of government for all the states really give the federal government power to determine the legitimacy of state governments?

All these questions came before the Court in a case involving ten million dollars originally paid to Texas by the United States government as a part of the 1850 Compromise. During the Civil War, the Confederate government of Texas spent the money to wage war against the United States. After Appomattox, the government of Texas wanted to take back the money spent by Confederate authorities. Understandably, the people who had sold Texas goods and services did not think they should give up the payment they had received for selling those goods and rendering the services. George W. White and John Chiles sued to keep the money. In his lawsuit, Chiles even claimed Texas had no right to sue in federal court as Texas had surrendered its status as a state of the United States when it seceded. And Chiles' lawyer added that even if the justices believed Texas continued to exist as a state, the government created by action of the United States Congress comprised no legitimate government. Chiles thus challenged the legitimacy of Congressional Reconstruction. If he had won his point, the Supreme Court would have declared Congressional Reconstruction unconstitutional.

The CHIEF JUSTICE delivered the opinion of the court.

The first inquiries to which our attention was directed by counsel, arose upon the allegations...of Chiles...that the State, having severed her relations with a majority of the States of the

Union, and having by her ordinance of secession attempted to throw off her allegiance to the Constitution and government of the United States, has so far changed her status as to be disabled from prosecuting suits in the National courts.

...The Articles of Confederation...solemnly declared [the Union] to "be perpetual." And when these Articles were found to be inadequate to the exigencies of the country, the Constitution was ordained "to form a more perfect Union." It is difficult to convey the idea of indissoluble unity more clearly than by these words. What can be indissoluble if a perpetual Union, made more perfect, is not?... The Constitution, in all its provisions, looks to an indestructible Union composed of indestructible States....

Considered therefore as transactions under the Constitution, the ordinance of secession, adopted by the convention and ratified by a majority of the citizens of Texas, and all the acts of her legislature intended to give effect to that ordinance, were absolutely null. They were utterly without operation in law. The obligations of the State, as a member of the Union, and of every citizen of the State, as a citizen of the United States, remained perfect and unimpaired.

...When the war closed, there was no government in the State except that which had been organized for the purpose of waging war against the United States. That government immediately disappeared. The chief functionaries left the State. Many of the subordinate officials followed their example. Legal responsibilities were annulled or greatly impaired. It was inevitable that great confusion should prevail. If order was maintained, it was where the good sense and virtue of the citizens gave support to local acting magistrates, or supplied more directly the needful restraints....

There being then no government in Texas in constitutional relations with the Union, it became the duty of the United States to provide for the restoration of such a government...the power to carry into effect the clause of guaranty is primarily a legislative power, and resides in Congress.

Under the fourth article of the Constitution, it rests with Congress to decide what government is the established one in a

State. For, as the United States guarantee to each State a republican government, Congress must necessarily decide what government is established in the State before it can determine whether it is republican or not....

The action of the President must therefore be considered as provisional, and in that light it seems to have been regarded by Congress. It was taken after the term of the 38th Congress had expired. The 39th Congress, which assembled in December, 1865, followed by the 40th Congress, which met in March, 1867, proceeded, after long deliberation, to adopt various measures for reorganization and restoration. These measures were embodied in proposed amendments to the Constitution, and in the acts known as the Reconstruction Acts, which have been so far carried into effect that a majority of the States which were engaged in the rebellion have been restored to their constitutional relations, under forms of government adjudged to be republican by Congress, through the admission of their "Senators and Representatives into the councils of the Union."...

That the bonds were the property of the State of Texas on the 11th of January, 1862, when the act prohibiting alienation without the indorsement of the governor was repealed, admits of no question, and is not denied. They came into her possession and ownership through public acts of the general government and of the State, which gave notice to all the world of the transaction consummated by them. And we think it clear that, if a State, by a public act of her legislature, imposes restrictions upon the alienation of her property, every person who takes a transfer of such property must be held affected by notice of them. Alienation in disregard of such restrictions can convey no title to the alienee.

In this case, however, it is said, that the restriction imposed by the act of 1851 was repealed by the act of 1862. And this is true if the act of 1862 can be regarded as valid. But was it valid?

What...was the character of the contract of the [Confederate] military board with White and Chiles?

That board, as we have seen, was organized not for the defence of the State against a foreign invasion or for its protection against domestic violence, within the meaning of these words as used in the National Constitution, but for the purpose, under the name of defence, of levying war against the United States. This purpose was undoubtedly unlawful, for the acts which it contemplated are, within the express definition of the Constitution, treasonable.

...Without entering at this time upon the inquiry whether any contract made by such a board can be sustained, we are obliged to say that...the contract...was...a contract in aid of the rebellion, and therefore void. And we cannot shut our eyes to the evidence which proves that the act of repeal was intended to aid rebellion by facilitating the transfer of these bonds....We can give no effect, therefore, to this repealing act.

It follows that the title of the State was not divested by the act of the insurgent government in entering into this contract....

On the whole case, therefore, our conclusion is that the State of Texas is entitled to the relief sought by her bill, and a decree must be made accordingly.

Source: 74 U.S. 700 (1868).

Reconstruction Amendments

During Reconstruction, the Constitution as a document changed more than at any other time in American history. No amendment has more profoundly changed the meaning of the Constitution than the Fourteenth.

After the Civil War some northern Republicans favored using the national government, strengthened and emboldened by the wartime experience, to protect citizens' rights from the states' bigotry. One newspaper editor concluded that the Civil War's one great lesson was that "the national citizenship must be paramount to the State." The Reconstruction amendments increased the power of the national government over the states.

The Fourteenth Amendment (1868)

Johnson's claims that the Civil Rights Act of 1866 violated the Constitution could be easily brushed aside by the moderate majority in Congress, but his veto message reminded many that this law could be repealed by some future Congress. Supporters of the 1866 Civil Rights Act could not be certain their work would stand forever unless they placed it in the Constitution. They did so in the Fourteenth Amendment.

John A. Bingham wrote section 1 of the Fourteenth Amendment. "I sought," he explained later, "to obtain for all *human beings...the precious right of life, liberty, and the pursuit of happiness." Deeply religious, Bingham believed he carried out God's work by writing the Fourteenth Amendment.*

The Fourteenth Amendment triumphantly repudiated the Supreme Court's infamous Dred Scott decision. Ultimately, this amendment served to nationalize the Bill of Rights, applying its provisions to the states. First, corporations, and then later civil rights groups and feminists relied heavily on this amendment for constitutional support.

SECT. 1. All persons born or naturalized in the United States, and subject to the jurisdiction thereof, are citizens of the United States and of the State wherein they reside. No State shall make or enforce any law which shall abridge the privileges or immunities of citizens of the United States; nor shall any State deprive any person of life, liberty, or property, without due process of law, nor deny any person within its jurisdiction the equal protection of the laws.

SECT. 2. Representatives shall be apportioned among the several States according to their respective numbers, counting the whole number of persons in each State, excluding Indians not taxed. But when the right to vote at any election for the choice of electors for President and Vice President of the United States, Representatives in Congress, the executive and judicial officers of a State, or the members of the legislature thereof, is denied to any of the male inhabitants of such State, being twenty-one years of age, and citizens of the United States, or in any way abridged, except for participation in rebellion or other crime, the basis of representation therein shall be reduced in the proportion which the number of such male citizens shall bear to the whole number of male citizens twenty-one years of age in such State.

SECT. 3. No person shall be a Senator or Representative in Congress, or elector of President and Vice President, or hold any office, civil or military, under the United States, or under any State, who, having previously taken an oath, as a member of Congress, or as an officer of the United States, or as a member of any State legislature, or as an executive or judicial officer of any State, to support the Constitution of the United States, shall have engaged in insurrection or rebellion against the same, or given aid or comfort to the enemies thereof. But Congress may, by a vote of two-thirds of each House, remove such disability.

SECT. 4 The validity of the public debt of the United States, authorized by law, including debts incurred for payment of pensions and bounties for services in suppressing insurrection or rebellion, shall not be questioned. But neither the United States nor any State shall assume or pay any debt or obligation incurred in aid of insurrection or rebellion against the United States, or any claim for the loss or emancipation of any slave; but all such debts, obligations, and claims shall be held illegal and void.

SECT 5. The Congress shall have power to enforce, by appropriate legislation, the provisions of this article.

Source: Francis Newton Thorpe, ed., *The Federal and State Constitutions, Colonial Charters and Other Organic Laws* (Washington, 1909), 1:31–32.

The Fifteenth Amendment (1870)

Congress debated black voting rights during its deliberations over the Thirteenth and Fourteenth Amendments. But voting rights had always been a particularly cherished state privilege. Republicans hesitated to interfere. White southern resistance hardened Republicans' determination to protect black suffrage through Constitutional amendment.

When southern state legislatures initially refused to ratify the Fourteenth Amendment, some Republicans became convinced that black voting must be federally protected. The 1867 Reconstruction law required black suffrage. In

1869 the House and Senate approved competing amendments, which had to be negotiated in conference. Congress approved and submitted the Fifteenth Amendment to the states on February 26. Many state legislatures were in session and dominated by Republicans when Congress sent them the amendment. Ratification came swiftly; on February 3, 1870, ratification was completed.

SECT. 1. The right of citizens of the United States to vote shall not be denied or abridged by the United States or by any State on account of race, color, or previous condition of servitude.

SECT. 2. The Congress shall have power to enforce this article by appropriate legislation.

Source: *The Constitution of the United State of America, as Amended,* 95th Congress, 1st Session, House Document No. 95-256 (Washington, 1978), 15.

6.

State Action and Civil Rights

After Congress wrote the three Civil War amendments and the states ratified them, the United States Supreme Court had to explain what had happened. These three amendments were the Constitutional fruits of the Civil War. By deciding their meaning, the Supreme Court also calculated the significance of that war. Some white Americans hoped that with the war's end, the federal government would shrink back to its pre-war state, allowing the states to once again do most of the governing. Other Americans, however, understood that for African Americans to enjoy even the most basic rights, including the right to live, the federal government would have to intervene forcefully on their behalf.

The Supreme Court proved a jealous guardian of states' rights and authorities. The Court decided that the states must retain the power to protect the health and safety of their citizens. Called the "police power," this authority had not been disturbed by the Civil War or the Constitutional amendments. The justices insisted that the Fourteenth Amendment did not allow Congress to regulate citizens directly but only through the states. When state legislatures passed a discriminatory law, the Congress could act against them. When individuals discriminated, the federal authority could do nothing—or so said the Supreme Court in 1875, 1882, and 1883.

Ku Klux Klan Act (1871)

Congress had to pass laws to enforce the Fourteenth Amendment's provisions. Samuel Shellabarger, an Ohio Republican, wrote the 1871 Ku Klux Klan Act. He thought that when states permitted discrimination, they violated the Fourteenth Amendment. In United States v. Cruikshank, *the Supreme Court disagreed, insisting that states had to actually pass a law to commit a state action, not just permit wrongdoing. Nonetheless, Shellabarger's law, called the "Klan Act" because it punished disguised mobs, is still the law today. In 1878, Congress made section 2 into section 5519 of the U.S. Code; it is now chapter 18, section 242. In 1951, Shellabarger's law became a more potent force when the Supreme Court reversed* United States v. Cruikshank *and decided that the Fourteenth Amendment covered private conspiracies. Because one part of the law makes it a crime to deprive "any class of persons"of equal protection of the laws, the Supreme Court has had to decide which groups in American society constitute a "class" entitled to federal protection. In 1997, the Court upheld the conviction of a state judge who had raped women in his judicial chambers (because he used the power of his office over women seeking custody of children and divorce settlements, he acted "under color of law"). By this decision, the Court defined women as a class of citizens deserving federal protection and made freedom from rape a national citizenship right.*

President Ulysses S. Grant used section 3 of Shellabarger's law to use troops against the Ku Klux Klan in South Carolina. Grant's soldiers proved very effective, breaking the back of the Klan in several counties.

An Act to enforce the Provisions of the Fourteenth Amendment of the Constitution of the United States, and for other Purposes.

Be it enacted by the Senate and House of Representatives of the United States of America in Congress assembled, That any person who, under color of any law, statute, ordinance, regulation, custom, or usage of any State shall subject, or cause to be subjected, any person within the jurisdiction of the United States to the deprivation of any rights, privileges, or immunities secured by the Constitution of the United States, shall, any such law, statute, ordinance, regulation, custom, or usage of the state to the contrary notwithstanding, be liable to the party injured in any action at law, suit in equity, or other proper proceeding for redress; such proceeding to be prosecuted in the several district or circuit courts....

SECT. 2. That if two or more persons within any State or Territory of the United States shall conspire together to...go in disguise upon the public highway or upon the premises of another for the purpose, either directly or indirectly, of depriving any person or any class of persons of the equal protection of the laws, or of equal privileges or immunities under the laws, or for the purpose of preventing or hindering the constituted authorities of any State from giving or securing to all persons within such State the equal protection of the laws, or shall conspire together for the purpose of in any manner impeding, hindering, obstructing, or defeating the due course of justice in any State or Territory, with intent to deny to any citizen of the United States the due and equal protection of the laws, or to injure any person in his person or his property for lawfully enforcing the right of any person or class of persons to the equal protection of the laws, or by force, intimidation, or threat to prevent any citizen of the United States lawfully entitled to vote from giving his support or advocacy in a lawful manner towards or in favor of the election of any lawfully qualified person as an elector of President or Vice-President of the United States, or as a member of Congress of the United States, or to injure any such citizen in his person or property on account of such support or advocacy, each and every person so offending shall be deemed guilty of a high crime, and, upon conviction thereof in any district or circuit court of the United States or district or supreme court of any Territory of the Untied States having jurisdiction of similar offences, shall be punished by a fine not less than five hundred nor more than five thousand dollars, or by imprisonment, with or without hard labor, as the court may determine, for a period of not less than six months nor more than six years, as the court may determine, or by both such fine and imprisonment as the court shall determine....

SECT. 3. That in all cases where insurrection, domestic violence, unlawful combinations, or conspiracies in any State shall so obstruct or hinder the execution of the laws thereof, and of the United States, as to deprive any portion or class of people of such

State of any of the rights, privileges, or immunities or protection, named in the Constitution and secured by this act, and the constituted authorities of such State shall either be unable to protect, or shall, from any cause, fail in or refuse protection of the people in such rights, such facts shall be deemed a denial by such State of the equal protection of the laws to which they are entitled under the Constitution of the United States; and in all such cases, or whenever any such insurrection, violence, unlawful combination, or conspiracy shall oppose or obstruct the laws of the United States or the due execution thereof, or impede or obstruct the due course of justice under the same, it shall be lawful for the President, and it shall be his duty to take such measures, by the employment of the militia or the land and naval forces of the United States, or of either, or by other means, as he may deem necessary for the suppression of such insurrection, domestic violence, or combinations....

Source: George P. Sanger, ed., *Statutes at Large and Proclamations of the United States* (Boston, 1873), 17:13–14.

Slaughterhouse Cases (1873)

Congressional action under the Fourteenth Amendment was just the first step. The Supreme Court had to interpret the new amendment's meaning. In 1873 the Supreme Court did this for the first time. On March 8, 1869, the Louisiana legislature had passed a law entitled "An Act to Protect the Health of the City of New Orleans, to Locate the Stock-Landings and Slaughter-Houses, and to Incorporate the Crescent City Live-Stock Landing and Slaughter-House Company." The new law created a butchering monopoly and prohibited rival butchers from operating outside the facilities of the Crescent City Live-Stock Landing and Slaughter-House Company.

Butchers thrown out of work by the Louisiana law filed three lawsuits that went to the Supreme Court: The Butchers' Benevolent Association of New Orleans v. The Crescent City Live-Stock Landing and Slaughter-House Company, Paul Esteben, L. Ruch, J. P. Rouede, W. Maylie, S. Firmberg, B. Beaubay, William Fagan, J. D. Broderick, N. Seibel, M. Lannes, J. Gitzinger, J. P. Aycock, D. Verges, The Live-Stock Dealers' and Butchers' Association of New Orleans and Charles Cavaroc v. The State of Louisiana, ex rel. S. Belden, Attorney General, and The Butchers' Benevolent Association of New Orleans v. The Crescent City Live-Stock Landing and Slaughter-House Company. *These cases are collectively known as the* Slaughterhouse Cases *and, in fact, that is the official name for this litigation.*

The butchers hired John Campbell to argue their suits before the Supreme Court. Campbell proved a brilliant choice. A former Supreme Court justice himself (an Alabamian, he resigned from the Court when his state seceded in 1861), he argued that the Civil War had changed the balance of power between the states and the national government. The Fourteenth Amendment made it unconstitutional for the states to encroach on citizens' national rights. Surely, he insisted, national citizens had the right to pursue their occupations free of interference by the states. The case pitted a former Confederate against a Supreme Court appointed by Lincoln, with the Confederate arguing for the most expansive reading of the new amendment. Campbell's ingenious argument almost succeeded. He persuaded four justices. The Slaughterhouse Cases *were the court's first opportunity to interpret the meaning of the new Fourteenth Amendment. The Court's decision limited the amendment's scope, meaning it would do little to protect the rights of the freed slaves for some time.*

MR. JUSTICE MILLER, now, April 14th, 1873, delivered the opinion of the court.

The power here exercised by the legislature of Louisiana is, in its essential nature, one which has been, up to the present period in the constitutional history of this country, always conceded to belong to the States, however it may now be questioned in some of its details.

...This is called the police power; and it is declared by Chief Justice Shaw that it is much easier to perceive and realize the existence and sources of it than to mark its boundaries, or prescribe limits to its exercise.

This power is, and must be from its very nature, incapable of any very exact definition or limitation. Upon it depends the security of social order, the life and health of the citizen, the comfort of an existence in a thickly populated community, the enjoyment of private and social life, and the beneficial use of property....

The regulation of the place and manner of conducting the slaughtering of animals, and the business of butchering within a city, and the inspection of the animals to be killed for meat, and of the meat afterwards, are among the most necessary and frequent exercises of this power. It is not, therefore, needed that we should seek for a comprehensive definition, but rather look for the proper source of its exercise....

Twelve articles of amendment were added to the Federal Constitution soon after the original organization of the government under it in 1789. Of these all but the last were adopted so soon afterwards as to justify the statement that they were practically contemporaneous with the adoption of the original; and the twelfth, adopted in eighteen hundred and three, was so nearly so as to have become, like all the others, historical and of another age. But within the last eight years three other articles of amendment of vast importance have been added by the voice of the people to that now venerable instrument.

The most cursory glance at these articles discloses a unity of purpose, when taken in connection with the history of the times, which cannot fail to have an important bearing on any question of doubt concerning their true meaning. Nor can such doubts, when any reasonably exist, be safely and rationally solved without a reference to that history; for in it is found the occasion and the necessity for recurring again to the great source of power in this country, the people of the States, for additional guarantees of human rights; additional powers to the Federal government; additional restraints upon those of the States. Fortunately that history is fresh within the memory of us all, and its leading features, as they bear upon the matter before us, free from doubt.

The institution of African slavery, as it existed in about half the States of the Union, and the contests pervading the public mind for many years, between those who desired its curtailment and ultimate extinction and those who desired additional safeguards for its security and perpetuation, culminated in the effort, on the part of most of the States in which slavery existed, to separate from the Federal government, and to resist its authority. This constituted the war of the rebellion, and whatever auxiliary causes may have contributed to bring about this war, undoubtedly the overshadowing and efficient cause was African slavery.

In that struggle slavery, as a legalized social relation, perished. It perished as a necessity of the bitterness and force of the conflict. When the armies of freedom found themselves upon the soil of slavery they could do nothing less than free the poor victims whose enforced servitude was the foundation of the quarrel. And when hard pressed in the contest these men (for they proved themselves men in that terrible crisis) offered their services and were accepted by thousands to aid in suppressing the unlawful rebellion, slavery was at an end wherever the Federal government succeeded in that purpose....

We repeat, then, in the light of this recapitulation of events, almost too recent to be called history, but which are familiar to us all; and on the most casual examination of the language of these amendments, no one can fail to be impressed with the one pervading purpose found in them all, lying at the foundation of each, and without which none of them would have been even suggested; we mean the freedom of the slave race, the security and firm establishment of that freedom, and the protection of the newly-made freeman and citizen from the oppressions of those who had formerly exercised unlimited dominion over him. It is true that only the fifteenth amendment, in terms, mentions the negro by speaking of his color and his slavery. But it is just as true that each of the other articles was addressed to the grievances of that race, and designed to remedy them as the fifteenth.

We do not say that no one else but the negro can share in this protection. Both the language and spirit of these articles are to have their fair and just weight in any question of construction. Undoubtedly while negro slavery alone was in the mind of the Congress which proposed the thirteenth article, it forbids any other kind of slavery, now or hereafter. If Mexican peonage or the Chinese coolie labor system shall develop slavery of the Mexican or Chinese race within our territory, this amendment may safely be trusted to make it void. And so if other rights are assailed by the States which properly and necessarily fall within the protection of these articles, that protection will apply, though the party interested may not be of African descent. But what we do say, and what we wish to be understood is, that in any fair and just construction of any section or phrase of these amendments, it is necessary to look to the purpose which we have said was the pervading spirit of them all, the evil which they were designed to remedy, and the process of continued addition to the Constitution, until that purpose was supposed to be accomplished, as far as constitutional law can accomplish it.

The first section of the fourteenth article, to which our attention is more specially invited, opens with a definition of citizenship—not only citizenship of the United States, but citizenship of the States. No such definition was previously found in the Constitution, nor had any attempt been made to define it by act of Congress. It had been the occasion of much discussion in the courts, by the executive departments, and in the public journals. It had been said by eminent judges that no man was a citizen of the United States, except as he was a citizen of one of the States composing the Union. Those, therefore, who had been born and resided always in the District of Columbia or in the Territories, though within the United States, were not citizens. Whether this proposition was sound or not had never been judicially decided. But it had been held by this court, in the celebrated Dred Scott case, only a few years before the outbreak of the civil war, that a man of African descent, whether a slave or not, was not and could not be a citizen of a State or of the United States. This decision, while it met the condemnation of some of the ablest statesmen and constitutional lawyers of the country, had never been overruled; and if it was to be accepted as a constitutional limitation of the right of citizenship, then all the negro race who had recently been made freemen, were still, not only not citizens, but were incapable of becoming so by anything short of an amendment to the Constitution.

To remove this difficulty primarily, and to establish a clear and comprehensive definition of citizenship which should declare what should constitute citizenship of the United States, and also citizenship of a State, the first clause of the first section was framed.

"All persons born or naturalized in the United States, and subject to the jurisdiction thereof, are citizens of the United States and of the State wherein they reside."

The first observation we have to make on this clause is, that it puts at rest both the questions which we stated to have been the subject of differences of opinion. It declares that persons may be citizens of the United States without regard to their citizenship of a particular State, and it overturns the Dred Scott decision by making all persons born within the United States and subject to its jurisdiction citizens of the United States. That its main purpose was to establish the citizenship of the negro can admit of no doubt. The phrase, "subject to its jurisdiction" was intended to exclude from its operation children of ministers, consuls, and citizens or subjects of foreign States born within the United States.

The next observation is more important in view of the arguments of counsel in the present case. It is, that the distinction between citizenship of the United States and citizenship of a State is clearly recognized and established. Not only may a man be a citizen of the United States without being a citizen of a State, but an important element is necessary to convert the former into the latter. He must reside within the State to make him a citizen of it, but it is only necessary that he should be born or naturalized in the United States to be a citizen of the Union.

It is quite clear, then, that there is a citizenship of the United States, and a citizenship of a State, which are distinct from each other, and which depend upon different characteristics or circumstances in the individual....

The constitutional provision there alluded to did not create those rights, which it called privileges and immunities of citizens of the States. It threw around them in that clause no security for the citizen of the State in which they were claimed or exercised. Nor did it profess to control the power of the State governments over the rights of its own citizens.

Its sole purpose was to declare to the several States, that whatever those rights, as you grant or establish them to your own citizens, or as you limit or qualify, or impose restrictions on their exercise, the same, neither more nor less, shall be the measure of the rights of citizens of other States within your jurisdiction.

It would be the vainest show of learning to attempt to prove by citations of authority, that up to the adoption of the recent amendments, no claim or pretence was set up that those rights depended on the Federal government for their existence or protection, beyond the very few express limitations which the Federal Constitution imposed upon the States—such, for instance, as the prohibition against ex post facto laws, bills of attainder, and laws impairing the obligation of contracts. But with the exception of these and a few other restrictions, the entire domain of the privileges and immunities of citizens of the States, as above defined, lay within the constitutional and legislative power of the States, and without that of the Federal government. Was it the purpose of the fourteenth amendment, by the simple declaration that no State should make or enforce any law which shall abridge the privileges and immunities of citizens of the United States, to transfer the security and protection of all the civil rights which we have mentioned, from the States to the Federal government? And where it is declared that Congress shall have the power to enforce that article, was it intended to bring within the power of Congress the entire domain of civil rights heretofore belonging exclusively to the States?

All this and more must follow, if the proposition of the plaintiffs in error be sound. For not only are these rights subject to the control of Congress whenever in its discretion any of them are supposed to be abridged by State legislation, but that body may also pass laws in advance, limiting and restricting the exercise of legislative power by the States, in their most ordinary and usual functions, as in its judgment it may think proper on all such subjects. And still further, such a construction followed by the reversal of the judgments of the Supreme Court of Louisiana in these cases, would constitute this court a perpetual censor upon all legislation of the States, on the civil rights of their own citizens, with authority to nullify such as it did not approve as consistent with those rights, as they existed at the time of the adoption of this amendment. The argument we admit is not always the most conclusive which is drawn from the consequences urged against the adoption of a particular construction of an instrument. But when, as in the case before us, these consequences are so serious, so far-reaching and pervading, so great a departure from the structure and spirit of our institutions; when the effect is to fetter and degrade the State governments by subjecting them to the control of Congress, in the exercise of powers heretofore universally conceded to them of the most ordinary and fundamental character; when in fact it radically changes the whole theory of the relations of the State and Federal governments to each other and of both these governments to the people; the argument has a force that is irresistible, in the absence of language which expresses such a purpose too clearly to admit of doubt.

We are convinced that no such results were intended by the Congress which proposed these amendments, nor by the legislatures of the States which ratified them.

Having shown that the privileges and immunities relied on in the argument are those which belong to citizens of the States as such, and that they are left to the State governments for security and protection, and not by this article placed under the special care of the Federal government, we may hold ourselves excused from defining the privileges and immunities of citizens of the United States which no State can abridge, until some case involving those privileges may make it necessary to do so.

But lest it should be said that no such privileges and immunities are to be found if those we have been considering are excluded, we venture to suggest some which owe their existence to the Federal government, its National character, its Constitution, or its laws.

...It is said to be the right of the citizen of this great country, protected by implied guarantees of its Constitution, "to come to the seat of government to assert any claim he may have upon that government, to transact any business he may have with it, to seek its protection, to share its offices, to engage in administering its functions. He has the right of free access to its seaports, through which all operations of foreign commerce are conducted, to the subtreasuries, land offices, and courts of justice in the several

States." And quoting from the language of Chief Justice Taney in another case, it is said "that for all the great purposes for which the Federal government was established, we are one people, with one common country, we are all citizens of the United States;" and it is, as such citizens, that their rights are supported in this court in *Crandall v. Nevada*.

Another privilege of a citizen of the United States is to demand the care and protection of the Federal government over his life, liberty, and property when on the high seas or within the jurisdiction of a foreign government. Of this there can be no doubt, nor that the right depends upon his character as a citizen of the United States. The right to peaceably assemble and petition for redress of grievances, the privilege of the writ of habeas corpus, are rights of the citizen guaranteed by the Federal Constitution. The right to use the navigable waters of the United States, however they may penetrate the territory of the several States, all rights secured to our citizens by treaties with foreign nations, are dependent upon citizenship of the United States, and not citizenship of a State. One of these privileges is conferred by the very article under consideration. It is that a citizen of the United States can, of his own volition, become a citizen of any State of the Union by a bona fide residence therein, with the same rights as other citizens of that State. To these may be added the rights secured by the thirteenth and fifteenth articles of amendment, and by the other clause of the fourteenth, next to be considered....

AFFIRMED.

MR. JUSTICE FIELD, dissenting:

I am unable to agree with the majority of the courts in these cases, and will proceed to state the reasons of my dissent from their judgment.

...The decree of Louis XVI, in 1776, abolished all monopolies of trades and all special privileges of corporations, guilds, and trading companies, and authorized every person to exercise, without restraint, his art, trade, or profession, and such has been the law of France and of her colonies ever since, and that law prevailed in Louisiana at the time of her cession to the United States. Since then, notwithstanding the existence in that State of the civil law as the basis of her jurisprudence, freedom of pursuit has been always recognized as the common right of her citizens. But were this otherwise, the fourteenth amendment secures the like protection to all citizens in that State against any abridgment of their common rights, as in other States. That amendment was intended to give practical effect to the declaration of 1776 of inalienable rights, rights which are the gift of the Creator, which the law does not confer, but only recognizes. If the trader in London could plead that he was a free citizen of that city against the enforcement to his injury of monopolies, surely under the fourteenth amendment every citizen of the United States should be able to plead his citizenship of the republic as a protection against any similar invasion of his privileges and immunities.

So fundamental has this privilege of every citizen to be free from disparaging and unequal enactments, in the pursuit of the ordinary avocations of life, been regarded, that few instances have arisen where the principle has been so far violated as to call for the interposition of the courts. But whenever this has occurred, with the exception of the present cases from Louisiana, which are the most barefaced and flagrant of all, the enactment interfering with the privilege of the citizen has been pronounced illegal and void. When a case under the same law, under which the present cases have arisen, came before the Circuit Court of the United States in the District of Louisiana, there was no hesitation on the part of the court in declaring the law, in its exclusive features, to be an invasion of one of the fundamental privileges of the citizen....

This equality of right, with exemption from all disparaging and partial enactments, in the lawful pursuits of life, throughout the whole country, is the distinguishing privilege of citizens of the United States. To them, everywhere, all pursuits, all professions, all avocations are open without other restrictions than such as are imposed equally upon all others of the same age, sex, and condition. The State may prescribe such regulations for every pursuit and calling of life as will promote the public health, secure the good order and advance the general prosperity of society, but when once prescribed, the pursuit or calling must be free to be followed by every citizen who is within the conditions designated, and will conform to the regulations. This is the fundamental idea upon which our institutions rest; and unless adhered to in the legislation of the country our government will be a republic only in name. The fourteenth amendment, in my judgment, makes it essential to the validity of the legislation of every State that this equality of right should be respected. How widely this equality has been departed from, how entirely rejected and trampled upon by the act of Louisiana, I have already shown. And it is to me a matter of profound regret that its validity is recognized by a majority of this court, for by it the right of free labor, one of the most sacred and imprescriptible rights of man, is violated....

MR. JUSTICE BRADLEY, also dissenting:

I concur in the opinion which has just been read by Mr. Justice Field; but desire to add a few observations for the purpose of more fully illustrating my views on the important question decided in these cases, and the special grounds on which they rest....

If a State legislature should pass a law prohibiting the inhabitants of a particular township, county, or city, from tanning leather or making shoes, would such a law violate any privileges or immunities of those inhabitants as citizens of the United States, or only their privileges and immunities as citizens of that particular State? Or if a State legislature should pass a law of caste, making all trades and professions, or certain enumerated trades and professions, hereditary, so that no one could follow any such trades or professions except that which was pursued by his father, would such a law violate the privileges and immunities of the people of that State as citizens of the United States, or only as citizens of the State? Would they have no redress but to appeal to the courts of that particular State?

This seems to me to be the essential question before us for consideration. And, in my judgment, the right of any citizen to follow whatever lawful employment he chooses to adopt (submitting himself to all lawful regulations) is one of his most valuable rights, and one which the legislature of a State cannot invade, whether restrained by its own constitution or not.

The right of a State to regulate the conduct of its citizens is undoubtedly a very broad and extensive one, and not to be lightly restricted. But there are certain fundamental rights which this right of regulation cannot infringe. It may prescribe the manner of their exercise, but it cannot subvert the rights themselves. I speak now of the rights of citizens of any free government. Granting for the present that the citizens of one government cannot claim the privileges of citizens in another government; that prior to the union of our North American States the citizens of one State could not claim the privileges of citizens in another State; or, that after the union was formed the citizens of the United States, as such, could not claim the privileges of citizens in any particular State; yet the citizens of each of the States and the citizens of the United States would be entitled to certain privileges and immunities as citizens, at the hands of their own government—privileges and immunities which their own governments respectively would be bound to respect and maintain. In this free country, the people of which inherited certain traditionary rights and privileges from their ancestors, citizenship means something. It has certain privileges and immunities attached to it which the government, whether restricted by express or implied limitations, cannot take away or impair. It may do so temporarily by force, but it cannot do so by right. And these privileges and immunities attach as well to citizenship of the United States as to citizenship of the States.

In my view, a law which prohibits a large class of citizens from adopting a lawful employment, or from following a lawful employment previously adopted, does deprive them of liberty as well as property, without due process of law. Their right of choice is a portion of their liberty; their occupation is their property. Such a law also deprives those citizens of the equal protection of the laws....

It is futile to argue that none but persons of the African race are intended to be benefited by this amendment. They may have been the primary cause of the amendment, but its language is general, embracing all citizens, and I think it was purposely so expressed.

The mischief to be remedied was not merely slavery and its incidents and consequences; but that spirit of insubordination and disloyalty to the National government which had troubled the country for so many years in some of the States, and that intolerance of free speech and free discussion which often rendered life and property insecure, and led to much unequal legislation. The amendment was an attempt to give voice to the strong National yearning for that time and that condition of things, in which American citizenship should be a sure guaranty of safety, and in which every citizen of the United States might stand erect on every portion of its soil, in the full enjoyment of every right and privilege belonging to a freeman, without fear of violence or molestation....

Source: 83 U.S. 36 (1873).

Bradwell v. the State (1873)

Myra Bradwell founded and published the Chicago Legal News and studied law with her husband, James B. Bradwell, probably in the 1850s or 1860s. At this time there were few female lawyers in the United States; the 1870 census found just five. Illinois law allowed any "person" of good character properly trained to practice law. Despite the statute, the Illinois Supreme Court refused to allow Myra Bradwell to become a lawyer. Bradwell went to the U.S. Supreme Court, claiming that her right to practice law was a privilege protected by the Fourteenth Amendment. The Supreme Court handed down its ruling in this case just one day after it ruled in the Slaughterhouse Cases. *When the Supreme Court finally did declare the states' sexual discriminations unconstitutional, in 1971, it used the equal protection clause of the Fourteenth Amendment, not its privileges and immunities clause.*

MR. JUSTICE MILLER delivered the opinion of the court.

...Counsel for the plaintiff in this court truly says that there are certain privileges and immunities which belong to a citizen of the United States as such; otherwise it would be nonsense for the fourteenth amendment to prohibit a State from abridging them, and he proceeds to argue that admission to the bar of a State of a person who possesses the requisite learning and character is one of those which a State may not deny.

In this latter proposition we are not able to concur with counsel. We agree with him that there are privileges and immunities belonging to citizens of the United States, in that relation and character, and that it is these and these alone which a State is forbidden to abridge. But the right to admission to practice in the courts of a State is not one of them.

Affirmed.

MR. JUSTICE BRADLEY:

I concur in the judgment of the court in this case, by which the judgment of the Supreme Court of Illinois is affirmed, but not for the reasons specified in the opinion just read.

The claim of the plaintiff, who is a married woman, to be admitted to practice as an attorney and counsellor-at-law, is based upon the supposed right of every person, man or woman, to engage in any lawful employment for a livelihood....

The claim that, under the fourteenth amendment of the Constitution, which declares that no State shall make or enforce any law which shall abridge the privileges and immunities of citizens of the United States, the statute law of Illinois, or the common law prevailing in that State, can no longer be set up as a barrier against the right of females to pursue any lawful employment for a livelihood (the practice of law included), assumes that it is one of the privileges and immunities of women as citizens to engage in any and every profession, occupation, or employment in civil life.

It certainly cannot be affirmed, as an historical fact, that this has ever been established as one of the fundamental privileges and immunities of the sex. On the contrary, the civil law, as well as nature herself, has always recognized a wide difference in the respective spheres and destinies of man and woman. Man is, or should be, woman's protector and defender. The natural and proper timidity and delicacy which belongs to the female sex evidently unfits it for many of the occupations of civil life. The constitution of the family organization, which is founded in the divine ordinance, as well as in the nature of things, indicates the domestic sphere as that which properly belongs to the domain and functions of womanhood. The harmony, not to say identity, of interests and views which belong, or should belong, to the family institution is repugnant to the idea of a woman adopting a distinct and independent career from that of her husband. So firmly fixed was this sentiment in the founders of the common law that it became a maxim of that system of jurisprudence that a woman had no legal existence separate from her husband, who was regarded as her head and representative in the social state; and, notwithstanding some recent modifications of this civil status, many of the special rules of law flowing from and dependent upon this cardinal principle still exist in full force in most States. One of these is, that a married woman is incapable, without her husband's consent, of making contracts which shall be binding on her or him. This very incapacity was one circumstance which the Supreme Court of Illinois deemed important in rendering a married woman incompetent fully to perform the duties and trusts that belong to the office of an attorney and counselor.

It is true that many women are unmarried and not affected by any of the duties, complications, and incapacities arising out of the married state, but these are exceptions to the general rule. The paramount destiny and mission of woman are to fulfill the noble and benign offices of wife and mother. This is the law of the Creator. And the rules of civil society must be adapted to the general constitution of things, and cannot be based upon exceptional cases.

The humane movements of modern society, which have for their object the multiplication of avenues for woman's advancement, and of occupations adapted to her condition and sex, have my heartiest concurrence. But I am not prepared to say that it is one of her fundamental rights and privileges to be admitted into every office and position, including those which require highly special qualifications and demanding special responsibilities. In the nature of things it is not every citizen of every age, sex, and condition that is qualified for every calling and position. It is the prerogative of the legislator to prescribe regulations founded on nature, reason, and experience for the due admission of qualified persons to professions and callings demanding special skill and confidence. This fairly belongs to the police power of the State; and, in my opinion, in view of the peculiar characteristics, destiny, and mission of woman, it is within the province of the legislature to ordain what offices, positions, and callings shall be filled and discharged by men, and shall receive the benefit of those energies and responsibilities, and that decision and firmness which are presumed to predominate in the sterner sex.

For these reasons I think that the laws of Illinois now complained of are not obnoxious to the charge of abridging any of the privileges and immunities of citizens of the United States.

Source: 83 U.S. 130 (1873).

United States v. Cruikshank (1876)

This case began in 1873 when fearful blacks fortified the little town of Colfax, Louisiana – they expected whites would attack them for their efforts to vote and hold political office. Whites did attack the town, overrunning the African Americans' fortifications and trapping them in the courthouse. Attacking whites forced an elderly black man to set fire to the building and then gunned down its occupants as they fled the flames. When whites captured some of the black defenders, they argued over whether to execute them or not. The pro-execution side won, and whites escorted the blacks out into a cotton field and shot them down.

When the U.S. Army arrived to restore order, they found dead African Americans scattered over the streets of Colfax and outside town as well. The state of Louisiana refused to prosecute the murderers, so a federal grand jury indicted 72 men under the 1870 Enforcement Act. The federal prosecutor took nine of these cases to trial in 1874. A jury found William Cruikshank and two others guilty. Cruikshank and his fellows appealed their convictions to the U.S. Supreme Court. The Supreme Court overturned their convictions, finding that the Fourteenth Amendment did not authorize the Enforcement Act. Crimes committed by individuals, outside state authority, were not covered by the Fourteenth Amendment, the Justices ruled. The amendment covered only state actions – actions officially authorized by the state legislature or courts. The Fourteenth Amendment, the Supreme Court decided, protected American citizens only from the states, not other citizens.

MR. CHIEF JUSTICE WAITE delivered the opinion of the court.

This case...presents for our consideration an indictment...based upon SECT. 6 of the Enforcement Act of May 31, 1870. That section is as follows:—

> That if two or more persons shall band or conspire together, or go in disguise upon the public highway, or upon the premises of another, with intent to violate any provision of this act, or to injure, oppress, threaten, or intimidate any citizen, with intent to prevent or hinder his free exercise and enjoyment of any right or privilege granted or secured to him by the constitution or laws of the United States, or because of his having exercised the same, such persons shall be held guilty of felony, and, on conviction thereof, shall be fined or imprisoned, or both, at the discretion of the court,—the fine not to exceed $5,000, and the imprisonment not to exceed ten years; and shall, moreover, be thereafter ineligible to, and disabled from holding, any office or place of honor, profit, or trust created by the constitution or laws of the United States.

...The fourteenth amendment prohibits a State from depriving any person of life, liberty, or property, without due process of law; but this adds nothing to the rights of one citizen against another. It simply furnishes an additional guaranty against any encroachment by the States upon the fundamental rights which belong to every citizen as a member of society....

The fourteenth amendment prohibits a State from denying to any person within its jurisdiction the equal protection of the laws; but this provision does not, any more than the one which precedes it, and which we have just considered, add any thing to the rights which one citizen has under the Constitution against another. The equality of the rights of citizens is a principle of republicanism.

Every republican government is in duty bound to protect all its citizens in the enjoyment of this principle, if within its power. That duty was originally assumed by the States; and it still remains there. The only obligation resting upon the United States is to see that the States do not deny the right. This the amendment guarantees, but no more. The power of the national government is limited to the enforcement of this guaranty....

We hold that the fifteenth amendment has invested the citizens of the United States with a new constitutional right, which is, exemption from discrimination in the exercise of the elective franchise on account of race, color, or previous condition of servitude. From this it appears that the right of suffrage is not a necessary attribute of national citizenship; but that exemption from discrimination in the exercise of that right on account of race, &c., is. The right to vote in the States comes from the States; but the right of exemption from the prohibited discrimination comes from the United States. The first has not been granted or secured by the Constitution of the United States; but the last has been.

Inasmuch, therefore, as it does not appear in these counts that the intent of the defendants was to prevent these parties from exercising their right to vote on account of their race, &c., it does not appear that it was their intent to interfere with any right granted or secured by the constitution or laws of the United States. We may suspect that race was the cause of the hostility; but that is not so averred. This is material to a description of the substance of the offence, and cannot be supplied by implication. Every thing essential must be charged positively, and not inferentially. The defect here is not in form, but in substance.

The order of the Circuit Court arresting the judgment upon the verdict is, therefore, affirmed; and the cause remanded, with instructions to discharge the defendants.

Source: 92 U.S. 542 (1876).

United States v. Harris (1882)

On August 14, 1876, a mob broke into the Crockett County, Tennessee, jail, extracted a man named P. M. Wells from his cell, and killed him. This crime violated the laws of Tennessee, but the state refused to prosecute the offenders. The United States Attorney, William W. Murray, a Union Army veteran from Georgia and a minor Republican politician, decided to pursue the members of the mob in federal court. He charged them with violating section two of the Ku Klux Klan Act of 1871. The law, based on the Fourteenth Amendment, made it a crime for "two or more persons" to "conspire or go in disguise upon the highway . . . for the purpose of depriving . . . any person . . . of the equal protection of the laws, or for the purpose of preventing or hindering the constituted authorities of any State or Territory from giving or securing to all persons . . . the equal protection of the laws . . . ." Murray believed that the mob, which included several persons named Harris, had conspired to prevent Tennessee from securing Wells in his right to protection while under arrest. Indicting the deputy sheriff in charge of the jail made the crime more obviously a "state action." The circuit judges hearing Murray's argument and reading his indictment could not agree among themselves on whether the Ku Klux Klan Act violated the Fourteenth Amendment or enforced its provisions.

The case went to the United States Supreme Court, giving the justices an opportunity to find that states had a duty to protect their arrested citizens from lynch mobs. Instead, the Court simply repeated their state action doctrine from United States v. Cruikshank, *ignoring Murray's argument. It seemed that even when a deputy sheriff – an employee of the state – cooperated with the mob, allowing a mob inside, no "state action" had occurred. The Supreme Court so completely dismissed Murray's argument that the official printed record does not actually say that the grand jury indicted the deputy, William A. Tucker or identify R.G. Harris as the sheriff of Crockett County. That information can only be extracted from the unpublished archival record of the case. To simply read the* Harris *decision fails to capture the significance of the case. Murray's original argument, recorded in his grand jury indictment, must be read as well.*

In the Circuit Court of the United States
Within and for the Western District of Tennessee
In the Sixth Judicial Circuit of the United States.

November 1876

The Grand Jurors of the United States within and for the Western District of Tennessee in the Sixth Judicial Circuit of the United

States duly elected, empanelled sworn and charged to inquire within and for said District in said Circuit upon their oaths present...that...R. G. Harris, E. D. Harris, James W. Harris, Tobe Harris, Milton Harris, Sidney Harris, Virgil M. Tucker, W. A. Tucker, A. J. Tucker, Samuel Hudgins, Nathan Brown, W. A. Powell, John Hunt, William Best, William Crandall, Charles L. Miller, Hugh McGavock, W. W. Hannell, A. J. Collinsworth, and S. W. Brassfield...within the jurisdiction of this court unlawfully and with force and arms did conspire together and with certain other evil disposed persons whose names are to the Grand Jurors aforesaid unknown then and there for the purpose of depriving one P. M. Wells, the said P.M. Wells then and there being a citizen of the United States and of the state of Tennessee of the equal protection of the laws, in this, to wit; that theretofore...the said P. M. Wells having been charged with the commission of a certain criminal offence against the laws of said state, the nature of which said criminal offence being to the Grand Jurors aforesaid unknown and having upon such charge been then and there duly arrested by the lawful and constituted authorities of said state, to wit, by one William A. Tucker, the said William A. Tucker then and there being a Deputy Sheriff of said county, and then and there acting as such; and the said P. M. Wells having been so then and there arrested as aforesaid, and being so as aforesaid under arrest, and in the custody of the said Deputy Sheriff, then and there aforesaid, then and there thereby and by virtue of the laws of said state became and was entitled to the due and equal protection of the said laws and was then and thereby entitled under and by virtue of and according the laws of said state to have his person protected from violence while he the said P. M. Wells was so then and there under arrest and in custody as aforesaid: And the Grand Jurors aforesaid upon their oaths aforesaid do further present that [the defendants named above] did...conspire together as aforesaid then and there for the purpose of depriving him the said P. M. Wells, of his right to the due and equal protection of the laws of said state and of his right to be protected in his person from violence while so there and there under arrest as aforesaid...unlawfully beating, bruising, wounding, and killing him the said P. M. Wells contrary to the form of the statute in such case made and provided against the peace and dignity of the United States of America.

MR. JUSTICE WOODS delivered the opinion of the court....

The language of the amendment does not leave this subject in doubt. When the State has been guilty of no violation of its provisions; when it has not made or enforced any law abridging the privileges or immunities of citizens of the United States; when no one of its departments has deprived any person of life, liberty, or property without due process of law, or denied to any person within its jurisdiction the equal protection of the laws; when, on the contrary, the laws of the State, as enacted by its legislative, and construed by its judicial, and administered by its executive departments, recognize and protect the rights of all persons, the amendment imposes no duty and confers no power upon Congress.

Source: 106 U.S. 629 (1882).

Civil Rights Cases (1883)

In 1875, Congress passed a law requiring the operators of hotels, restaurants, and theaters not to discriminate on the basis of race. This law came before the Supreme Court in a series of cases grouped together and called, collectively, "the Civil Rights Cases." Perhaps the most interesting came from New York's Grand Opera House, where the brother of John Wilkes Booth performed, very successfully. "I am jamming the Grand Opera House," Edwin Booth gloated. In November 1897, a black journalist named William R. Davis, Jr., hired a small white boy to buy two tickets for Booth's play. When Davis presented his tickets, the doorkeeper pronounced them "no good." Davis filed a criminal complaint against the doorkeeper, Samuel Singleton. Singleton's lawyer argued that the 1875 federal law "interferes with the right of the state of New York to provide the means under which the citizens of the state have the power to control and protect their rights in respect to private property."

Bradley's opinion includes notorious language that, from our point of view, disgraced the reputation of the Court. At one point he called blacks "the special favorite of the laws." He tried to disconnect racial discrimination from slavery by declaring that it ***"would be running the slavery argument into the ground to make it apply to every act of discrimination which a person may see fit to make as to the guests he will entertain."*** *Like many Republicans, and white people generally, Bradley believed that once slavery had ended, blacks should quickly assume the full burdens of citizenship and protect their own rights for themselves with no help from federal authorities.*

The Civil Rights Cases *broke like a shockwave across black America. Leaders organized protests against this latest evidence that the Fourteenth Amendment would not, after all, make them fully American citizens with federally protected rights.*

MR. JUSTICE BRADLEY delivered the opinion of the court.

It is obvious that the primary and important question in all the cases is the constitutionality of the law: for if the law is unconstitutional none of the prosecutions can stand.

The sections of the law referred to provide as follows:

> SECT. 1. That all persons within the jurisdiction of the United States shall be entitled to the full and equal enjoyment of the accommodations, advantages, facilities, and privileges of inns, public conveyances on land or water, theatres, and other places of public amusement; subject only to the conditions and limitations established by law, and applicable alike to citizens of every race and color, regardless of any previous condition of servitude.
>
> SECT. 2. That any person who shall violate the foregoing section by denying to any citizen, except for reasons by law applicable to citizens of every race and color, and regardless of any previous condition of servitude, the full enjoyment of any of the accommodations, advantages, facilities, or privileges in said section enumerated, or by aiding or inciting such denial, shall for every such offence forfeit and pay the sum of five hundred dollars to the person aggrieved thereby, to be recovered in an action of debt, with full costs; and shall also, for every such offence, be deemed guilty of a misdemeanor, and, upon conviction thereof, shall be fined not less than five hundred nor more than one thousand dollars, or shall be imprisoned not less than thirty days nor more than one year: Provided, That all persons may elect to sue

> for the penalty aforesaid, or to proceed under their rights at common law and by State statutes; and having so elected to proceed in the one mode or the other, their right to proceed in the other jurisdiction shall be barred. But this provision shall not apply to criminal proceedings, either under this act or the criminal law of any State: And provided further, That a judgment for the penalty in favor of the party aggrieved, or a judgment upon an indictment, shall be a bar to either prosecution respectively.

Are these sections constitutional?

The first section of the Fourteenth Amendment (which is the one relied on), after declaring who shall be citizens of the United States, and of the several States, is prohibitory in its character, and prohibitory upon the States. It declares that:

> No State shall make or enforce any law which shall abridge the privileges or immunities of citizens of the United States; nor shall any State deprive any person of life, liberty, or property without due process of law; nor deny to any person within its jurisdiction the equal protection of the laws.

It is State action of a particular character that is prohibited. Individual invasion of individual rights is not the subject-matter of the amendment. It has a deeper and broader scope. It nullifies and makes void all State legislation, and State action of every kind, which impairs the privileges and immunities of citizens of the United States, or which injures them in life, liberty or property without due process of law, or which denies to any of them the equal protection of the laws....It does not authorize Congress to create a code of municipal law for the regulation of private rights; but to provide modes of redress against the operation of State laws, and the action of State officers executive or judicial, when these are subversive of the fundamental rights specified in the amendment. Positive rights and privileges are undoubtedly secured by the Fourteenth Amendment; but they are secured by way of prohibition against State laws and State proceedings affecting those rights and privileges, and by power given to Congress to legislate for the purpose of carrying such prohibition into effect:

and such legislation must necessarily be predicated upon such supposed State laws or State proceedings, and be directed to the correction of their operation and effect....

And so in the present case, until some State law has been passed, or some State action through its officers or agents has been taken, adverse to the rights of citizens sought to be protected by the Fourteenth Amendment, no legislation of the United States under said amendment, nor any proceeding under such legislation, can be called into activity: for the prohibitions of the amendment are against State laws and acts done under State authority....

In this connection it is proper to state that civil rights, such as are guaranteed by the Constitution against State aggression, cannot be impaired by the wrongful acts of individuals, unsupported by State authority in the shape of laws, customs, or judicial or executive proceedings. The wrongful act of an individual, unsupported by any such authority, is simply a private wrong, or a crime of that individual; an invasion of the rights of the injured party, it is true, whether they affect his person, his property, or his reputation; but if not sanctioned in some way by the State, or not done under State authority, his rights remain in full force, and may presumably be vindicated by resort to the laws of the State for redress. An individual cannot deprive a man of his right to vote, to hold property, to buy and sell, to sue in the courts, or to be a witness or a juror; he may, by force or fraud, interfere with the enjoyment of the right in a particular case; he may commit an assault against the person, or commit murder, or use ruffian violence at the polls, or slander the good name of a fellow citizen; but, unless protected in these wrongful acts by some shield of State law or State authority, he cannot destroy or injure the right; he will only render himself amenable to satisfaction or punishment; and amenable therefore to the laws of the State where the wrongful acts are committed. Hence, in all those cases where the Constitution seeks to protect the rights of the citizen against discriminative and unjust laws of the State by prohibiting such laws, it is not individual offences, but abrogation and denial of rights, which it denounces, and for which it clothes the Congress with power to provide a remedy. This abrogation and denial of rights, for which the States alone were or could be responsible, was the great seminal and fundamental wrong which was intended to be remedied. And the remedy to be provided must necessarily be predicated upon that wrong. It must assume that in the cases provided for, the evil or wrong actually committed rests upon some State law or State authority for its excuse and perpetration....

The only question under the present head, therefore, is, whether the refusal to any persons of the accommodations of an inn, or a public conveyance, or a place of public amusement, by an individual, and without any sanction or support from any State law or regulation, does inflict upon such persons any manner of servitude, or form of slavery, as those terms are understood in this country?...

Now, conceding, for the sake of the argument, that the admission to an inn, a public conveyance, or a place of public amusement, on equal terms with all other citizens, is the right of every man and all classes of men, is it any more than one of those rights which the states by the Fourteenth Amendment are forbidden to deny to any person? And is the Constitution violated until the denial of the right has some State sanction or authority? Can the act of a mere individual, the owner of the inn, the public conveyance or place of amusement, refusing the accommodation, be justly regarded as imposing any badge of slavery or servitude upon the applicant, or only as inflicting an ordinary civil injury, properly cognizable by the laws of the State, and presumably subject to redress by those laws until the contrary appears?

After giving to these questions all the consideration which their importance demands, we are forced to the conclusion that such an act of refusal has nothing to do with slavery or involuntary servitude, and that if it is violative of any right of the party, his redress is to be sought under the laws of the State; or if those laws are adverse to his rights and do not protect him, his remedy will be found in the corrective legislation which Congress has adopted, or may adopt, for counteracting the effect of State laws, or State action, prohibited by the Fourteenth Amendment. It would be running the slavery argument into the ground to make it apply to every act of discrimination which a person may see fit to make as to the guests he will entertain, or as to the people he will take into his coach or cab or car, or admit to his concert or theatre, or deal with in other matters of intercourse or business. Innkeepers and public carriers, by the laws of all the States, so far as we are aware, are bound, to the extent of their facilities, to furnish proper accommodation to all unobjectionable persons who in good faith apply for them. If the laws themselves make any unjust discrimination, amenable to the prohibitions of the Fourteenth Amendment, Congress has full power to afford a remedy under that amendment and in accordance with it.

When a man has emerged from slavery, and by the aid of beneficent legislation has shaken off the inseparable concomitants of that state, there must be some stage in the progress of his elevation when he takes the rank of a mere citizen, and ceases to be the special favorite of the laws, and when his rights as a citizen, or a man, are to be protected in the ordinary modes by which other men's rights are protected. There were thousands of free colored people in this country before the abolition of slavery, enjoying all the essential rights of life, liberty and property the same as white citizens; yet no one, at that time, thought that it was any invasion of his personal status as a freeman because he was not admitted to all the privileges enjoyed by white citizens, or because he was subjected to discriminations in the enjoyment of accommodations in inns, public conveyances and places of amusement. Mere discriminations on account of race or color were not regarded as badges of slavery....

On the whole we are of opinion, that no countenance of authority for the passage of the law in question can be found in either the Thirteenth or Fourteenth Amendment of the Constitution; and no other ground of authority for its passage being suggested, it must necessarily be declared void, at least so far as its operation in the several States is concerned.

And it is so ordered.

MR. JUSTICE HARLAN dissenting.

The opinion in these cases proceeds, it seems to me, upon grounds entirely too narrow and artificial. I cannot resist the conclusion that the substance and spirit of the recent amendments of the Constitution have been sacrificed by a subtle and ingenious verbal criticism....

The Thirteenth Amendment, it is conceded, did something more than to prohibit slavery as an institution, resting upon distinctions of race, and upheld by positive law. My brethren admit that it established and decreed universal civil freedom throughout the United States. But did the freedom thus established involve nothing more than exemption from actual slavery? Was nothing more intended than to forbid one man from owning another as property?...

I am of the opinion that such discrimination practiced by corporations and individuals in the exercise of their public or quasi-public functions is a badge of servitude the imposition of which Congress may prevent under its power, by appropriate legislation, to enforce the Thirteenth Amendment; and, consequently, without reference to its enlarged power under the Fourteenth Amendment, the act of March 1, 1875, is not, in my judgment, repugnant to the Constitution....

The assumption that this amendment consists wholly of prohibitions upon State laws and State proceedings in hostility to its provisions, is unauthorized by its language. The first clause of the first section—"All persons born or naturalized in the United States, and subject to the jurisdiction thereof, are citizens of the United States, and of the State wherein they reside"—is of a distinctly affirmative character. In its application to the colored race, previously liberated, it created and granted, as well citizenship of the United States, as citizenship of the State in which they respectively resided. It introduced all of that race, whose ancestors had been imported and sold as slaves, at once, into the political community known as the "People of the United States." They became, instantly, citizens of the United States, and of their respective States. Further, they were brought, by this supreme act of the nation, within the direct operation of that provision of the Constitution which declares that "the citizens of each State shall be entitled to all privileges and immunities of citizens in the several States."...

My brethren say, that when a man has emerged from slavery, and by the aid of beneficent legislation has shaken off the inseparable concomitants of that state, there must be some stage in the progress of his elevation when he takes the rank of a mere citizen, and ceases to be the special favorite of the laws, and when his rights as a citizen, or a man, are to be protected in the ordinary modes by which other men's rights are protected. It is, I submit, scarcely just to say that the colored race has been the special favorite of the laws. The statute of 1875, now adjudged to be unconstitutional, is for the benefit of citizens of every race and color. What the nation through Congress, has sought to accomplish in reference to that race, is—what had already been done in every State of the Union for the white race—to secure and protect rights belonging to them as freemen and citizens; nothing more. It was not deemed enough "to help the feeble up, but to support him after." The one underlying purpose of congressional legislation has been to enable the black race to take the rank of mere citizens. The difficulty has been to compel a recognition of the legal right of the black race to take the rank of citizens, and to secure the enjoyment of privileges belonging, under the law, to them as a component part of the people for whose welfare and happiness government is ordained. At every step, in this direction, the nation has been confronted with class tyranny, which a contemporary English historian says is, of all tyrannies, the most intolerable, "for it is ubiquitous in its operation, and weighs, perhaps, most heavily on those whose obscurity or distance would withdraw them from the notice of a single despot." To-day, it is the colored race which is denied, by corporations and individuals wielding public authority, rights fundamental in their freedom and citizenship. At some future time, it may be that some other race will fall under the ban of race discrimination. If the constitutional amendments be enforced, according to the intent with which, as I conceive, they were adopted, there cannot be, in this republic, any class of human beings in practical subjection to another class, with power in the latter to dole out to the former just such privileges as they may choose to grant. The supreme law of the land has decreed that no authority shall be exercised in this country upon the basis of discrimination, in respect of civil rights, against freemen and citizens because of their race, color, or previous condition of servitude. To that decree—for the due enforcement of which, by appropriate legislation, Congress has been invested with express power—every one must bow, whatever may have been, or whatever now are, his individual views as to the wisdom or policy, either of the recent changes in the fundamental law, or of the legislation which has been enacted to give them effect.

For the reasons stated I feel constrained to withhold my assent to the opinion of the court.

Source: 109 U.S. 3 (1883).

T. Thomas Fortune and Constitutional Rights (1884)

The Supreme Court sought to minimize the impact of the Fourteenth Amendment. But its language remained available for use by oppressed peoples. When the Supreme Court left black citizens' rights and even their lives to the none-too-tender mercies of the states, some voices did rise in protest. T. Thomas Fortune, a black journalist based in New York, emerged to challenge what the Supreme Court had done. His speech delivered January 10, 1884, at the Putnam Phalanx armory used the rhetoric of the Constitution to challenge white racism. Determining the meaning of the Constitution is a task never solely in the hands of lawyers.

The black men of this republic have a herculean labor to perform. They need not look to others, to men and to parties, to perform it for them. The South has already wrenched from us the freedom and power of the ballot, and the doors of courts of law have been slammed in our faces. Star chamber justice has been instituted throughout the South, and mob and ruffianly outlaws execute the decree of the star chamber. The criminal is denied the protection of the law; the innocent have no immunity from violent taking off; the laborer is defrauded of his honest wage, and our women are reduced to indignities which would arouse the vengeance of a savage. The South is now under the influence of a reign of terror. The usual processes of the law are suspended and individual license and hatred are the standards by which black men must measure the volume of their security of life and property....

The State denies us protection, and the National Government says it has no jurisdiction, so that the black citizens of the South are absolutely without the rule of the law. What shall they do? Where shall they turn for succor or protection? What champion have they on the wave of politics...to present their grievances and urge with matchless zeal and eloquence that impartial justice shall be done?...

I know that it has become the fashion to hoot out of the politics of the North the race question; I know that men and parties have entered into compact to treat with silence and indifference the wails of sorrow and distress that come up hourly from our southland; I know that the country is drifting back to the view of the States Rights doctrines where Calhoun and Webster left off, and to ignore the power of the National Government as expressed in the XIVth and XVth Amendment to the Constitution—the essence of our four years of bloody internecine conflict—these things I know and feel to be the essence of the policy inaugurated by Mr. R. B. Hayes, President, of Ohio, and perpetuated since by each President. This policy was more fully outlined by the Supreme Court of the United States in declaring the unconstitutionality of the Ku-Klux law and the Civil Rights law—decisions which deny that Congress has power to enforce, by appropriate legislation, the civil and political rights of individual members of States, although explicitly conferred in the amendments outgrowing from the surrender of Robert E. Lee at Appomattox. But I affirm it to-night...that the citizen of the United States is greater than the citizen of the State; that the laws of the United States are more sovereign than the laws of the States in the matter of rights of citizens. In confirmation of my position, I appeal to the Constitution of the United States, which declares that "no State shall make or enforce any law which shall abridge the privileges or immunities of citizens of the United States, nor shall any State deprive any person of life, liberty or property without due process of law;" and that the "right of citizens of the United States to vote shall not be denied or abridged by the United States or any State." ...Will any man, even a judge of the Supreme Court, have the impudence to declare that the Constitution of the United States does not empower Congress with authority to protect citizens in their civil and political rights?...Strange as it may appear, the Supreme Court of the United States has denied the authority of the Congress of the Nation in these very fundamental particulars. And I have the courage here to-night...to declare the Supreme Court to be at fault, and to appeal from its arbiter dictum, as was done in the decision of Chief Justice Taney, in 1856, and more forcibly in 1860. I care not to where that appeal leads. If it leads to another such conflict as the one which gibbeted treason at Appomattox, let it come. Better that tons of treasure and millions of lives were sacrificed on the field of battle than that the infamous principle should be established that there was one citizen of this grand republic who had not equal and inalienable rights with each and every one of his fellow-citizens. That the just laws incorporated in the Constitution of our country shall have full and ample vindication; that lawlessness may be throttled at Danville, Virginia, and in Copiah County, Mississippi, I appeal to the honest sentiment of the country; I appeal to the courage and manhood and intelligence of the race, and I trust that I shall not appeal in vain. We ask for no special favor; we ask for no law reared upon subterfuge or chicanery; we ask for no particular immunity on account of race, we ask simply for justice; we demand justice, pure and simple, and though it be delayed for a quarter of a century, *justice we will have*! ...Let us agitate! *agitate*! AGITATE! until the protest shall awake the nation from its indifference....

Source: *New York Globe*, January 19, 1884.

Isaiah T. Montgomery at the Mississippi Constitutional Convention (1890)

In 1890, Mississippi held a state constitutional convention for the express purpose of disenfranchising the state's black voters. In the immediate aftermath of the Civil War, black political leaders had emerged to present their claims for freedom. So many attended the state's 1868 constitutional convention that racist wags dubbed it the "black and tan convention." By 1890, whites had violently squelched such leaders, driving them underground. Mississippi's leading politicians candidly announced that they wanted to "devise such measures, consistent with the Constitution of the United States, as will enable us to maintain a home government, under control of the white people of the state." Delegates devised a scheme designed to circumvent the Fourteenth and Fifteenth Amendments in a way that would not invite federal intervention in the state. Section 243 set "A uniform poll tax of two dollars, to be used in aid of the common schools, and for no other purpose," on "every male inhabitant of this State between the ages of twenty-one and sixty years." Persons unable to pay the tax, could not vote. The next section specified that every voter "be able to read any section of the constitution of this State; or he shall be able to understand the same when read to him, or give a reasonable interpretation thereof." Though seemingly race neutral, everyone understood that this scheme would allow registrars to keep black would-be voters away from the polls. This scheme became known as the Mississippi Plan. The Supreme Court declared it constitutional and other states followed suit. Soon few African Americans voted.

Only one African American attended the 1890 constitutional convention as a delegate, Isaiah T. Montgomery. Montgomery survived in Mississippi by speaking only very guardedly in the presence of whites. Nonetheless, Montgomery lectured his fellow delegates on the travails of black Mississippians. Montgomery endorsed the proposed voting restrictions as an improvement over the violent methods white Mississippians had been using to prevent black voting.

I. T. MONTGOMERY: Sometimes, Mr. President, as I gaze o'er our broad acres, my heart would rejoice in the progress and glory of Mississippi, but a feeling of sadness represses my exaltation, as the unanswerable question arises: How much life? how much of privation, sorrow and toil, has it cost my people? perchance every acre represents a grave and every furrow a tear. And what have they by way of recompense?...

My mission here is to bridge a chasm that has been widening and deepening for a generation; to divert a maelstrom that threatens destructions to you and yours, while it promises no enduring prosperity to me and mine....

Sir, we are well aware, that our Race has not yet attained the high plane of moral, intellectual and political excellence common to yours. But it is our privilege to press onward and upward. We accord you a generous need of praise for the assistance you have afforded. But you have suffered your prejudices to set the bounds and limits to our progress. Therefore, we still lack confidence to your professions of good will. It is this lack of confidence in any adjustment of our political economy proposed by you, that keeps up the Race solidity.

Mr. President, without a restoration of confidence, I can see no solution of this great problem. Without its solution, the work of this Convention will prove but a temporary expedient unworthy of the dignified principles that called it into being. While the silent and irrepressible conflict between the races has progressed. The condition of the State has languished. Her Treasury has been neglected. While the energies of her best citizens have been wasted in a needless conflict....

According to the most reliable estimates I have been able to procure...the present population of the State consists of:

Negroes	940,424
Whites	594,453
Total	1,543,877
Of which the black voters number	189,884
Of which the white voters number	118,890
Negro majority	70,994

Owing to the conditions herein specifically set forth, this vote, though nominally classed as Republican and Democratic, is practically divided up on the Race line.

The white people determined that the best interests of the state, and their own protection demanded that they should rule. This rule being generally fixed and arbitrary, virtually amounts to a domination with a fixed purpose to repress the negro vote. The methods employed to produce this result have introduced into the body politic every form of demoralization. Bloodshed, bribery, ballot stuffing, corruption, and perjury stalk unblushingly through the land. The good people of Mississippi stand aghast at the spectacle. The wail comes up from thousands of hearts in mute appeal to this Convention.

"Oh, how the mighty has fallen!"

Mr. President, this, in brief, is the problem [we face]....

[I]n the presence of the grave responsibilities resting upon this Convention, I shall support the Committee report. To quote the language of a leading negro statesman, I will say, "It is the Ship; all else is an Open, Raging, Tempestuous Sea."...

If we are to adhere to the belief that there exists a Supreme Arbiter of the destiny of Nations, we must also accept the opinion that by His decree these two races have been brought together on Southern soil.

That by His decree they must march on together for all time, so far as the mind of man can foresee.

Will not this same guiding power adjust their relations of the future as they march together evolving new and greater triumphs of progressive civilization?

Mr. Chairman, and gentlemen: In conclusion I again propound the great question? "Is our sacrifice accepted? Shall the great question be settled?"...

Your reply will cause their hearts to throb with joy, and break forth in the glad song of confidence, peace and good will, or it will cause them to gather their armor closer about, and with higher resolve press forward to the impending conflict.

In the name of God our common Father, in the name of humanity and the future hopes of our common country, I press the question...home to your conscience and to your hearts. What answer.

Source: *Vicksburg Evening Post*, September 18, 1890.

Plessy v. Ferguson (1896)

In 1890 Louisiana passed a law "to Promote the Comfort of Passengers." This statute required railroads to put separate cars on trains for blacks or to partition existing cars into white and black sections. When African Americans wanted to test the constitutionality of the new law, they did so with the complicity of railroads. "They want to help us," one black leader wrote, "but dread public opinion." The train companies did not want the expense of added train cars and partitions. On June 7, 1892, Homer Adolph Plessy boarded a car reserved for whites. By arrangement, authorities arrested him. In court, Plessy argued that he had been denied his privileges as an American citizen as well as the equal protection of the law.

It was Plessy's misfortune that he argued his case in the heyday of scientific racism. The best scientists in America, at the most prestigious universities, had "proven" black people physically inferior to whites. In 1884, the future dean of Harvard's Lawrence Scientific School justified disenfranchisement of blacks on the basis of their "animal nature." The chairman of the faculty of the University of Virginia thought blacks' education should be limited to "a Sunday-school training." Historian William H. Dunning thought allowing blacks voting rights had been a "reckless species of statecraft." Sociologist William Graham Sumner doubted government could change folkways.

MR. JUSTICE BROWN, after stating the case, delivered the opinion of the court.

This case turns upon the constitutionality of an act of the General Assembly of the State of Louisiana, passed in 1890, providing for separate railway carriages for the white and colored races.

The first section of the statute enacts "that all railway companies carrying passengers in their coaches in this State, shall provide equal but separate accommodations for the white, and colored races, by providing two or more passenger coaches for each passenger train, or by dividing the passenger coaches by a partition so as to secure separate accommodations…."

The object of the amendment was undoubtedly to enforce the absolute equality of the two races before the law, but in the nature of things it could not have been intended to abolish distinctions based upon color, or to enforce social, as distinguished from political equality, or a commingling of the two races upon terms unsatisfactory to either. Laws permitting, and even requiring, their separation in places where they are liable to be brought into contact do not necessarily imply the inferiority of either race to the other, and have been generally, if not universally, recognized as within the competency of the state legislatures in the exercise of their police power. The most common instance of this is connected with the establishment of separate schools for white and colored children, which has been held to be a valid exercise of the legislative power even by courts of States where the political rights of the colored race have been longest and most earnestly enforced....

While we think the enforced separation of the races, as applied to the internal commerce of the State, neither abridges the privileges or immunities of the colored man, deprives him of his property without due process of law, nor denies him the equal protection of the laws, within the meaning of the Fourteenth Amendment, we are not prepared to say that the conductor, in assigning passengers to the coaches according to their race, does not act at his peril, or that the provision of the second section of the act, that denies to the passenger compensation in damages for a refusal to receive him into the coach in which he properly belongs, is a valid exercise of the legislative power. Indeed, we understand it to be conceded by the State's attorney, that such part of the act as exempts from liability the railway company and its officers is unconstitutional. The power to assign to a particular coach obviously implies the power to determine to which race the passenger belongs, as well as the power to determine who, under the laws of the particular State, is to be deemed a white, and who a colored person. This question, though indicated in the brief of the plaintiff in error, does not properly arise upon the record in this case, since the only issue made is as to the unconstitutionality of the act, so far as it requires the railway to provide separate accommodations, and the conductor to assign passengers according to their race.

It is claimed by the plaintiff in error that, in any mixed community, the reputation of belonging to the dominant race, in this instance the white race, is property, in the same sense that a right of action, or of inheritance, is property. Conceding this to be so, for the purposes of this case, we are unable to see how this statute deprives him of, or in any way affects his right to, such property. If he be a white man and assigned to a colored coach, he may have his action for damages against the company for being deprived of his so called property. Upon the other hand, if he be a colored man and be so assigned, he has been deprived of no property, since he is not lawfully entitled to the reputation of being a white man.

In this connection, it is also suggested by the learned counsel for the plaintiff in error that the same argument that will justify the state legislature in requiring railways to provide separate accommodations for the two races will also authorize them to require separate cars to be provided for people whose hair is of a certain color, or who are aliens, or who belong to certain nationalities, or to enact laws requiring colored people to walk upon one side of the street, and white people upon the other, or requiring white men's houses to be painted white, and colored men's black, or their vehicles or business signs to be of different colors, upon the theory that one side of the street is as good as the other, or that a house or vehicle of one color is as good as one of another color. The reply to all this is that every exercise of the police power must be reasonable, and extend only to such laws as are enacted in good faith for the promotion for the public good, and not for the annoyance or oppression of a particular class....

So far, then, as a conflict with the Fourteenth Amendment is concerned, the case reduces itself to the question whether the statute of Louisiana is a reasonable regulation, and with respect to this there must necessarily be a large discretion on the part of the legislature. In determining the question of reasonableness it is at liberty to act with reference to the established usages, customs and traditions of the people, and with a view to the promotion of their comfort, and the preservation of the public peace and good order. Gauged by this standard, we cannot say that a law which authorizes or even requires the separation of the two races in public conveyances is unreasonable, or more obnoxious to the Fourteenth Amendment than the acts of Congress requiring separate schools for colored children in the District of Columbia, the constitutionality of which does not seem to have been questioned, or the corresponding acts of state legislatures.

We consider the underlying fallacy of the plaintiff's argument to consist in the assumption that the enforced separation of the two races stamps the colored race with a badge of inferiority. If this be so, it is not by reason of anything found in the act, but solely because the colored race chooses to put that construction upon it. The argument necessarily assumes that if, as has been more than once the case, and is not unlikely to be so again, the colored race should become the dominant power in the state legislature, and should enact a law in precisely similar terms, it would thereby relegate the white race to an inferior position. We imagine that the white race, at least, would not acquiesce in this assumption. The argument also assumes that social prejudices may be overcome by legislation, and that equal rights cannot be secured to the negro except by an enforced commingling of the two races. We cannot accept this proposition. If the two races are to meet upon terms of social equality, it must be the result of natural affinities, a mutual appreciation of each other's merits and a voluntary consent of individuals....

The judgment of the court below is, therefore,

AFFIRMED.

MR. JUSTICE HARLAN dissenting.

...The Thirteenth Amendment does not permit the withholding or the deprivation of any right necessarily inhering in freedom. It not only struck down the institution of slavery as previously existing in the United States, but it prevents the imposition of any burdens or disabilities that constitute badges of slavery or servitude. It decreed universal civil freedom in this country. This court has so adjudged. But that amendment having been found inadequate to the protection of the rights of those who had been in slavery, it was followed by the Fourteenth Amendment, which added greatly to the dignity and glory of American citizenship, and to the security of personal liberty, by declaring that "all persons born or naturalized in the United States, and subject to the jurisdiction thereof, are citizens of the United States and of the State wherein they reside," and that "no State shall make or enforce any law which shall abridge the privileges or immunities of citizens of the United States; nor shall any State deprive any person of life, liberty or property without due process of law, nor deny to any person within its jurisdiction the equal protection of the laws." These two amendments, if enforced according to their true intent and meaning, will protect all the civil rights that pertain to freedom and citizenship. Finally, and to the end that no citizen should be denied, on account of his race, the privilege of participating in the political control of his country, it was declared by the Fifteenth Amendment that "the right of citizens of the United States to vote shall not be denied or abridged by the United States or by any State on account of race, color or previous condition of servitude."

These notable additions to the fundamental law were welcomed by the friends of liberty throughout the world. They removed the race line from our governmental systems....

The white race deems itself to be the dominant race in this country. And so it is, in prestige, in achievements, in education, in wealth and in power. So, I doubt not, it will continue to be for all time, if it remains true to its great heritage and holds fast to the principles of constitutional liberty. But in view of the Constitution, in the eye of the law, there is in this country no superior, dominant, ruling class of citizens. There is no caste here. Our Constitution is color-blind, and neither knows nor tolerates classes among citizens. In respect of civil rights, all citizens are equal before the law. The humblest is the peer of the most powerful. The law regards man as man, and takes no account of his surroundings or of his color when his civil rights as guaranteed by the supreme law of the land are involved. It is, therefore, to be regretted that this high tribunal, the final expositor of the fundamental law of the land, has reached the conclusion that it is competent for a State to regulate the enjoyment by citizens of their civil rights solely upon the basis of race.

In my opinion, the judgment this day rendered will, in time, prove to be quite as pernicious as the decision made by this tribunal in the Dred Scott case. It was adjudged in that case that the descendants of Africans who were imported into this country and sold as slaves were not included nor intended to be included under the word "citizens" in the Constitution, and could not claim any of the rights and privileges which that instrument provided for and secured to citizens of the United States; that at the time of the adoption of the Constitution they were "considered as a subordinate and inferior class of beings, who had been subjugated by the dominant race, and, whether emancipated or not, yet remained subject to their authority, and had no rights or privileges but such as those who held the power and the government might choose to grant them." The recent amendments of the Constitution, it was supposed, had eradicated these principles from our institutions. But it seems that we have yet, in some of the States, a dominant race—a superior class of citizens, which assumes to regulate the enjoyment of civil rights, common to all citizens, upon the basis of race. The present decision, it may well be apprehended, will not only stimulate aggressions, more or less brutal and irritating, upon the admitted rights of colored citizens, but will encourage the belief that it is possible, by means of state enactments, to defeat the beneficent purposes which the people of the United States had in view when they adopted the recent amendments of the Constitution, by one of which the blacks of this country were made citizens of the United States and of the States in which they respectively reside, and whose privileges and immunities, as citizens, the States are forbidden to abridge. Sixty millions of whites are in no danger from the presence here of eight millions of blacks. The destinies of the two races, in this country, are indissolubly linked together, and the interests of both require that the common government of all shall not permit the seeds of race hate to be planted under the sanction of law. What can more certainly arouse race hate, what more certainly create and perpetuate a feeling of distrust between these races, than state enactments, which, in fact, proceed on the ground that colored citizens are so inferior and degraded that they cannot be allowed to sit in public coaches occupied by white citizens? That, as all will admit, is the real meaning of such legislation as was enacted in Louisiana.

The sure guarantee of the peace and security of each race is the clear, distinct, unconditional recognition by our governments, National and State, of every right that inheres in civil freedom, and of the equality before the law of all citizens of the United States without regard to race....

There is a race so different from our own that we do not permit those belonging to it to become citizens of the United States. Persons belonging to it are, with few exceptions, absolutely excluded from our country. I allude to the Chinese race. But by the statute in question, a Chinaman can ride in the same passenger coach with white citizens of the United States, while citizens of the black race in Louisiana, many of whom, perhaps, risked their lives for the preservation of the Union, who are entitled, by law, to participate in the political control of the State and nation, who are not excluded, by law or by reason of their race, from public stations of any kind, and who have all the legal rights that belong to white citizens, are yet declared to be criminals, liable to imprisonment, if they ride in a public coach occupied by citizens of the white race. It is scarcely just to say that a colored citizen should not object to occupying a public coach assigned to his own race. He does not object, nor, perhaps, would he object to separate coaches for his race, if his rights under the law were recognized. But he objects, and ought never to cease objecting to the proposition, that citizens of the white and black races can be adjudged criminals because they sit, or claim the right to sit, in the same public coach on a public highway.

The arbitrary separation of citizens, on the basis of race, while they are on a public highway, is a badge of servitude wholly inconsistent with the civil freedom and the equality before the law established by the Constitution. It cannot be justified upon any legal grounds....

I am of opinion that the statute of Louisiana is inconsistent with the personal liberty of citizens, white and black, in that State, and hostile to both the spirit and letter of the Constitution of the United States. If laws of like character should be enacted in the several States of the Union, the effect would be in the highest degree mischievous. Slavery, as an institution tolerated by law would, it is true, have disappeared from our country, but there would remain a power in the States, by sinister legislation, to interfere with the full enjoyment of the blessings of freedom; to regulate civil rights, common to all citizens, upon the basis of race; and to place in a condition of legal inferiority a large body of American citizens, now constituting a part of the political community called the People of the United States, for whom, and by whom through representatives, our government is administered. Such a system is inconsistent with the guarantee given by the Constitution to each State of a republican form of government, and may be stricken down by Congressional action, or by the courts in the discharge of their solemn duty to maintain the supreme law of the land, anything in the constitution or laws of any State to the contrary notwithstanding.

For the reasons stated, I am constrained to withhold my assent from the opinion and judgment of the majority.

Source: 163 U.S. 537 (1896).

APPENDIX

Constitution of the United States

We the People of the United States, in Order to form a more perfect Union, establish Justice, insure domestic Tranquility, provide for the common defence, promote the general Welfare, and secure the Blessings of Liberty to ourselves and our Posterity, do ordain and establish this Constitution for the United States of America.

ARTICLE I

SECTION 1. All legislative Powers herein granted shall be vested in a Congress of the United States, which shall consist of a Senate and House of Representatives.

SECTION 2. The House of Representatives shall be composed of Members chosen every second Year by the People of the several States, and the Electors in each State shall have the Qualifications requisite for Electors of the most numerous Branch of the State Legislature.

No Person shall be a Representative who shall not have attained to the Age of twenty five Years, and been seven Years a Citizen of the United States, and who shall not, when elected, be an Inhabitant of that State in which he shall be chosen.

Representatives and direct Taxes shall be apportioned among the several States which may be included within this Union, according to their respective Numbers, which shall be determined by adding to the whole Number of free Persons, including those bound to Service for a Term of Years, and excluding Indians not taxed, three fifths of all other Persons. The actual Enumeration shall be made within three Years after the first Meeting of the Congress of the United States, and within every subsequent Term of ten Years, in such Manner as they shall by Law direct. The Number of Representatives shall not exceed one for every thirty Thousand, but each State shall have at Least one Representative;

and until such enumeration shall be made, the State of New Hampshire shall be entitled to chuse three, Massachusetts eight, Rhode-Island and Providence Plantations one, Connecticut five, New-York six, New Jersey four, Pennsylvania eight, Delaware one, Maryland six, Virginia ten, North Carolina five, South Carolina five, and Georgia three.

When vacancies happen in the Representation from any State, the Executive Authority thereof shall issue Writs of Election to fill such Vacancies.

The House of Representatives shall chuse their Speaker and other Officers; and shall have the sole Power of Impeachment.

SECTION 3. The Senate of the United States shall be composed of two Senators from each State, chosen by the Legislature thereof, for six Years; and each Senator shall have one Vote.

Immediately after they shall be assembled in Consequence of the first Election, they shall be divided as equally as may be into three Classes. The Seats of the Senators of the first Class shall be vacated at the Expiration of the second Year, of the second Class at the Expiration of the fourth Year, and of the third Class at the Expiration of the sixth Year, so that one third may be chosen every second Year; and if Vacancies happen by Resignation, or otherwise, during the Recess of the Legislature of any State, the Executive thereof may make temporary Appointments until the next Meeting of the Legislature, which shall then fill such Vacancies.

No Person shall be a Senator who shall not have attained to the Age of thirty Years, and been nine Years a Citizen of the United States, and who shall not, when elected, be an Inhabitant of that State for which he shall be chosen.

The Vice President of the United States shall be President of the Senate, but shall have no Vote, unless they be equally divided.

The Senate shall chuse their other Officers, and also a President pro tempore, in the Absence of the Vice President, or when he shall exercise the Office of President of the United States.

The Senate shall have the sole Power to try all Impeachments. When sitting for that Purpose, they shall be on Oath or Affirmation. When the President of the United States is tried, the Chief

Justice shall preside: And no Person shall be convicted without the Concurrence of two thirds of the Members present.

Judgment in Cases of Impeachment shall not extend further than to removal from Office, and disqualification to hold and enjoy any Office of honor, Trust or Profit under the United States: but the Party convicted shall nevertheless be liable and subject to Indictment, Trial, Judgment and Punishment, according to Law.

SECTION 4. The Times, Places and Manner of holding Elections for Senators and Representatives, shall be prescribed in each State by the Legislature thereof; but the Congress may at any time by Law make or alter such Regulations, except as to the Places of chusing Senators.

The Congress shall assemble at least once in every Year, and such Meeting shall be on the first Monday in December, unless they shall by Law appoint a different Day.

SECTION 5. Each House shall be the Judge of the Elections, Returns and Qualifications of its own Members, and a Majority of each shall constitute a Quorum to do Business; but a smaller Number may adjourn from day to day, and may be authorized to compel the Attendance of absent Members, in such Manner, and under such Penalties as each House may provide.

Each House may determine the Rules of its Proceedings, punish its Members for disorderly Behaviour, and, with the Concurrence of two thirds, expel a Member.

Each House shall keep a Journal of its Proceedings, and from time to time publish the same, excepting such Parts as may in their Judgment require Secrecy; and the Yeas and Nays of the Members of either House on any question shall, at the Desire of one fifth of those Present, be entered on the Journal.

Neither House, during the Session of Congress, shall, without the Consent of the other, adjourn for more than three days, nor to any other Place than that in which the two Houses shall be sitting.

SECTION 6. The Senators and Representatives shall receive a Compensation for their Services, to be ascertained by Law, and paid out of the Treasury of the United States. They shall in all Cases, except Treason, Felony and Breach of the Peace, be privileged from Arrest during their Attendance at the Session of their respective Houses, and in going to and returning from the same; and for any Speech or Debate in either House, they shall not be questioned in any other Place.

No Senator or Representative shall, during the Time for which he was elected, be appointed to any civil Office under the Authority of the United States, which shall have been created, or the Emoluments whereof shall have been encreased during such time; and no Person holding any Office under the United States, shall be a Member of either House during his Continuance in Office.

SECTION 7. All Bills for raising Revenue shall originate in the House of Representatives; but the Senate may propose or concur with Amendments as on other Bills.

Every Bill which shall have passed the House of Representatives and the Senate, shall, before it become a Law, be presented to the President of the United States; If he approve he shall sign it, but if not he shall return it, with his Objections to that House in which it shall have originated, who shall enter the Objections at large on their Journal, and proceed to reconsider it. If after such Reconsideration two thirds of that House shall agree to pass the Bill, it shall be sent, together with the Objections, to the other House, by which it shall likewise be reconsidered, and if approved by two thirds of that House, it shall become a Law. But in all such Cases the Votes of both Houses shall be determined by yeas and Nays, and the Names of the Persons voting for and against the Bill shall be entered on the Journal of each House respectively. If any Bill shall not be returned by the President within ten Days (Sundays excepted) after it shall have been presented to him, the Same shall be a Law, in like Manner as if he had signed it, unless the Congress by their Adjournment prevent its Return, in which Case it shall not be a Law.

Every Order, Resolution, or Vote to which the Concurrence of the Senate and House of Representatives may be necessary (except on a question of Adjournment) shall be presented to the President of the United States; and before the Same shall take Effect, shall be approved by him, or being disapproved by him, shall be repassed by two thirds of the Senate and House of Representatives, according to the Rules and Limitations prescribed in the Case of a Bill.

SECTION 8. The Congress shall have Power To lay and collect Taxes, Duties, Imposts and Excises, to pay the Debts and provide for the common Defence and general Welfare of the United States; but all Duties, Imposts and Excises shall be uniform throughout the United States;

To borrow Money on the credit of the United States;

To regulate Commerce with foreign Nations, and among the several States, and with the Indian Tribes;

To establish an uniform Rule of Naturalization, and uniform Laws on the subject of Bankruptcies throughout the United States;

To coin Money, regulate the Value thereof, and of foreign Coin, and fix the Standard of Weights and Measures;

To provide for the Punishment of counterfeiting the Securities and current Coin of the United States;

To establish Post Offices and post Roads;

To promote the Progress of Science and useful Arts, by securing for limited Times to Authors and Inventors the exclusive Right to their respective Writings and Discoveries;

To constitute Tribunals inferior to the Supreme Court;

To define and punish Piracies and Felonies committed on the high Seas, and Offences against the Law of Nations;

To declare War, grant Letters of Marque and Reprisal, and make Rules concerning Captures on Land and Water;

To raise and support Armies, but no Appropriation of Money to that Use shall be for a longer Term than two Years;

To provide and maintain a Navy;

To make Rules for the Government and Regulation of the land and naval Forces;

To provide for calling forth the Militia to execute the Laws of the Union, suppress Insurrections and repel Invasions;

To provide for organizing, arming, and disciplining, the Militia, and for governing such Part of them as may be employed in the Service of the United States, reserving to the States respectively, the Appointment of the Officers, and the Authority of training the Militia according to the discipline prescribed by Congress;

To exercise exclusive Legislation in all Cases whatsoever, over such District (not exceeding ten Miles square) as may, by Cession of particular States, and the Acceptance of Congress, become the Seat of the Government of the United States, and to exercise like Authority over all Places purchased by the Consent of the Legislature of the State in which the Same shall be, for the Erection of Forts, Magazines, Arsenals, dock-Yards, and other needful Buildings;—And

To make all Laws which shall be necessary and proper for carrying into Execution the foregoing Powers, and all other Powers vested by this Constitution in the Government of the United States, or in any Department or Officer thereof.

SECTION 9. The Migration or Importation of such Persons as any of the States now existing shall think proper to admit, shall not be prohibited by the Congress prior to the Year one thousand eight hundred and eight, but a Tax or duty may be imposed on such Importation, not exceeding ten dollars for each Person.

The Privilege of the Writ of Habeas Corpus shall not be suspended, unless when in Cases of Rebellion or Invasion the public Safety may require it.

No Bill of Attainder or ex post facto law shall be passed.

No Capitation, or other direct, Tax shall be laid, unless in Proportion to the Census or Enumeration herein before directed to be taken.

No Tax or Duty shall be laid on Articles exported from any State.

No Preference shall be given by any Regulation of Commerce or Revenue to the Ports of one State over those of another: nor shall Vessels bound to, or from, one State, be obliged to enter, clear, or pay Duties in another.

No Money shall be drawn from the Treasury, but in Consequence of Appropriations made by Law; and a regular Statement and Account of the Receipts and Expenditures of all public Money shall be published from time to time.

No Title of Nobility shall be granted by the United States: And no Person holding any Office of Profit or Trust under them, shall, without the Consent of the Congress, accept of any present, Emolument, Office, or Title, of any kind whatever, from any King, Prince, or foreign State.

SECTION 10. No State shall enter into any Treaty, Alliance, or Confederation; grant Letters of Marque and Reprisal; coin Money; emit Bills of Credit; make any Thing but gold and silver Coin a Tender in Payment of Debts; pass any Bill of Attainder, ex post facto Law, or Law impairing the Obligation of Contracts, or grant any Title of Nobility.

No State shall, without the Consent of the Congress, lay any Imposts or Duties on Imports or Exports, except what may be absolutely necessary for executing it's inspection Laws: and the net Produce of all Duties and Imposts, laid by any State on Imports or Exports, shall be for the Use of the Treasury of the United States; and all such Laws shall be subject to the Revision and Controul of the Congress.

No State shall, without the Consent of Congress, lay any Duty of Tonnage, keep Troops, or Ships of War in time of Peace, enter into any Agreement or Compact with another State, or with a foreign Power, or engage in War, unless actually invaded, or in such imminent Danger as will not admit of delay.

ARTICLE II

SECTION 1. The executive Power shall be vested in a President of the United States of America. He shall hold his Office during the Term of four Years, and, together with the Vice President, chosen for the same Term, be elected, as follows

Each State shall appoint, in such Manner as the Legislature thereof may direct, a Number of Electors, equal to the whole Number of Senators and Representatives to which the State may be entitled in the Congress: but no Senator or Representative, or

Person holding an Office of Trust or Profit under the United States, shall be appointed an Elector.

The Electors shall meet in their respective States, and vote by Ballot for two Persons, of whom one at least shall not be an Inhabitant of the same State with themselves. And they shall make a List of all the Persons voted for, and of the Number of Votes for each; which List they shall sign and certify, and transmit sealed to the Seat of the Government of the United States, directed to the President of the Senate. The President of the Senate shall, in the Presence of the Senate and House of Representatives, open all the Certificates, and the Votes shall then be counted. The Person having the greatest Number of Votes shall be the President, if such Number be a Majority of the whole Number of Electors appointed; and if there be more than one who have such Majority, and have an equal Number of Votes, then the House of Representatives shall immediately chuse by Ballot one of them for President; and if no Person have a Majority, then from the five highest on the List the said House shall in like Manner chuse the President. But in chusing the President, the Votes shall be taken by States, the Representation from each State having one Vote; a quorum for this Purpose shall consist of a Member or Members from two thirds of the States, and a Majority of all the States shall be necessary to a Choice. In every Case, after the Choice of the President, the Person having the greatest Number of Votes of the Electors shall be the Vice President. But if there should remain two or more who have equal Votes, the Senate shall chuse from them by Ballot the Vice President.

The Congress may determine the Time of chusing the Electors, and the Day on which they shall give their Votes; which Day shall be the same throughout the United States.

No Person except a natural born Citizen, or a Citizen of the United States, at the time of the Adoption of this Constitution, shall be eligible to the Office of President; neither shall any Person be eligible to that Office who shall not have attained to the Age of thirty five Years, and been fourteen Years a Resident within the United States.

In Case of the Removal of the President from Office, or of his Death, Resignation, or Inability to discharge the Powers and Duties of the said Office, the Same shall devolve on the Vice President, and the Congress may by Law provide for the Case of Removal, Death, Resignation or Inability, both of the President and Vice President, declaring what Officer shall then act as President, and such Officer shall act accordingly, until the Disability be removed, or a President shall be elected.

The President shall, at stated Times, receive for his Services, a Compensation, which shall neither be encreased nor diminished during the Period for which he shall have been elected, and he shall not receive within that Period any other Emolument from the United States, or any of them.

Before he enter on the Execution of his Office, he shall take the following Oath or Affirmation:—"I do solemnly swear (or affirm) that I will faithfully execute the Office of President of the United States, and will to the best of my Ability, preserve, protect and defend the Constitution of the United States."

SECTION 2. The President shall be Commander in Chief of the Army and Navy of the United States, and of the Militia of the several States, when called into the actual Service of the United States; he may require the Opinion, in writing, of the principal Officer in each of the executive Departments, upon any Subject relating to the Duties of their respective Offices, and he shall have Power to grant Reprieves and Pardons for Offences against the United States, except in Cases of Impeachment.

He shall have Power, by and with the Advice and Consent of the Senate, to make Treaties, provided two thirds of the Senators present concur; and he shall nominate, and by and with the Advice and Consent of the Senate, shall appoint Ambassadors, other public Ministers and Consuls, Judges of the supreme Court, and all other Officers of the United States, whose Appointments are not herein otherwise provided for, and which shall be established by Law: but the Congress may by Law vest the Appointment of such inferior Officers, as they think proper, in the President alone, in the Courts of Law, or in the Heads of Departments.

The President shall have Power to fill up all Vacancies that may happen during the Recess of the Senate, by granting Commissions which shall expire at the End of their next Session.

SECTION 3. He shall from time to time give to the Congress Information of the State of the Union, and recommend to their Consideration such Measures as he shall judge necessary and expedient; he may, on extraordinary Occasions, convene both Houses, or either of them, and in Case of Disagreement between them, with Respect to the Time of Adjournment, he may adjourn them to such Time as he shall think proper; he shall receive Ambassadors and other public Ministers; he shall take Care that the Laws be faithfully executed, and shall Commission all the Officers of the United States.

SECTION 4. The President, Vice President and all civil Officers of the United States, shall be removed from Office on Impeachment for, and Conviction of, Treason, Bribery, or other high Crimes and Misdemeanors.

ARTICLE III

SECTION 1. The judicial Power of the United States, shall be vested in one supreme Court, and in such inferior Courts as the Congress may from time to time ordain and establish. The Judges, both of the supreme and inferior Courts, shall hold their Offices during good Behaviour, and shall, at stated Times, receive for their Services, a Compensation, which shall not be diminished during their Continuance in Office.

SECTION 2. The judicial Power shall extend to all Cases, in Law and Equity, arising under this Constitution, the Laws of the United States, and Treaties made, or which shall be made, under their Authority;—to all Cases affecting Ambassadors, other public Ministers and Consuls;—to all Cases of admiralty and maritime Jurisdiction;—to Controversies to which the United States shall be a Party;—to Controversies between two or more States;—between a State and Citizens of another State;—between Citizens of different States, —between Citizens of the same State claiming Lands under Grants of different States, and between a State, or the Citizens thereof, and foreign States, Citizens or Subjects.

In all Cases affecting Ambassadors, other public Ministers and Consuls, and those in which a State shall be Party, the supreme Court shall have original Jurisdiction. In all the other Cases before mentioned, the supreme Court shall have appellate Jurisdiction, both as to Law and Fact, with such Exceptions, and under such Regulations as the Congress shall make.

The Trial of all Crimes, except in Cases of Impeachment, shall be by Jury; and such Trial shall be held in the State where the said Crimes shall have been committed; but when not committed within any State, the Trial shall be at such Place or Places as the Congress may by Law have directed.

SECTION 3. Treason against the United States, shall consist only in levying War against them, or in adhering to their Enemies, giving them Aid and Comfort. No Person shall be convicted of Treason unless on the Testimony of two Witnesses to the same overt Act, or on Confession in open Court.

The Congress shall have Power to declare the Punishment of Treason, but no Attainder of Treason shall work Corruption of Blood, or Forfeiture except during the Life of the Person attainted.

ARTICLE IV

SECTION 1. Full Faith and Credit shall be given in each State to the public Acts, Records, and judicial Proceedings of every other State. And the Congress may by general Laws prescribe the Manner in which such Acts, Records and Proceedings shall be proved, and the Effect thereof.

SECTION 2. The Citizens of each State shall be entitled to all Privileges and Immunities of Citizens in the several States.

A Person charged in any State with Treason, Felony, or other Crime, who shall flee from Justice, and be found in another State, shall on Demand of the executive Authority of the State from which he fled, be delivered up, to be removed to the State having Jurisdiction of the Crime.

No Person held to Service or Labour in one State, under the Laws thereof, escaping into another, shall, in Consequence of any Law or Regulation therein, be discharged from such Service or Labour, but shall be delivered up on Claim of the Party to whom such Service or Labour may be due.

SECTION 3. New States may be admitted by the Congress into this Union; but no new State shall be formed or erected within the Jurisdiction of any other State; nor any State be formed by the Junction of two or more States, or Parts of States, without the Consent of the Legislatures of the States concerned as well as of the Congress.

The Congress shall have Power to dispose of and make all needful Rules and Regulations respecting the Territory or other Property belonging to the United States; and nothing in this Constitution shall be so construed as to Prejudice any Claims of the United States, or of any particular State.

SECTION 4. The United States shall guarantee to every State in this Union a Republican Form of Government, and shall protect each of them against Invasion; and on Application of the Legislature, or of the Executive (when the Legislature cannot be convened) against domestic Violence.

ARTICLE V

The Congress, whenever two thirds of both Houses shall deem it necessary, shall propose Amendments to this Constitution, or, on the Application of the Legislatures of two thirds of the several States, shall call a Convention for proposing Amendments, which, in either Case, shall be valid to all Intents and Purposes, as Part of this Constitution, when ratified by the Legislatures of three fourths of the several States, or by Conventions in three fourths thereof, as the one or the other Mode of Ratification may be proposed by the Congress; Provided that no Amendment which may be made prior to the Year One thousand eight hundred and eight shall in any Manner affect the first and fourth Clauses in the Ninth Section of the first Article; and that no State, without its Consent, shall be deprived of its equal Suffrage in the Senate.

ARTICLE VI

All Debts contracted and Engagements entered into, before the Adoption of this Constitution, shall be as valid against the United States under this Constitution, as under the Confederation.

This Constitution, and the Laws of the United States which shall be made in Pursuance thereof; and all Treaties made, or which shall be made, under the Authority of the United States, shall be the supreme Law of the Land; and the Judges in every State shall be bound thereby, any Thing in the Constitution or Laws of any State to the Contrary notwithstanding.

The Senators and Representatives before mentioned, and the Members of the several State Legislatures, and all executive and judicial Officers, both of the United States and of the several States, shall be bound by Oath or Affirmation, to support this Constitution; but no religious Test shall ever be required as a Qualification to any Office or public Trust under the United States.

ARTICLE VII

The Ratification of the Conventions of nine States, shall be sufficient for the Establishment of this Constitution between the States so ratifying the Same.

Amendment I (1791)

Congress shall make no law respecting an establishment of religion, or prohibiting the free exercise thereof; or abridging the freedom of speech, or of the press; or the right of the people peaceably to assemble, and to petition the government for a redress of grievances.

Amendment II (1791)
A well regulated militia, being necessary to the security of a free state, the right of the people to keep and bear arms, shall not be infringed.

Amendment III (1791)
No soldier shall, in time of peace be quartered in any house, without the consent of the owner, nor in time of war, but in a manner to be prescribed by law.

Amendment IV (1791)
The right of the people to be secure in their persons, houses, papers, and effects, against unreasonable searches and seizures, shall not be violated, and no warrants shall issue, but upon probable cause, supported by oath or affirmation, and particularly describing the place to be searched, and the persons or things to be seized.

Amendment V (1791)
No person shall be held to answer for a capital, or otherwise infamous crime, unless on a presentment or indictment of a grand jury, except in cases arising in the land or naval forces, or in the militia, when in actual service in time of war or public danger; nor shall any person be subject for the same offense to be twice put in jeopardy of life or limb; nor shall be compelled in any criminal case to be a witness against himself, nor be deprived of life, liberty, or property, without due process of law; nor shall private property be taken for public use, without just compensation.

Amendment VI (1791)
In all criminal prosecutions, the accused shall enjoy the right to a speedy and public trial, by an impartial jury of the state and district wherein the crime shall have been committed, which district shall have been previously ascertained by law, and to be informed of the nature and cause of the accusation; to be confronted with the witnesses against him; to have compulsory process for obtain-

ing witnesses in his favor, and to have the assistance of counsel for his defense.

Amendment VII (1791)
In suits at common law, where the value in controversy shall exceed twenty dollars, the right of trial by jury shall be preserved, and no fact tried by a jury, shall be otherwise reexamined in any court of the United States, than according to the rules of the common law.

Amendment VIII (1791)
Excessive bail shall not be required, nor excessive fines imposed, nor cruel and unusual punishments inflicted.

Amendment IX (1791)
The enumeration in the Constitution, of certain rights, shall not be construed to deny or disparage others retained by the people.

Amendment X (1791)
The powers not delegated to the United States by the Constitution, nor prohibited by it to the states, are reserved to the states respectively, or to the people.

Amendment XI (1798)
The judicial power of the United States shall not be construed to extend to any suit in law or equity, commenced or prosecuted against one of the United States by citizens of another state, or by citizens or subjects of any foreign state.

Amendment XII (1804)
The electors shall meet in their respective states and vote by ballot for President and Vice-President, one of whom, at least, shall not be an inhabitant of the same state with themselves; they shall name in their ballots the person voted for as President, and in distinct ballots the person voted for as Vice-President, and they shall make distinct lists of all persons voted for as President, and of all persons voted for as Vice-President, and of the number of votes for each, which lists they shall sign and certify, and transmit

sealed to the seat of the government of the United States, directed to the President of the Senate;—The President of the Senate shall, in the presence of the Senate and House of Representatives, open all the certificates and the votes shall then be counted;—the person having the greatest number of votes for President, shall be the President, if such number be a majority of the whole number of electors appointed; and if no person have such majority, then from the persons having the highest numbers not exceeding three on the list of those voted for as President, the House of Representatives shall choose immediately, by ballot, the President. But in choosing the President, the votes shall be taken by states, the representation from each state having one vote; a quorum for this purpose shall consist of a member or members from two-thirds of the states, and a majority of all the states shall be necessary to a choice. And if the House of Representatives shall not choose a President whenever the right of choice shall devolve upon them, before the fourth day of March next following, then the Vice-President shall act as President, as in the case of the death or other constitutional disability of the President. The person having the greatest number of votes as Vice-President, shall be the Vice-President, if such number be a majority of the whole number of electors appointed, and if no person have a majority, then from the two highest numbers on the list, the Senate shall choose the Vice-President; a quorum for the purpose shall consist of two-thirds of the whole number of Senators, and a majority of the whole number shall be necessary to a choice. But no person constitutionally ineligible to the office of President shall be eligible to that of Vice-President of the United States.

Amendment XIII (1865)

SECTION 1. Neither slavery nor involuntary servitude, except as a punishment for crime whereof the party shall have been duly convicted, shall exist within the United States, or any place subject to their jurisdiction.

SECTION 2. Congress shall have power to enforce this article by appropriate legislation.

Amendment XIV (1868)

SECTION 1. All persons born or naturalized in the United States, and subject to the jurisdiction thereof, are citizens of the United States and of the state wherein they reside. No state shall make or enforce any law which shall abridge the privileges or immunities of citizens of the United States; nor shall any state deprive any person of life, liberty, or property, without due process of law; nor deny to any person within its jurisdiction the equal protection of the laws.

SECTION 2. Representatives shall be apportioned among the several states according to their respective numbers, counting the whole number of persons in each state, excluding Indians not taxed. But when the right to vote at any election for the choice of electors for President and Vice President of the United States, Representatives in Congress, the executive and judicial officers of a state, or the members of the legislature thereof, is denied to any of the male inhabitants of such state, being twenty-one years of age, and citizens of the United States, or in any way abridged, except for participation in rebellion, or other crime, the basis of representation therein shall be reduced in the proportion which the number of such male citizens shall bear to the whole number of male citizens twenty-one years of age in such state.

SECTION 3. No person shall be a Senator or Representative in Congress, or elector of President and Vice President, or hold any office, civil or military, under the United States, or under any state, who, having previously taken an oath, as a member of Congress, or as an officer of the United States, or as a member of any state legislature, or as an executive or judicial officer of any state, to support the Constitution of the United States, shall have engaged in insurrection or rebellion against the same, or given aid or comfort to the enemies thereof. But Congress may by a vote of two-thirds of each House, remove such disability.

SECTION 4. The validity of the public debt of the United States, authorized by law, including debts incurred for payment of pensions and bounties for services in suppressing insurrection or rebellion, shall not be questioned. But neither the United States nor any state shall assume or pay any debt or obligation incurred in aid of insurrection or rebellion against the United States, or any claim for the loss or emancipation of any slave; but all such debts, obligations and claims shall be held illegal and void.

SECTION 5. The Congress shall have power to enforce, by appropriate legislation, the provisions of this article.

Amendment XV (1870)

SECTION 1. The right of citizens of the United States to vote shall not be denied or abridged by the United States or by any state on account of race, color, or previous condition of servitude.

SECTION 2. The Congress shall have power to enforce this article by appropriate legislation.

Amendment XVI (1913)

The Congress shall have power to lay and collect taxes on incomes, from whatever source derived, without apportionment among the several states, and without regard to any census of enumeration.

Amendment XVII (1913)

The Senate of the United States shall be composed of two Senators from each state, elected by the people thereof, for six years; and each Senator shall have one vote. The electors in each state shall have the qualifications requisite for electors of the most numerous branch of the state legislatures.

When vacancies happen in the representation of any state in the Senate, the executive authority of such state shall issue writs of election to fill such vacancies: Provided, that the legislature of any state may empower the executive thereof to make temporary appointments until the people fill the vacancies by election as the legislature may direct.

This amendment shall not be so construed as to affect the election or term of any Senator chosen before it becomes valid as part of the Constitution.

Amendment XVIII (1919)

SECTION 1. After one year from the ratification of this article the manufacture, sale, or transportation of intoxicating liquors within, the importation thereof into, or the exportation thereof from the United States and all territory subject to the jurisdiction thereof for beverage purposes is hereby prohibited.

SECTION 2. The Congress and the several states shall have concurrent power to enforce this article by appropriate legislation.

SECTION 3. This article shall be inoperative unless it shall have been ratified as an amendment to the Constitution by the legislatures of the several states, as provided in the Constitution, within seven years from the date of the submission hereof to the states by the Congress.

Amendment XIX (1920)

The right of citizens of the United States to vote shall not be denied or abridged by the United States or by any state on account of sex.

Congress shall have power to enforce this article by appropriate legislation.

Amendment XX (1933)

SECTION 1. The terms of the President and Vice President shall end at noon on the 20th day of January, and the terms of Senators and Representatives at noon on the 3d day of January, of the years in which such terms would have ended if this article had not been ratified; and the terms of their successors shall then begin.

SECTION 2. The Congress shall assemble at least once in every year, and such meeting shall begin at noon on the 3d day of January, unless they shall by law appoint a different day.

SECTION 3. If, at the time fixed for the beginning of the term of the President, the President elect shall have died, the Vice President elect shall become President. If a President shall not have been chosen before the time fixed for the beginning of his term, or if the President elect shall have failed to qualify, then the Vice President elect shall act as President until a President shall have qualified; and the Congress may by law provide for the case wherein neither

a President elect nor a Vice President elect shall have qualified, declaring who shall then act as President, or the manner in which one who is to act shall be selected, and such person shall act accordingly until a President or Vice President shall have qualified.
SECTION 4. The Congress may by law provide for the case of the death of any of the persons from whom the House of Representatives may choose a President whenever the right of choice shall have devolved upon them, and for the case of the death of any of the persons from whom the Senate may choose a Vice President whenever the right of choice shall have devolved upon them.
SECTION 5. Sections 1 and 2 shall take effect on the 15th day of October following the ratification of this article.
SECTION 6. This article shall be inoperative unless it shall have been ratified as an amendment to the Constitution by the legislatures of three-fourths of the several states within seven years from the date of its submission.

Amendment XXI (1933)
SECTION 1. The eighteenth article of amendment to the Constitution of the United States is hereby repealed.
SECTION 2. The transportation or importation into any state, territory, or possession of the United States for delivery or use therein of intoxicating liquors, in violation of the laws thereof, is hereby prohibited.
SECTION 3. This article shall be inoperative unless it shall have been ratified as an amendment to the Constitution by conventions in the several states, as provided in the Constitution, within seven years from the date of the submission hereof to the states by the Congress.

Amendment XXII (1951)
SECTION 1. No person shall be elected to the office of the President more than twice, and no person who has held the office of President, or acted as President, for more than two years of a term to which some other person was elected President shall be elected to the office of the President more than once. But this article shall not apply to any person holding the office of President when this arti-

cle was proposed by the Congress, and shall not prevent any person who may be holding the office of President, or acting as President, during the term within which this article becomes operative from holding the office of President or acting as President during the remainder of such term.

SECTION 2. This article shall be inoperative unless it shall have been ratified as an amendment to the Constitution by the legislatures of three-fourths of the several states within seven years from the date of its submission to the states by the Congress.

Amendment XXIII (1961)

SECTION 1. The District constituting the seat of government of the United States shall appoint in such manner as the Congress may direct:

A number of electors of President and Vice President equal to the whole number of Senators and Representatives in Congress to which the District would be entitled if it were a state, but in no event more than the least populous state; they shall be in addition to those appointed by the states, but they shall be considered, for the purposes of the election of President and Vice President, to be electors appointed by a state; and they shall meet in the District and perform such duties as provided by the twelfth article of amendment.

SECTION 2. The Congress shall have power to enforce this article by appropriate legislation.

Amendment XXIV (1964)

SECTION 1. The right of citizens of the United States to vote in any primary or other election for President or Vice President, for electors for President or Vice President, or for Senator or Representative in Congress, shall not be denied or abridged by the United States or any state by reason of failure to pay any poll tax or other tax.

SECTION 2. The Congress shall have power to enforce this article by appropriate legislation.

Amendment XXV (1967)

SECTION 1. In case of the removal of the President from office or of his death or resignation, the Vice President shall become President.

SECTION 2. Whenever there is a vacancy in the office of the Vice President, the President shall nominate a Vice President who shall take office upon confirmation by a majority vote of both Houses of Congress.

SECTION 3. Whenever the President transmits to the President pro tempore of the Senate and the Speaker of the House of Representatives his written declaration that he is unable to discharge the powers and duties of his office, and until he transmits to them a written declaration to the contrary, such powers and duties shall be discharged by the Vice President as Acting President.

SECTION 4. Whenever the Vice President and a majority of either the principal officers of the executive departments or of such other body as Congress may by law provide, transmit to the President pro tempore of the Senate and the Speaker of the House of Representatives their written declaration that the President is unable to discharge the powers and duties of his office, the Vice President shall immediately assume the powers and duties of the office as Acting President.

Thereafter, when the President transmits to the President pro tempore of the Senate and the Speaker of the House of Representatives his written declaration that no inability exists, he shall resume the powers and duties of his office unless the Vice President and a majority of either the principal officers of the executive department or of such other body as Congress may by law provide, transmit within four days to the President pro tempore of the Senate and the Speaker of the House of Representatives their written declaration that the President is unable to discharge the powers and duties of his office. Thereupon Congress shall decide the issue, assembling within forty-eight hours for that purpose if not in session. If the Congress, within twenty-one days after receipt of the latter written declaration, or, if Congress is not in session, within twenty-one days after Congress is required to assemble, determines by two-thirds vote of both Houses that the President is unable to discharge the powers and duties of his office, the Vice President shall continue to discharge the same as Acting President; otherwise, the President shall resume the powers and duties of his office.

Amendment XXVI (1971)
SECTION 1. The right of citizens of the United States, who are 18 years of age or older, to vote, shall not be denied or abridged by the United States or any state on account of age.
SECTION 2. The Congress shall have the power to enforce this article by appropriate legislation.

Amendment XXVII (1992)
No law varying the compensation for the services of the Senators and Representatives shall take effect until an election of Representatives shall have intervened.

Constitution of the Confederate States (1861)

We, the people of the Confederate States, each State acting in its sovereign and independent character, in order to form a permanent federal government, establish justice, insure domestic tranquility, and secure the blessings of liberty to ourselves and our posterity—invoking the favor and guidance of Almighty God—do ordain and establish this Constitution for the Confederate States of America.

ARTICLE I

SECTION 1. All legislative powers herein delegated shall be vested in a Congress of the Confederate States, which shall consist of a Senate and House of Representatives.

SECTION 2. The House of Representatives shall be composed of members chosen every second year by the people of the several States; and the electors in each State shall be citizens of the Confederate States, and have the qualifications requisite for electors of the most numerous branch of the State Legislature; but no person of foreign birth, not a citizen of the Confederate States, shall be allowed to vote for any officer, civil or political, State or Federal.

No person shall be a Representative who shall not have attained the age of twenty-five years, and be a citizen of the Confederate States, and who shall not when elected, be an inhabitant of that State in which he shall be chosen.

Representatives and direct taxes shall be apportioned among the several States, which may be included within this Confederacy, according to their respective numbers, which shall be determined by adding to the whole number of free persons, including those bound to service for a term of years, and excluding Indians not taxed, three-fifths of all slaves. The actual enumeration shall be made within three years after the first meeting of the Congress of the Confederate States, and within every subsequent term of ten years, in such manner as they shall by law direct. The number of Representatives shall not exceed one for every fifty thousand, but each State shall have at least one Representative; and until such enumeration shall be made, the State of South Carolina shall be entitled to choose six; the State of Georgia ten; the State of Alabama nine; the State of Florida two; the State of Mississippi seven; the State of Louisiana six; and the State of Texas six.

When vacancies happen in the representation from any State the executive authority thereof shall issue writs of election to fill such vacancies.

The House of Representatives shall choose their Speaker and other officers; and shall have the sole power of impeachment; except that any judicial or other Federal officer, resident and acting solely within the limits of any State, may be impeached by a vote of two-thirds of both branches of the Legislature thereof.

SECTION 3. The Senate of the Confederate States shall be composed of two Senators from each State, chosen for six years by the Legislature thereof, at the regular session next immediately preceding the commencement of the term of service; and each Senator shall have one vote.

Immediately after they shall be assembled, in consequence of the first election, they shall be divided as equally as may be into three classes. The seats of the Senators of the first class shall be vacated at the expiration of the second year; of the second class at the expiration of the fourth year; and of the third class at the expiration of the sixth year; so that one-third may be chosen every second year; and if vacancies happen by resignation, or other wise, during the recess of the Legislature of any State, the Executive thereof may make temporary appointments until the next meeting of the Legislature, which shall then fill such vacancies.

No person shall be a Senator who shall not have attained the age of thirty years, and be a citizen of the Confederate States; and who shall not, then elected, be an inhabitant of the State for which he shall be chosen.

The Vice President of the Confederate States shall be president of the Senate, but shall have no vote unless they be equally divided.

The Senate shall choose their other officers; and also a president pro tempore in the absence of the Vice President, or when he shall exercise the office of President of the Confederate states.

The Senate shall have the sole power to try all impeachments. When sitting for that purpose, they shall be on oath or affirmation. When the President of the Confederate States is tried, the Chief Justice shall preside; and no person shall be convicted without the concurrence of two-thirds of the members present.

Judgment in cases of impeachment shall not extend further than to removal from office, and disqualification to hold any office of honor, trust, or profit under the Confederate States; but the party convicted shall, nevertheless, be liable and subject to indictment, trial, judgment, and punishment according to law.

SECTION 4. The times, places, and manner of holding elections for Senators and Representatives shall be prescribed in each State by the Legislature thereof, subject to the provisions of this Constitution; but the Congress may, at any time, by law, make or alter such regulations, except as to the times and places of choosing Senators.

The Congress shall assemble at least once in every year; and such meeting shall be on the first Monday in December, unless they shall, by law, appoint a different day.

SECTION 5. Each House shall be the judge of the elections, returns, and qualifications of its own members, and a majority of each shall constitute a quorum to do business; but a smaller number may adjourn from day to day, and may be authorized to compel the attendance of absent members, in such manner and under such penalties as each House may provide.

Each House may determine the rules of its proceedings, punish its members for disorderly behavior, and, with the concurrence of two-thirds of the whole number, expel a member.

Each House shall keep a journal of its proceedings, and from time to time publish the same, excepting such parts as may in their judgment require secrecy; and the yeas and nays of the members of either House, on any question, shall, at the desire of one-fifth of those present, be entered on the journal.

Neither House, during the session of Congress, shall, without the consent of the other, adjourn for more than three days, nor to any other place than that in which the two Houses shall be sitting.

SECTION 6. The Senators and Representatives shall receive a compensation for their services, to be ascertained by law, and paid out of the Treasury of the Confederate States. They shall, in all cases, except treason, felony, and breach of the peace, be privileged from arrest during their attendance at the session of their respective Houses, and in going to and returning from the same; and for any speech or debate in either House, they shall not be questioned in any other place. Senator or Representative shall, during the time for which he was elected, be appointed to any civil office under the authority of the Confederate States, which shall have been created, or the emoluments whereof shall have been increased during such time; and no person holding any office under the Confederate States shall be a member of either House during his continuance in office. But Congress may, by law, grant to the principal officer in each of the Executive Departments a seat upon the floor of either House, with the privilege of discussing any measures appertaining to his department.

SECTION 7. All bills for raising revenue shall originate in the House of Representatives; but the Senate may propose or concur with amendments, as on other bills.

Every bill which shall have passed both Houses, shall, before it becomes a law, be presented to the President of the Confederate States; if he approve, he shall sign it; but if not, he shall return it, with his objections, to that House in which it shall have originated, who shall enter the objections at large on their journal, and proceed to reconsider it. If, after such reconsideration, two-thirds of that House shall agree to pass the bill, it shall be sent, together with the objections, to the other House, by which it shall likewise be reconsidered, and if approved by two-thirds of that House, it shall become a law. But in all such cases, the votes of both Houses shall be determined by yeas and nays, and the names of the persons voting for and against the bill shall be entered on the journal of each House respectively. If any bill shall not be returned by the President within ten days (Sundays excepted) after it shall have been presented to him, the same shall be a law, in like manner as if he had signed it, unless the Congress, by their adjournment, prevent its return; in which case it shall not be a law. The President may approve any appropriation and disapprove any other appropriation in the same bill. In such case he shall, in signing the bill, designate the appropriations disapproved; and shall return a copy of such appropriations, with his objections, to the House in which the bill shall have originated; and the same proceedings shall then be had as in case of other bills disapproved by the President.

Every order, resolution, or vote, to which the concurrence of both Houses may be necessary (except on a question of adjournment) shall be presented to the President of the Confederate States; and before the same shall take effect, shall be approved by him; or, being disapproved by him, shall be repassed by two-thirds of both Houses, according to the rules and limitations prescribed in case of a bill.

SECTION 8. The Congress shall have power—

To lay and collect taxes, duties, imposts, and excises for revenue, necessary to pay the debts, provide for the common defense, and carry on the Government of the Confederate States; but no bounties shall be granted from the Treasury; nor shall any duties or taxes on importations from foreign nations be laid to promote or foster any branch of industry; and all duties, imposts, and excises shall be uniform throughout the Confederate States.

To borrow money on the credit of the Confederate States.

To regulate commerce with foreign nations, and among the several States, and with the Indian tribes; but neither this, nor any other clause contained in the Constitution, shall ever be construed to delegate the power to Congress to appropriate money for any internal improvement intended to facilitate commerce; except for the purpose of furnishing lights, beacons, and buoys, and other aids to navigation upon the coasts, and the improvement of harbors and the removing of obstructions in river navigation; in all which cases such duties shall be laid on the navigation facilitated thereby as may be necessary to pay the costs and expenses thereof.

To establish uniform laws of naturalization, and uniform laws on the subject of bankruptcies, throughout the Confederate States; but no law of Congress shall discharge any debt contracted before the passage of the same.

To coin money, regulate the value thereof, and of foreign coin, and fix the standard of weights and measures.

To provide for the punishment of counterfeiting the securities and current coin of the Confederate States.

To establish post offices and post routes; but the expenses of the Post Office Department, after the Ist day of March in the year of our Lord eighteen hundred and sixty-three, shall be paid out of its own revenues.

To promote the progress of science and useful arts, by securing for limited times to authors and inventors the exclusive right to their respective writings and discoveries.

To constitute tribunals inferior to the Supreme Court.

To define and punish piracies and felonies committed on the high seas, and offenses against the law of nations.

To declare war, grant letters of marque and reprisal, and make rules concerning captures on land and water.

To raise and support armies; but no appropriation of money to that use shall be for a longer term than two years.

To provide and maintain a navy.

To make rules for the government and regulation of the land and naval forces.

To provide for calling forth the militia to execute the laws of the Confederate States, suppress insurrections, and repel invasions.

To provide for organizing, arming, and disciplining the militia, and for governing such part of them as may be employed in the service of the Confederate States; reserving to the States, respectively, the appointment of the officers, and the authority of training the militia according to the discipline prescribed by Congress.

To exercise exclusive legislation, in all cases whatsoever, over such district (not exceeding ten miles square) as may, by cession of one or more States and the acceptance of Congress, become the seat of the Government of the Confederate States; and to exercise like authority over all places purchased by the consent of the Legislature of the State in which the same shall be, for the erection of forts, magazines, arsenals, dockyards, and other needful buildings; and

To make all laws which shall be necessary and proper for carrying into execution the foregoing powers, and all other powers vested by this Constitution in the Government of the Confederate States, or in any department or officer thereof.

SECTION 9. The importation of negroes of the African race from any foreign country other than the slaveholding States or Territories of the United States of America, is hereby forbidden; and Congress is required to pass such laws as shall effectually prevent the same.

Congress shall also have power to prohibit the introduction of slaves from any State not a member of, or Territory not belonging to, this Confederacy.

The privilege of the writ of habeas corpus shall not be suspended, unless when in cases of rebellion or invasion the public safety may require it.

No bill of attainder, ex post facto law, or law denying or impairing the right of property in negro slaves shall be passed.

No capitation or other direct tax shall be laid, unless in proportion to the census or enumeration hereinbefore directed to be taken.

No tax or duty shall be laid on articles exported from any State, except by a vote of two-thirds of both Houses.

No preference shall be given by any regulation of commerce or revenue to the ports of one State over those of another.

No money shall be drawn from the Treasury, but in consequence of appropriations made by law; and a regular statement and account of the receipts and expenditures of all public money shall be published from time to time.

Congress shall appropriate no money from the Treasury except by a vote of two-thirds of both Houses, taken by yeas and nays, unless it be asked and estimated for by some one of the heads of departments and submitted to Congress by the President; or for the purpose of paying its own expenses and contingencies; or for the payment of claims against the Confederate States, the justice of which shall have been judicially declared by a tribunal for the investigation of claims against the Government, which it is hereby made the duty of Congress to establish.

All bills appropriating money shall specify in Federal currency the exact amount of each appropriation and the purposes for which it is made; and Congress shall grant no extra compensation to any public contractor, officer, agent, or servant, after such contract shall have been made or such service rendered.

No title of nobility shall be granted by the Confederate States; and no person holding any office of profit or trust under them shall, without the consent of the Congress, accept of any present, emolument, office, or title of any kind whatever, from any king, prince, or foreign state.

Congress shall make no law respecting an establishment of religion, or prohibiting the free exercise thereof; or abridging the freedom of speech, or of the press; or the right of the people peaceably to assemble and petition the Government for a redress of grievances.

A well-regulated militia being necessary to the security of a free State, the right of the people to keep and bear arms shall not be infringed.

No soldier shall, in time of peace, be quartered in any house without the consent of the owner; nor in time of war, but in a manner to be prescribed by law.

The right of the people to be secure in their persons, houses, papers, and effects, against unreasonable searches and seizures, shall not be violated; and no warrants shall issue but upon probable cause, supported by oath or affirmation, and particularly describing the place to be searched and the persons or things to be seized.

No person shall be held to answer for a capital or otherwise infamous crime, unless on a presentment or indictment of a grand jury, except in cases arising in the land or naval forces, or in the militia, when in actual service in time of war or public danger; nor shall any person be subject for the same offense to be twice put in jeopardy of life or limb; nor be compelled, in any criminal case, to be a witness against himself; nor be deprived of life, liberty, or property without due process of law; nor shall private property be taken for public use, without just compensation.

In all criminal prosecutions the accused shall enjoy the right to a speedy and public trial, by an impartial jury of the State and district wherein the crime shall have been committed, which district shall have been previously ascertained by law, and to be informed of the nature and cause of the accusation; to be confronted with the witnesses against him; to have compulsory process for obtaining witnesses in his favor; and to have the assistance of counsel for his defense.

In suits at common law, where the value in controversy shall exceed twenty dollars, the right of trial by jury shall be preserved; and no fact so tried by a jury shall be otherwise reexamined in any court of the Confederacy, than according to the rules of common law.

Excessive bail shall not be required, nor excessive fines imposed, nor cruel and unusual punishments inflicted.

Every law, or resolution having the force of law, shall relate to but one subject, and that shall be expressed in the title.

SECTION 10. No State shall enter into any treaty, alliance, or confederation; grant letters of marque and reprisal; coin money; make anything but gold and silver coin a tender in payment of debts; pass any bill of attainder, or ex post facto law, or law impairing the obligation of contracts; or grant any title of nobility.

No State shall, without the consent of the Congress, lay any imposts or duties on imports or exports, except what may be absolutely necessary for executing its inspection laws; and the net produce of all duties and imposts, laid by any State on imports, or exports, shall be for the use of the Treasury of the Confederate States; and all such laws shall be subject to the revision and control of Congress.

No State shall, without the consent of Congress, lay any duty on tonnage, except on seagoing vessels, for the improvement of its rivers and harbors navigated by the said vessels; but such duties shall not conflict with any treaties of the Confederate States with foreign nations; and any surplus revenue thus derived shall, after making such improvement, be paid into the common treasury. Nor shall any State keep troops or ships of war in time of peace, enter into any agreement or compact with another State, or with a foreign power, or engage in war, unless actually invaded, or in such imminent danger as will not admit of delay. But when any river divides or flows through two or more States they may enter into compacts with each other to improve the navigation thereof.

ARTICLE II

SECTION 1. The executive power shall be vested in a President of the Confederate States of America. He and the Vice President shall hold their offices for the term of six years; but the President shall not be re-eligible. The President and Vice President shall be elected as follows:

Each State shall appoint, in such manner as the Legislature thereof may direct, a number of electors equal to the whole number of Senators and Representatives to which the State may be entitled in the Congress; but no Senator or Representative or person holding an office of trust or profit under the Confederate States shall be appointed an elector.

The electors shall meet in their respective States and vote by ballot for President and Vice President, one of whom, at least, shall not be an inhabitant of the same State with themselves; they shall name in their ballots the person voted for as President, and in distinct ballots the person voted for as Vice President, and they shall make distinct lists of all persons voted for as President, and of all persons voted for as Vice President, and of the number of votes for each, which lists they shall sign and certify, and transmit, sealed, to the seat of the Government of the Confederate States, directed to the President of the Senate; the President of the Senate shall, in the presence of the Senate and House of Representatives, open all the certificates, and the votes shall then be counted; the person having the greatest number of votes for President shall be the President, if such number be a majority of the whole number of electors appointed; and if no person have such majority, then from the persons having the highest numbers, not exceeding three, on the list of those voted for as President, the House of Representatives shall choose immediately, by ballot, the President. But in choosing the President the votes shall be taken by States—the representation from each State having one vote; a quorum for this purpose shall consist of a member or members from two-thirds of the States, and a majority of all the States shall be necessary to a choice. And if the House of Representatives shall not choose a President, whenever the right of choice shall devolve upon them, before the 4th day of March next following, then the Vice President shall act as President, as in case of the death, or other constitutional disability of the President.

The person having the greatest number of votes as Vice President shall be the Vice President, if such number be a majority of the whole number of electors appointed; and if no person have a majority, then, from the two highest numbers on the list, the Senate shall choose the Vice President; a quorum for the purpose shall consist of two-thirds of the whole number of Senators, and a majority of the whole number shall be necessary to a choice.

But no person constitutionally ineligible to the office of President shall be eligible to that of Vice President of the Confederate States.

The Congress may determine the time of choosing the electors, and the day on which they shall give their votes; which day shall be the same throughout the Confederate States.

No person except a natural-born citizen of the Confederate States, or a citizen thereof at the time of the adoption of this Constitution, or a citizen thereof born in the United States prior to the 20th of December, 1860, shall be eligible to the office of President; neither shall any person be eligible to that office who shall not have attained the age of thirty-five years, and been fourteen years a resident within the limits of the Confederate States, as they may exist at the time of his election.

In case of the removal of the President from office, or of his death, resignation, or inability to discharge the powers and duties of said office, the same shall devolve on the Vice President; and the Congress may, by law, provide for the case of removal, death, resignation, or inability, both of the President and Vice President, declaring what officer shall then act as President; and such officer shall act accordingly until the disability be removed or a President shall be elected.

The President shall, at stated times, receive for his services a compensation, which shall neither be increased nor diminished during the period for which he shall have been elected; and he shall not receive within that period any other emolument from the Confederate States, or any of them.

Before he enters on the execution of his office he shall take the following oath or affirmation:

> I do solemnly swear (or affirm) that I will faithfully execute the office of President of the Confederate States, and will, to the best

of my ability, preserve, protect, and defend the Constitution thereof.

SECTION 2. The President shall be Commander-in-Chief of the Army and Navy of the Confederate States, and of the militia of the several States, when called into the actual service of the Confederate States; he may require the opinion, in writing, of the principal officer in each of the Executive Departments, upon any subject relating to the duties of their respective offices; and he shall have power to grant reprieves and pardons for offenses against the Confederate States, except in cases of impeachment.

He shall have power, by and with the advice and consent of the Senate, to make treaties; provided two-thirds of the Senators present concur; and he shall nominate, and by and with the advice and consent of the Senate shall appoint, ambassadors, other public ministers and consuls, judges of the Supreme Court, and all other officers of the Confederate States whose appointments are not herein otherwise provided for, and which shall be established by law; but the Congress may, by law, vest the appointment of such inferior officers, as they think proper, in the President alone, in the courts of law, or in the heads of departments.

The principal officer in each of the Executive Departments, and all persons connected with the diplomatic service, may be removed from office at the pleasure of the President. All other civil officers of the Executive Departments may be removed at any time by the President, or other appointing power, when their services are unnecessary, or for dishonesty, incapacity, inefficiency, misconduct, or neglect of duty; and when so removed, the removal shall be reported to the Senate, together with the reasons therefor.

The President shall have power to fill all vacancies that may happen during the recess of the Senate, by granting commissions which shall expire at the end of their next session; but no person rejected by the Senate shall be reappointed to the same office during their ensuing recess.

SECTION 3. The President shall, from time to time, give to the Congress information of the state of the Confederacy, and recommend to their consideration such measures as he shall judge necessary and expedient; he may, on extraordinary occasions, convene both Houses, or either of them; and in case of disagreement between them, with respect to the time of adjournment, he may adjourn them to such time as he shall think proper; he shall receive ambassadors and other public ministers; he shall take care that the laws be faithfully executed, and shall commission all the officers of the Confederate States.

SECTION 4. The President, Vice President, and all civil officers of the Confederate States, shall be removed from office on impeachment for and conviction of treason, bribery, or other high crimes and misdemeanors.

ARTICLE III

SECTION 1. The judicial power of the Confederate States shall be vested in one Supreme Court, and in such inferior courts as the Congress may, from time to time, ordain and establish. The judges, both of the Supreme and inferior courts, shall hold their offices during good behavior, and shall, at stated times, receive for their services a compensation which shall not be diminished during their continuance in office.

SECTION 2. The judicial power shall extend to all cases arising under this Constitution, the laws of the Confederate States, and treaties made, or which shall be made, under their authority; to all cases affecting ambassadors, other public ministers and consuls; to all cases of admiralty and maritime jurisdiction; to controversies to which the Confederate States shall be a party; to controversies between two or more States; between a State and citizens of another State, where the State is plaintiff; between citizens claiming lands under grants of different States; and between a State or the citizens thereof, and foreign states, citizens, or subjects; but no State shall be sued by a citizen or subject of any foreign state.

In all cases affecting ambassadors, other public ministers and consuls, and those in which a State shall be a party, the Supreme

Court shall have original jurisdiction. In all the other cases before mentioned, the Supreme Court shall have appellate jurisdiction both as to law and fact, with such exceptions and under such regulations as the Congress shall make.

The trial of all crimes, except in cases of impeachment, shall be by jury, and such trial shall be held in the State where the said crimes shall have been committed; but when not committed within any State, the trial shall be at such place or places as the Congress may by law have directed.

SECTION 3. Treason against the Confederate States shall consist only in levying war against them, or in adhering to their enemies, giving them aid and comfort. No person shall be convicted of treason unless on the testimony of two witnesses to the same overt act, or on confession in open court.

The Congress shall have power to declare the punishment of treason; but no attainder of treason shall work corruption of blood, or forfeiture, except during the life of the person attainted.

ARTICLE IV

SECTION 1. Full faith and credit shall be given in each State to the public acts, records, and judicial proceedings of every other State; and the Congress may, by general laws, prescribe the manner in which such acts, records, and proceedings shall be proved, and the effect thereof.

SECTION 2. The citizens of each State shall be entitled to all the privileges and immunities of citizens in the several States; and shall have the right of transit and sojourn in any State of this Confederacy, with their slaves and other property; and the right of property in said slaves shall not be thereby impaired.

A person charged in any State with treason, felony, or other crime against the laws of such State, who shall flee from justice, and be found in another State, shall, on demand of the executive authority of the State from which he fled, be delivered up, to be removed to the State having jurisdiction of the crime.

No slave or other person held to service or labor in any State or Territory of the Confederate States, under the laws thereof, escaping or unlawfully carried into another, shall, in consequence of any law or regulation therein, be discharged from such service or labor; but shall be delivered up on claim of the party to whom such slave belongs; or to whom such service or labor may be due.

SECTION 3. Other States may be admitted into this Confederacy by a vote of two-thirds of the whole House of Representatives and two-thirds of the Senate, the Senate voting by States; but no new State shall be formed or erected within the jurisdiction of any other State, nor any State be formed by the junction of two or more States, or parts of States, without the consent of the Legislatures of the States concerned, as well as of the Congress.

The Congress shall have power to dispose of and make all needful rules and regulations concerning the property of the Confederate States, including the lands thereof.

The Confederate States may acquire new territory; and Congress shall have power to legislate and provide governments for the inhabitants of all territory belonging to the Confederate States, lying without the limits of the several Sates; and may permit them, at such times, and in such manner as it may by law provide, to form States to be admitted into the Confederacy. In all such territory the institution of negro slavery, as it now exists in the Confederate States, shall be recognized and protected by Congress and by the Territorial government; and the inhabitants of the several Confederate States and Territories shall have the right to take to such Territory any slaves lawfully held by them in any of the States or Territories of the Confederate States.

The Confederate States shall guarantee to every State that now is, or hereafter may become, a member of this Confederacy, a republican form of government; and shall protect each of them against invasion; and on application of the Legislature (or of the Executive when the Legislature is not in session) against domestic violence.

ARTICLE V

SECTION 1. Upon the demand of any three States, legally assembled in their several conventions, the Congress shall summon a convention of all the States, to take into consideration such amendments to the Constitution as the said States shall concur in suggesting at the time when the said demand is made; and should any of the proposed amendments to the Constitution be agreed on by the said convention—voting by States—and the same be ratified by the Legislatures of two-thirds of the several States, or by conventions in two-thirds thereof—as the one or the other mode of ratification may be proposed by the general convention—they shall thenceforward form a part of this Constitution. But no State shall, without its consent, be deprived of its equal representation in the Senate.

ARTICLE VI

SECTION 1. The Government established by this Constitution is the successor of the Provisional Government of the Confederate States of America, and all the laws passed by the latter shall continue in force until the same shall be repealed or modified; and all the officers appointed by the same shall remain in office until their successors are appointed and qualified, or the offices abolished.

SECTION 2. All debts contracted and engagements entered into before the adoption of this Constitution shall be as valid against the Confederate States under this Constitution, as under the Provisional Government.

SECTION 3. This Constitution, and the laws of the Confederate States made in pursuance thereof, and all treaties made, or which shall be made, under the authority of the Confederate States, shall be the supreme law of the land; and the judges in every State shall be bound thereby, anything in the constitution or laws of any State to the contrary notwithstanding.

SECTION 4. The Senators and Representatives before mentioned, and the members of the several State Legislatures, and all executive and judicial officers, both of the Confederate States and of the several States, shall be bound by oath or affirmation to support this Constitution; but no religious test shall ever be required as a qualification to any office or public trust under the Confederate States.

SECTION 5. The enumeration, in the Constitution, of certain rights shall not be construed to deny or disparage others retained by the people of the several States.

SECTION 6. The powers not delegated to the Confederate States by the Constitution, nor prohibited by it to the States, are reserved to the States, respectively, or to the people thereof.

ARTICLE VII

The ratification of the conventions of five States shall be sufficient for the establishment of this Constitution between the States so ratifying the same.

When five States shall have ratified this Constitution, in the manner before specified, the Congress under the Provisional Constitution shall prescribe the time for holding the election of President and Vice President; and for the meeting of the Electoral College; and for counting the votes, and inaugurating the President. They shall, also, prescribe the time for holding the first election of members of Congress under this Constitution, and the time for assembling the same. Until the assembling of such Congress, the Congress under the Provisional Constitution shall continue to exercise the legislative powers granted them; not extending beyond the time limited by the Constitution of the Provisional Government.

Adopted unanimously by the Congress of the Confederate States of South Carolina, Georgia, Florida, Alabama, Mississippi, Louisiana, and Texas, sitting in convention at the capitol, in the city of Montgomery, Ala., on the eleventh day of March, in the year eighteen hundred and sixty-one.

HOWELL COBB,
President of the Congress

South Carolina: R. Barnwell Rhett, C. G. Memminger, Wm. Porcher Miles, James Chesnut, Jr., R. W. Barnwell, William W. Boyce, Lawrence M. Keitt, T. J. Withers.
Georgia: Francis S. Bartow, Martin J. Crawford, Benjamin H. Hill, Thos. R. R. Cobb.
Florida: Jackson Morton, J. Patton Anderson, Jas. B. Owens.
Alabama: Richard W. Walker, Robt. H. Smith, Colin J. McRae, William P. Chilton, Stephen F. Hale, David P. Lewis, Tho. Fearn, Jno. Gill Shorter, J. L. M. Curry.
Mississippi: Alex. M. Clayton, James T. Harrison, William S. Barry, W. S. Wilson, Walker Brooke, W. P. Harris, J. A. P. Campbell.
Louisiana: Alex. de Clouet, C. M. Conrad, Duncan F. Kenner, Henry Marshall.
Texas: John Hemphill, Thomas N. Waul, John H. Reagan, Williamson S. Oldham, Louis T. Wigfall, John Gregg, William Beck Ochiltree.

GLOSSARY

amici curiae. Friend of the court. Someone not directly involved in a court case can sometimes make an argument as a friend of the court.

bills of attainder. Punishment by legislative enactment rather than through the courts.

certiorari. A writ from a superior court to a subordinate court asking for a record of the case. Persons desiring to have their case heard by the Supreme Court ask the Court for a writ of certiorari, meaning they want the Court to get a copy of the case record so they can hear the case.

citizenship. Not defined until the Fourteenth Amendment. As of 1868, a citizen is anyone "born or naturalized in the United States, and subject to the jurisdiction thereof."

chancery. A court of equity—following jurisprudence based on fairness rather than following the common law.

cloture. A parliamentary device for closing unlimited debate in the United States Senate, calling the question at hand to an immediate vote. See filibuster.

common law. Judge-made law common to the realm. This is law not passed by any legislature but emerges from judicial precedents.

constitutionalism. A constitution is a set of rules limiting the power of government and the people acting through their government. Constitutionalism is the belief that one is limited by a constitution.

coverture. The status of a married woman legally subsuming her personhood under the authority of her husband.

democracy. Madison defined democracy as a system of government where every citizen participates in making public decisions.

duces tecum. A writ demanding that someone bring documents or evidence to court.

executive order. The president can issue an executive order which, when published in the Federal Register, has the force of law.

ex parte. Apart from. A judicial proceeding involving only one party.

ex post facto. Done after the fact. An ex post facto law seeks to punish crimes committed before passage of the law.

federalism. A system of government whereby sovereignty is divided, with provincial authorities having authority over some questions.

filibuster. In the U.S. Senate members have the right of unlimited debate. A speech designed to circumvent another issue from taking the floor and thus stop action is called a filibuster.

habeas corpus. Have the body. This is a writ allowing a prisoner to challenge his or her incarceration by forcing his or her jailors to appear in court with evidence justifying the imprisonment.

judicial review. When the Supreme Court examines a law to determine if it is constitutional or not, it judicially reviews the law.

libel. To damage the reputation of another through writing or print is to libel them.

natural law. Law emerging from nature rather than from legislative or judicial process.

penumbras. Something shadowy or indefinite. The Supreme Court has found rights implied or suggested in the Bill of Rights in addition to those overtly articulated.

per curiam. By the court. A decision said to be issued by the whole court rather than any particular judge.

police power. The states' powers to make and enforce laws for the health and safety of their citizens.

Political Action Committee (PAC). A fundraising group.

republic. A system of government where the citizens elect a few to make decisions for the whole. Madison contrasted this with a democracy, where citizens make decisions.

sovereignty. Ultimate power in government.

stare decisis. The rule that courts should obey their precedents.

writ of mandamus. A writ commanding someone or some agency to do something.

INDEX

TEACHING TEXTS IN LAW AND POLITICS

David Schultz, *General Editor*

The new series Teaching Texts in Law and Politics is devoted to textbooks that explore the multidimensional and multidisciplinary areas of law and politics. Special emphasis will be given to textbooks written for the undergraduate classroom. Subject matters to be addressed in this series include, but will not be limited to: constitutional law; civil rights and liberties issues; law, race, gender, and gender orientation studies; law and ethics; women and the law; judicial behavior and decision-making; legal theory; comparative legal systems; criminal justice; courts and the political process; and other topics on the law and the political process that would be of interest to undergraduate curriculum and education. Submission of single-author and collaborative studies, as well as collections of essays are invited.

Authors wishing to have works considered for this series should contact:

Peter Lang Publishing
Acquisitions Department
275 Seventh Avenue, 28th floor
New York, New York 10001

To order other books in this series, please contact our Customer Service Department at:

800-770-LANG (within the U.S.)
(212) 647-7706 (outside the U.S.)
(212) 647-7707 FAX

or browse online by series at:

WWW.PETERLANGUSA.COM